ABOUT THE AUTHOR

Pete May has been a freelance journalist since 1987 and has contributed to *The Guardian*, *The Observer*, *The Independent*, *Time Out*, *Loaded*, *Midweek* and numerous other publications. His books include *There's A Hippo In My Cistern*, *Rent Boy*, *Hammers in the Heart*, *West Ham: Irons in the Soul*, *Flying So High: West Ham's Cup Finals* and *Sunday Muddy Sunday*. Having been brought up as an Essex Man, he now lives in north London with his wife, two daughters and a large collection of football programmes.

THE JOY OF ESSEX

Welcome to ESSEX

TRAVELS THROUGH GOD'S OWN COUNTY

PETE MAY

The Robson Press

First published in Great Britain in 2012 by
The Robson Press (an imprint of Biteback Publishing Ltd)
Westminster Tower
3 Albert Embankment
London SE1 7SP
Copyright © Pete May 2012

ISBN 978-1-84954-423-8

10 9 8 7 6 5 4 3 2 1

A CIP catalogue record for this book is available from the British Library.

Set in Sabon and Helvetica Neue

Printed and bound in Great Britain by
CPI Group (UK) Ltd, Croydon CR0 4YY

ACKNOWLEDGEMENTS

My apologies to everyone who has put up with my being an Essex anorak for the last year or so and endured endless trips to the far East. Thanks to *The Independent*, *The Guardian*, *Midweek*, the *Essex Chronicle*, the BBC and Radio Essex for publishing and broadcasting my thoughts on the county, and particularly to Iain Dale at Biteback Publishing for taking a punt on this book and Jessica Feehan at the Robson Press for her fine editing.

Help and advice on Essexology has come from many quarters. Special thanks to Phill Jupitus for giving up a day to show me sunshine on Leigh, and also David Nicholls for the Brian as Pip quote, Robert Halfon MP for his thoughts on Harlow, Kevin Diver for the Tilbury Fort tour and Katie Mumford and all at Wilkin & Sons in Tiptree. Others I'm indebted to include David and Nishani Kampfner, Jacqui Burke, Gavin Hadland, Nigel Morris, Chris the Scouser, John Curren, Katie Dawson, Sarah Speight, Big Joe, Nick Toms, Paul Garrett, Alison O'Brien, John Young, Robert Walker and Oxana Bondyuk.

My daughters Lola and Nell provided vital research into *TOWIE* and helped me explore several areas of Essex and sample the chip shops. I owe a debt of gratitude to my wife Nicola Baird for proofreading, advice, photography, endurance, having lunch in Chigwell, tea in Clacton and dinner in Colchester and, of course, being born in Chelmsford.

And finally, thanks to my late parents Sheila and Dennis May for raising me as an Essex Man.

CONTENTS

THE JOY OF ESSEX

Essex Man was twenty-two on 7 October 2012. Wanna make something of it? Well, yes actually. Twenty-two years on, something strange has happened: Essex is still the most iconic county in the UK and the essence of Essex is everywhere.

In 2011 Harry Judd, of pop-rock band McFly, from Chelmsford won *Strictly Come Dancing* and Essex claimed the entire top three of *I'm A Celebrity* – winner Dougie Poynter (Judd's bandmate) from Corringham, Mark Wright from Abridge and Fatima Whitbread from Shenfield. Winners of *The X Factor* Little Mix included Jesy Nelson from Romford, while Southend's The Horrors and Jessie J, another Romford girl, had huge musical success.

From Russell Brand and Jamie Oliver to Phill Jupitus, Alan Davies and Ray Winstone (home bar, gaff in Roydon, Essex, and a brilliant turn as Magwitch in *Great Expectations*), via the runaway success of TV series *Gavin and Stacey* and films such as *Made in Dagenham*, *Sex & Drugs & Rock & Roll* and *Oil City Confidential*, Essex is in danger of getting well cultured.

Everyone thinks they have an idea of Essex. For twenty-plus years we've been fascinated by the Thames Delta, as Dr Feelgood memorably termed their Canvey Island hinterland. Could there be something more than a good joke involved?

The word Essex comes from the early Middle Ages and is derived from East Seaxe, meaning the East Saxons. East Seaxe sounds like a heavy metal band from Dagenham and is a suitably hard moniker for the old county. In the glory days of Essex it had all the lands east of the river Lea before Greater London started lopping bits off. Even the site of Thames Ironworks in Canning Town, the shipyard where the works team eventually became West Ham United, was once in Essex.

The first reference to 'Essex Man' was in a piece entitled 'Maggie's mauler' on the Comment page of the *Sunday Telegraph*, edited by Sir Peregrine Worsthorne, on 7 October 1990. There was no byline, although we now know the author was Simon Heffer, a right-wing iconoclast who has lived in Essex all his life.

The *Telegraph* profile described Essex Man as 'young, industrious, mildly brutish and culturally barren', and, of course, 'breathtakingly right-wing'. He wanted to own a Rottweiler and didn't like foreigners or books. The accompanying illustration featured a bull-necked young man in a shiny suit standing outside his bought council house with a satellite dish on the roof and a new motor outside.

Essex Man was useful shorthand for why Thatcherism was successful, thought Heffer: 'The barrow boy who uses instinct and energy rather than contacts and education ... He is unencumbered by any "may the best man win" philosophy. He expects to win whether he's the best man or not.'

It described a cultural phenomenon. Aspirational working-class East Enders had made a bit of dosh and moved out to Essex, leaving war-damaged homes behind for 'Stalinist' new towns like Harlow and Basildon. As manufacturing and dock jobs went, the children of the old East Enders found jobs in the City and the used car lots of the Southend Arterial Road.

Heffer continued his observations with a snapshot of travelling home on commuter trains:

> When one walks through the City most evenings the pools of vomit into which one may step have usually been put there by Essex man, whose greatly enhanced wealth has exceeded his breeding in terms of alcoholic capacity. The late night trains from Liverpool Street are not lacking drunks, though Essex Man's sense of decency means he is usually sick before boarding.

Heffer later described his moment of Essex epiphany in an interview for the political blog *Iain Dale's Diary*:

> I was with my wife on a train sitting outside Liverpool Street station, it would have been late September 1990. We were going to a very sad event, the funeral of Sir Peregrine Worsthorne's first wife, of whom we were enormously fond.

Liverpool Street was just being rebuilt in those days and there were always huge delays going in there, and as we sat patiently in our funeral garb waiting to get into the station, there was an 'Essex man', a 'geezer', sitting opposite me. He was late for work. He was on a mobile telephone, which in those days were huge, and he was conducting a very animated conversation. The entire carriage could hear him saying: 'Yeah I can't get in, I'm stuck, but you've got to do this deal and that deal, get on a phone, do this, do that, do this.'

I said to my dear wife when we got off the train, although I didn't really want to be part of his business conversation, it was really symbolic of how things had changed. Because when I was a boy living in a little village in Essex most of the people who lived in our village were either farm labourers or they worked in industrial nurseries. Hardly anybody went to London to work.

I said to my wife: 'You know that is what's happened. That bloke is absolutely synonymous with this change...' Anyway, we get to the funeral and we're talking to [the journalist] Frank Johnson about this. He said: 'You've spotted a social phenomenon here!' I said: 'What, you mean Essex Man?' He said: 'Write it, do it!' So I went away and wrote it, and I was astonished by the reaction to it.

It was a brilliant piece of journalism, snobbish, overstated, but with enough truth for the phrase Essex Man to enter the *Oxford English Dictionary.*

For someone like me, who grew up in Brentwood, it seemed all too familiar. Essex Man and Essex Girl stereotypes became a national craze. Essex Man's missus was a blonde wearing white stilettos, and the subject of jokes such as 'How does an Essex Girl turn off the light after sex? She kicks shut the car door.'

Today newspaper ran an Essex Man cartoon. In one, Essex Man asks a fellow passenger on the train if there's a buffet. There isn't, so Essex Man declares, 'Well, you'll just have to go thirsty then, mate!' as he sips his can of lager.

The country became gripped by Essex mania. Ten days after the Essex Man feature appeared, Phill Jupitus (then Porky the Poet), fanzine editor Richard Edwards and I made it onto BBC *South East News* having formed the spoof Essex Liberation Front, whose motto was 'Liberty, equality, Tiptree jam!' We held a press conference at a pub in Stratford telling the BBC that we were making a unilateral declaration of independence for Essex. We claimed that our government in exile would soon restore culture to the new nation and fund itself through sales of Tiptree jam and marmalade. Earlier we had ceremonially burned a copy of *Arena* and a pair of furry dice in Epping Forest, which made a two-page feature in *Midweek*, a free magazine for (sometimes vomiting) commuters. Mention Essex and it pushes media buttons.

There have been many extensions of the Essex Man caricature, such as Mondeo Man, Worcester Woman, White Van Man, something that is almost certainly linked to the English class system too. When toffs get a bit of money they still wear frayed shirts and plead poverty due to school fees. They'd never have a personalised number plate. Whereas the working class made good flaunting their cash was considered much more vulgar. It's possible that Essex Man made it permissible to laugh at the white working class again, leading to chav jokes and *Little Britain*'s Vicky Pollard. But none of these labels have stuck like Essex Man, and there was enough truth in it for it to have entered the national lexicon.

The prototype for Essex Man had been germinating for many years. In 1990, Mick Bunnage (later Dr Mick in *Loaded* magazine) described the county as 'the Jacuzzi of the soul' in an *Arena* piece entitled 'Essex, innit?' I, too, have a claim to contributing to early Essexology. In January 1989 my feature 'Essex appeal' appeared in *Midweek*. The strapline read, 'Darrens, Sharons and the enduring charms of the A13 ... Essex is to culture what Bob Monkhouse is to sincerity.' It cited Romford's Hollywood nightclub, stilettos worn without tights whatever the weather, current joint-chairman of West Ham David Sullivan, right-wing Billericay MPs Harvey Proctor and Teresa Gorman, and Chingford's Thatcherite MP Norman 'on your bike' Tebbit: 'Politically most residents of Essex think of Thatcherism as a temporary left-wing aberration that the Tory party will soon discard in favour of public executions and compulsory repatriation.'

A year earlier, Harry Enfield had produced his Loadsamoney character, a plasterer hollering, 'Oi you! Shut your mouth and look at my wad!' When Loadsamoney drove into the countryside and shouted

'Oi! Get this place developed up!' it could only have been in Essex. Or perhaps it was the great Ian Dury who really identified the first Essex Man way back in 1977, with songs like 'Blockheads' about boy racers in black and orange cars and 'Billericay Dickie', on the sexploits of a libidinous brickie.

Whatever the origins of Essex Man, he's no longer seen as exclusively nasty, short and brutish. He's cuddlier today, no longer exclusively right wing having flirted with Blair and the coalition. He's also a lot funnier.

Self-deprecating Essex humour is in the ascendant. The environs of the A13 and the merging of new money with a lack of cultural nous has produced many top comedians.

Russell Brand from Grays – a reformed sex addict and 'Billericay Dickie' clone – fulfilled the ultimate Essex Man fantasy when he persuaded his then-girlfriend Katy Perry to pose in a West Ham basque at the MTV awards, while Brand's fellow Essex comedians Phill Jupitus, Alan Davies and Lee Evans are fixtures on our TV screens. Davies achieved great comic mileage on Channel 4's *Alan Davies' Teenage Revolution,* returning to his mockney Loughton roots and meeting up in the Winston Churchill pub with one of the 'Debden Skins' who terrorised his middle-class mates. Even Matt Smith on *Doctor Who* ended up too Essexy for his Tardis, lodging with James Corden and playing Sunday league football in one episode.

In 2000 Jamie Oliver certainly played up his roots in the introduction of *The Naked Chef Returns.* 'Blimey, what a year!' he wrote. 'As you can imagine, being the youngest chef on the block, having a bestselling book as well as a cracking television series, not to mention being a bit scruffy and coming from Essex, I have come in for a bit of stick from folk...' His cooking manifesto was as in-yer-face as Essex itself: 'This book isn't about cheffy food. It's for normal people.' When *Jamie's Great Britain* was published in 2012 he was still featuring the Essex border sign near Clavering on the inside cover montage.

Low culture is infiltrating high culture. You might expect Essex resident Germaine Greer to be horrified by Essex Girls, but in 2006 she wrote in *The Observer*:

> The Essex girl is a working-class heroine surviving in a post-proletarian world ... Chantelle [Houghton] and Jodie Marsh both did the Essex girl proud in the *Big Brother* house, Jodie by refusing to droop under relentless bullying and Chantelle by winning. Essex girls, who turn middle-class notions of distinction on their heads, are anti-celebrities.

In 2010 the ITV2 docusoap *The Only Way Is Essex* was an unexpected success, winning a BAFTA YouTube Audience award. Nanny Pat, Mark 'Mr Essex' Wright, Lauren Goodger, Kirk Norcross, James 'Arg' Argent, Lydia Bright and Joey Essex became icons of the celebrity magazines. Essex argot became hip, with a nation suddenly learning the art of the vajazzle and terms such as 'jel', 'babe', 'shu' up!' and 'are you mugging me off?'

In politics it was felt there was a vacancy for an Essex

Man in David Cameron's inner circle after the resignation of ex-*News of the World* editor Andy Coulson in January 2011. The Wickford-born Coulson might not have been the best advert for Essex after the phone-hacking scandal, but it was striking how many commentators felt that a bunch of old Etonians needed a down-to-earth Essex geezer alongside all that Bullingdon Club stuff. Indeed, Defence Secretary Philip Hammond, a former pupil of Shenfield School and self-made millionaire, already has much influence with the old Etonians at the top of the Tory party.

On *BBC News*, Nick Robinson emphasised that Andy Coulson was an 'Essex boy' and that he was valuable to the 'posh boys' in the Cabinet, because he provided a direct link to working-class core Tory voters in deepest Essex. *The Guardian*, meanwhile, described Coulson as an 'Essex Man' who was brought up in a council house and had a 'street-smart background born of Beauchamps comprehensive in Wickford'. While Cameron and George Osborne were at Oxford University, Coulson was at the *Basildon Evening Echo* before graduating to *The Sun*'s 'Bizarre' page. It's interesting how deep the Essex stereotype has penetrated the media: an Essex comprehensive now equates to 'street-smart'.

Admittedly, the old stereotype is hard to shake off. In 2009 Labour MP David Taylor was in trouble for asking Tessa Jowell if events such as throwing the white high heels and putting the medallion on might encourage Essex people to participate in the Olympics. Yet today Essex can laugh at its image too. A few years ago

Basildon erected a huge tongue-in-cheek Hollywood-style sign on the A127. Any visit brings some comical 'only in Essex' moments. It might be an unsubtle place, but it does seem we're succumbing to Essex appeal. Which isn't surprising, as the sons and daughters of Essex Man now run much of the media. Public school might teach soft skills, but in Essex hard skills such as drive, hunger, humour and a refusal to worry if you call the drawing room the lounge have brought big rewards, and indeed bonuses for turning the banks into upmarket bookies.

Why write a book on Essex? Well, a county with so much baggage – mainly leopard-print or mockodile – surely deserves investigation. And from a personal viewpoint, Essex made me the man I am today. The death of your parents inevitably results in a period of reflection and a desire to explore the haunts of your youth.

As a young man my peers would laugh at Essex's more absurd stereotypes of furry dice in done-up Cortinas. It was a place you escaped from. Yet over the years I realised that despite leaving the county and living in London, most of my lasting friendships were with my Essex peers. And returning to many of the scenes of my early years brought the revelation that Essex wasn't a bad place at all; in fact, it was rather special. My humour was fashioned by Essex, and much of my career in journalism had been spent chronicling the astonishing array of Essex talent done good.

Slowly an idea emerged. To travel along the Thames Delta and into the heart of Essex, to catch a flavour of Essexuality. There was Chigwell, the markets of Romford, the *TOWIE* town of Brentwood, Billericay (home of the eponymous Dickie), and a trawl along the Thames Estuary taking in Dagenham, Grays, Basildon, Canvey Island and Southend. There would also be an exploration of inner Essex, from Chelmsford and on towards Tiptree, the Tendring Peninsula and Colchester, the original capital of England.

My definition of Essex would be deliberately loose. Some areas like Romford and Dagenham are technically in London boroughs, or on the tube, like Chigwell and Upminster, but all are indelibly Essex in spirit.

Essex is where the city and country merge. Away from the Thames Estuary, Essex has wide skies, sea, marshes and estuaries, and the Essex tundra is just as deserving of chronicling as the more exotic destinations of, say, the Solomon Islands or Papua New Guinea. What is the anthropological significance of the indigenous people of Essex and their totemic nail salons, spray-tans and vajaz-zles? Is the only way Essex or is there another way? My plan was to find out.

1

IS THIS THE ONLY WAY IN ESSEX?

'Chavs top the toffs,' declared the *Daily Mirror*. Essex had only gone and won a BAFTA. This unlikeliest of events occurred in May 2011 as *The Only Way Is Essex* beat upmarket *Downton Abbey* to win a BAFTA YouTube Audience award – thus proving that Essex is well telegenic.

Amy Childs gave a moving acceptance speech: 'Shu' up!' While Joey Essex was presumably still wondering who this Bafta bloke was.

Page three of *The Sun* trumpeted: 'The only hooray is Essex!' *TOWIE*, as it rapidly became known in the celeb mags, was an unexpected TV hit, winning a million viewers and doubling that number online. It created a new genre of reality TV. It was real people with real emotions, though, as the opening credits read by Essex's Denise Van Outen explained: 'This programme contains flash cars, big watches and false boobs. The tans you see may be fake but the people are all real, although some of what they do has been set up purely for your entertainment.'

Many of the *TOWIE* cast had already attempted to

break into the world of reality TV and most already knew each other and frequented the same nightspots. So it was fairly easy for makers Lime Pictures to assemble the group in a merging of documentary and drama. The shoots were plotted in advance and suggestions made to the cast as to what they should discuss, but the results were gloriously unpredictable. Everyone in Essex, it seemed, was just one shot away from blubbing, proposing, fronting someone up or going 'mental'.

Daran Little, producer of the first series, explained the show's structured reality technique to *The Guardian*:

> If there's a boy and a girl in a scene, you'll pull them over individually and you'll say: 'Right, in this scene I want you to ask her what she did last night.' Because I know what she did last night, but he doesn't. Then we start the scene and they just talk it through and if it gets a bit dry, we'll stop and pull them to one side and we'll say: 'How do you feel about him asking you that? Because I think you feel more emotional about it. I think you're pulling something back. Do you think it's fair that he's asking you this?'

The show centred around the gridlocked love life of the lupine Mark Wright, a handsome estuary werewolf disguised as a club promoter, tempting on-off lover of nine years Lauren Goodger – along with Lucy, Sam and numerous other lovelies – with his gym-toned body. Mark's sister Jess, a singer with girl group Lola, also featured heavily, along with his blonde mum Carol and splendid Nanny Pat, a real old East Ender who spent her holidays in a caravan, not in Marbella, and was constantly proffering pampered grandson Mark her legendary sausage plait.

Mark was faithfully attended by his 'wingman', the dopey but loveable James 'Arg' Argent, a wannabe Brat Packer in a bow tie, hopelessly besotted with the nice but demanding Lydia Bright and constantly fighting his urge to eat steak baguettes. Throughout *TOWIE* viewers enjoyed Arg's unofficial bromance with best mate Mark.

The early star of the series was Amy Childs. With her big eyes, curves and enhanced breasts, she looked like a real life Jessica Rabbit from the film *Who Framed Roger Rabbit*. Apparently she spent her time working as a beautician in a pink parlour when not looking for glamour-modelling work. Amy soon proved herself an inadvertent comic star by saying things like 'Where's north London?' and 'Where's Essex, is it in south London?'

Amy might not have known the meaning of certain words, but she wasn't scared to ask and was fiercely driven. You sensed she was possibly cleverer than she let on, after all she appeared to be running her own salon and interviewing for staff. Besides, you have to admire the ambition of someone who could bill herself as an 'eyelash technician'. At one point Amy was confronted by Lydia for alleged flirting with Arg. 'Are you having a go at me in my salon?' enquired Amy, with a forcefulness that made Ray Winstone look as soft as Arg's jelly belly.

Alongside Amy was the feline Sam Faiers, an Essex blonde who, along with her mum and sister Billie, ran

Minnies boutique in Brentwood. Sam had an attractive, controlled steeliness that was ultimately to see off even lothario Mark. Together, Amy Childs and Sam Faiers appeared to be 1990s Essex Girls personified with their girly East End accents intoning words like 'luvverley' and 'togevver'.

A superb moment came when Sam told Amy over a large glass of rosé that the term Essex Girl was 'actually in the dictionary'. Amy asked if it meant glamorous, then reacted in shock: 'What it right slags us off ... shu' up! You're having me on! I thought it meant like classy...' Sam replied, 'It's like stilettos and men.'

With admirable precision Amy got to the nub of the issue, asking: 'The person that's obviously done the dictionary, who is it? I'm being serious. Is he from Essex or is he from wherever, like the north or Manchester? If they were from Essex they wouldn't write that.'

Into this mix was lobbed Kirk Norcross, whose dad Mick is the owner of Sugar Hut nightclub in Brentwood High Street. Kirk had a likeable Essex wit, even if Mick was to admit, 'You are spoilt!' when his son received a BMW for his birthday, along with a private funfair in his back garden for his party.

Initially Kirk was dating Amy, telling her without any hint of irony that blokes will always chat her up because 'you have fake boobs and you look really nice'. Silicon Valley was no longer in San Francisco but Brentwood.

Feisty Lauren Goodger was initially an Essex Woman scorned. The first show saw Lauren having a birthday treat of diamonds encrusted on her below bikini line area by beautician Amy in what was termed a 'vajazzle' – a word soon to enter the national consciousness. Like many of those granddaughters of East End matriarchs she wasn't to be messed with either. At the end of her birthday party, eyeing dodgy Mark flirting with Sam, Lauren was filmed declaring, 'I'll f**king knock her out the door!' Once they had got engaged, again, Lauren pushed Mark in the swimming pool after he banned her from attending one of his events, a swimwear party. You'd certainly have backed the *TOWIE* girls to land a TKO against Mark, Arg, Kirk and co.

The homophobic Essex Man of Simon Heffer's profile had moved on in his sexual politics too. Mark Wright and Kirk Norcross posed on the front of *Attitude* magazine in their pants and were quite happy to be lusted after by men. In the interview both emphasised their tolerance of all sexualities. And Harry Derbidge, the gayest man in Essex, could invariably be found in cousin Amy's pink beauty parlour. Flash 'Arry was soon to coin a national catchphrase with his lisped 'Shu' up!' Camp humour had been added to the Essex repertoire. Harry's seventeenth birthday party at a plush Essex country club had an air of *The Decline and Fall of the Roman Empire* about it. Harry dressed as Lady Gaga and was carried in by four semi-naked male hunks as *TOWIE* met *Caligula*.

By series two there was another addition, Joey Essex, a character described by the *Daily Mirror* as a man enduring a 'daily battle with sentience'. Joey attempted to chat up Mark's ex Lucy Mecklenburgh by saying that he was interested in politics. When Lucy asked who the

Prime Minister was, Joey answered, 'What, the Prime Minister of Essex?' before singularly failing to identify David Cameron. At the pub quiz he thought the Isle of Wight was the longest pleasure pier in Britain rather than Southend. There was a heated debate outside Jess's party about the fact that Richard is short for Dick (a fact new to Joey) and some great motoring banter as Kirk explained to Joey what horsepower was (Kirk jokes the horses go in the boot) and how all cars have red brake lights.

Joey wore trainers two sizes too small so they didn't crumple in the middle, along with 1980s nylon shorts. He liked his blow-dried hair and just about everything else to look 'reem'. Yet he managed to be not only a Shakespearian fool in reem clothes, but also strangely loveable. There was also a tragic element to his story, when it was later revealed that his mother had committed suicide when he was a child. Clearly there was something down those tight shorts – despite Joey and cousin Chloe confusing the sun and moon he still got to snog both Sam and Jess. Maybe he really will become Prime Minister of Essex.

Initially, it was easy to fear the programme would be voyeuristic, laughing at thick people in Essex. And it did indeed have its share of Essex stereotypes. *TOWIE* had more orange skin than you could shake a tanning lamp at. Plus lots of pink beauty parlours, tattoos, gyms, lingerie shoots, BMWs, £3,000 watches and the Sugar Hut nightclub.

In one sense the young stars were caricatures. They

were *nouveau riche* and had loadsamoney (or at least their parents did), spent mainly on clothes, cars, cocktails and vajazzles. But there was a lot more to *TOWIE* than laughing at Essex. The show had what *The Guardian* termed 'an emotional warmth' that its imitators lacked. Yes, the cast were told to do certain things by the producers, but their reactions seemed, unless they were brilliant thespians, utterly genuine. There was something universal about the dreams and mistakes of these young people. You could watch macho Kirk blubbing after dumping Lauren Pope one moment, and then Lauren Goodger looking bemused as Mark Wright produced an engagement ring.

TOWIE got its timing right too. The year 2010 was something of an *annus mirabilis* – and no, that's not a beauty treatment connected to a vajazzle – for Essex. The county was the setting for three films that year, *Made in Dagenham*, *Sex & Drugs & Rock & Roll* and *Oil City Confidential*. Garrulous Stacey 'Oh my gosh!' Solomon from Dagenham had followed *X Factor* stardom by winning *I'm a Celebrity ... Get Me Out of Here!*, Basildon-born Kara Tointon triumphed in *Strictly Come Dancing* and painter and decorator Matt Cardle from Halstead was victorious in that year's *The X Factor*, while apparently getting up to some Mark Wright-style antics with make-up assistants too.

Another factor that ensured cult status was the marvellous Essex argot. While street Londoners were speaking Jafrican, here there was a peculiar cock-er-ney merged with Californian – even though the *TOWIE* lot had probably never set foot in the East End, unlike Mark's Nanny Pat and the rest of the cast's geezerish dads.

The vajazzle was the most memorable addition to the English language, along with its male counterpart, the pejazzle. From my own upbringing in Brentwood it was easy to recall such phrases as 'well out of order', referring to a perceived injustice, and 'the 'ump', aka the hump, referring to someone being annoyed. A new mangling of the dialect emerged with a jealous Kirk asking Amy, 'Are you mugging me off?', meaning are you treating me as a mug by chatting to other geezers.

Camp Harry had cornered the glottal-stop free 'Shu' up!' and Amy loved 'Oh my gawd!' and 'Obviously!', obviously. And there was a renaissance of the non-PC 'mental' when Lauren's sister Nicola berated her for accepting Mark's engagement ring. While in the form of Mark 'Mr Essex' Wright, *Carry On* met Ian Dury in the form of phrases such as 'you doughnut!', 'rotters', Arg's 'burger nips' (large nipples) and the greeting 'Oi! Oi!'

It was English but not as we knew it. By series two we saw Mark speculating that his sister Jess had got 'the raving hump' because he didn't agree with her having a boob job. Arg was wailing, 'Talk about digging me out, Lyd!' while Kirk was talking about 'fronting up the geezer' and recommending his old man Mick to Gemma with a memorable definition of Essex class: 'He's a right gentleman, a geezer … he's everything!'

Joey Essex coined 'reem' for anything that was cool or looked good like his 'reem hair' or the 'reem nights' he promoted at Sugar Hut. The *TOWIE* girls popularised 'glamping' (glamorous camping) and added 'jel' for jealous and 'Marbs' for Marbella to the nation's lexicon.

Everything was 'well' or 'proper'. Before the pub quiz someone said of Maria, 'She's well intelligent – she's got GCSEs and everything!'

No wonder it was cult TV. You could have digging me out, mugging me off, raving humps, fronting up geezers, and right gentlemen in one episode, not to mention painted trotters on Mr Darcy the Vietnamese pig.

Another hit with viewers was the intrinsic, sharp wit of Essex hiding beneath the lack of general knowledge. That unscripted, self-effacing Essex humour added much to the *TOWIE* formula. When Kirk drew up to the kerb in the new Range Rover that his dad had just bought him and Amy declared, 'Kirk, you can't sleep with a car!' Kirk replied, 'Dunno, I can give it a right good go!' Mark joked to Arg as they rode white horses to his engagement party, 'This is our *Brokeback Mountain* moment!' Amy described one of her spray-tans as 'the Oompa-Loompa', while Lydia Bright revealed that after watching herself on TV she thought she looked like 'a big orange balloon'.

Even the formidable Lauren Goodger told *The Sun*, 'I also think we don't take ourselves that seriously. With all the catchphrases we are almost taking the piss out of being from Essex. We have humour which other similar shows don't have.'

Everything about *TOWIE* was right, even the adverts for sponsors Wink Bingo and Cymex. A series that allowed itself to be sponsored by a cream for cold sores couldn't be taking itself that seriously. Did Cymex's PR people spot a correlation between Herpes Simplex and lots of snogging at Sugar Hut and Faces? It might not have been the most romantic of sponsors, but like Essex itself, Cymex did what it said on the tube.

Of course, the series provoked criticism too, much of it from outraged residents of Essex, who formed Facebook protest sites. Daphne Field, founder of The Essex Women's Advisory Group, an organisation set up to counter Essex Girl stereotyping, told the *Sunday Telegraph*:

> I actually felt sorry for the cast, having to go on screen and do it. What can be good about trying to tell young people that life is all about expensive clothes and no morals? I know it's supposed to be entertainment but there's a serious side to all this. We've got businesses in Essex that can't attract female staff because women feel uncomfortable saying they're from here.

The paper also quoted Jeremy Lucas, Essex County Council's Head of Culture and Heritage, saying that the show 'undermines everything we've tried to do, to give a broader, better picture of life in the county'.

There was certainly too much plastic surgery talk, with Chloe deciding to have a bottom boost and even Arg pondering a tooth job, although this was only reflecting a national obsession among insecure celebrity-obsessed young people.

But 2.5 million viewers watched the first episode. Clearly the public liked something about *TOWIE*. In a revealing quote to *Attitude*, Kirk Norcross said: 'We're all working, every one of us works, every one of us gets up early and goes to work. Mark, I can't stand him, but he gets up early to go to work too. That's what people should see about us. We work as hard as everyone else.' And perhaps that was the biggest factor in the public's love for the show: celebs who took to their roles as if they were asphalters, glazers or roofers.

It's a very Essex thing this work ethic. The Prodigy's Leeroy Thornhill, brought up in Barking, ploughed all his royalties into doing up a period windmill in Terling, near Chelmsford. After leaving the band it seems most of his fire-starting was in the hearth of his front room, complete with floor cushions imported from Dubai. He bought the windmill for £350,000 and had it on the market for £850,000 in 2010. 'I could have drunk or wasted that money like other musicians, but instead I have made my nest-egg and I am very proud of it,' said the 6'7" keyboard player and dancer from 'the scariest dance group in the world'.

My friend Jacqui Burke, who grew up in Romford and is now a lawyer, reflected the national mood in her views on *TOWIE*'s Essex girls:

> I think a lot of girls tended to dress showier when I was growing up there thirty years ago. You were very much a follower of fashion, and by the time a trend had permeated its way down to Essex it could be found on every clothes stall in Romford Market, so would never be what you could describe as 'classy' and so became the norm.

Now things have changed: there's still that hankering towards showiness (some things are hard to shake off!) but now it seems to be on new terms with this new Essex breed appearing to be in charge of it, not reacting to it. I love it! The Essex way of talking, dressing and acting is just a style of the moment and to those who want to indulge in it, good luck to them! Essex comes across now as essentially light-hearted and glamorous and a breath of fresh air.

Soon the stars of *TOWIE* were in *OK!*, *Heat* and numerous other celebrity magazines virtually every issue. Nanny Pat even got her own column in *Now!* magazine. The *TOWIE* cast represented the hunger and desire to succeed that epitomised early entrepreneurial Essex Man. There was something endearingly old-fashioned about their commitment to hard graft – not on the docks or chemical works of the East End, but toiling on the typeface of the celeb mags.

Amy was happy to admit that she liked the paparazzi. The *TOWIE* stars embraced the tabloids with gusto. Most of the female cast appeared in their undies for *Zoo* magazine, Mark and Lauren were pictured in *OK!* in muddy eighteenth-century military uniforms, while *The Sun* reported endless rumours that Lauren and Mark's relationship was only for the sake of the media. When *The Only Way Is Essex* made the 'Short Cuts' column in *The Guardian* you knew it was bigger than Arg's steak baguette.

The *TOWIE* participants wanted to be famous for

being famous and were happy to admit it. No pretensions and complaints about media intrusion. Just as Jamie Oliver wasn't scared of working hard on sorting school dinners, so the *TOWIE* stars believed that you did a job and you put the hours in.

By the end of 2010 *The Times* was booking its writers in for up-market vajazzles. Amy Childs was mates with Peter Andre and on the cover of *FHM*. And Essex had its own royal engagement when Mark Wright and Lauren Goodger spoofed Will and Kate for an Essex royal wedding shoot in *Now!* entitled 'The Only Way is ... Windsor'. The pair were pictured wearing identical clothes to Kate and Wills, just days after the royal engagement, and they made a fine royal couple when poshed up. Possibly Amy could have become a vajazzler by royal appointment. Lauren told the *Daily Mail*, 'Kate's going to look lovely, isn't she? I'd like to Essex her up a bit, though, give her a blow-dry, a bit of fake tan from my range. Get her nails done, some fake eyelashes, little miniskirt, she'd love it!'

Tourism in Essex experienced an unlikely boom, with Brentwood's Posthouse packed with northerners on stag weekends, out for a bit of Essexuality. There were even *TOWIE* coach tours on offer taking in Sheesh, the King William IV, Sugar Hut and the tanning salons of Buckhurst Hill.

Simon Heffer might have been gratified to know that despite the *TOWIE* phenomenon, the cuddlier Essex Man and Essex Girl hadn't changed that much. In his original Essex Man profile in the *Sunday Telegraph*, Heffer wrote of vomiting on the trains home from Liverpool Street. As if to back Heffer up, at the end of the second series of *TOWIE*, a photo appeared of Arg chundering at the show's wrap party. He later tweeted, 'I got paralytic at the *TOWIE* wrap party, Debbie took me home and I puked up all over her car!!!! Hahahaha.'

Meanwhile, Amy Childs revealed her new, soon to be ex, boyfriend Joe Hurlock in the pages of *New!* magazine. Frank Lampard-lookalike Joe said of their first date, 'I was propping her up as we left the bar. I struggled to find a taxi driver who would take us home and when I did, she was sick in his cab.' Amy added, 'I can't believe I did that. I drank three bottles of wine because I was nervous.'

In an inspired piece of programming, as a teaser to series three *The Only Way Is Essex* teamed up with *Most Haunted*. The cast was abandoned in the tunnels of Coalhouse Fort in Tilbury, once used to defend the Thames. Mark, Arg, Harry, Joey, Sam and Amy and jumpy presenter Yvette Fielding spent ninety minutes squealing, whining and crying, 'Oh my God!' and generally displaying cowardice beyond the call of duty. As Ghostbusters they were about as effective as Mark would be on a women's studies course. No wonder that poltergeist was angry – would you want to see the Thames defended by *TOWIE*? The best moments were Amy's sustained use of the F word when something grabbed her hair and Joey Essex's inadvertent impersonation of Shaggy in *Scooby Doo*. Yikes!

As series three approached in the autumn of 2011

there were signs of strain among the *TOWIE* cast. The tabloids claimed they had only been paid £50 a day for the first series, though most had profited from numerous endorsements. As in the finest vajazzle, sooner or later the crystals become detached. Amy Childs was the first to depart the show. She had her own show lined up, *It's All About Amy*, on Channel 5, and immediately appeared on *Celebrity Big Brother*. The guest bookings duly arrived in her agent's inbox and she probably chose the right time to leave *TOWIE*.

Amy had a lot of front, in more ways than one. Like most Essex folk, she had enough banter to match the lads on the quiz show circuit. On *Never Mind the Buzzcocks* she could easily compete with the likes of Frankie Boyle, host Greg Davies and Tinchy Stryder, who rapidly made Amy an offer of both a pejazzle session and marriage. She even survived saying that at her private school in Essex she 'come first in elocution'.

Amy will go far – possibly as a chat show hostess or the next Barbara Windsor. In November 2011, Childs opened a beauty salon in Brentwood High Street and it soon had a nine-week waiting list.

Inevitably the stars' new celebrity provoked jealousy and sadly violence from some miscreants. Lauren Goodger also opened a salon in Chigwell that had its window smashed and was a victim of Twitter trolls, and *TOWIE* made tabloid headlines when Sam and Billie Faiers were attacked by a girl gang outside the Jet Black nightclub in the West End. '*TOWIE*'s Sam is beaten unconscious and left for dead,' read the front page of the

Daily Star; *The Sun* ran the headline 'They were like wild animals: *TOWIE* sisters tell of vicious girl-gang attack' over a picture of the bruised sisters, with Billie holding her bruised lip and Sam in a neck-brace. The pair had been set upon when they left the nightclub and Sam's £2,500 Mulberry handbag and phone were stolen. The story was that Sam had later agreed to meet the person who had stolen her phone in Repton Park, Chigwell, but when she arrived the gang then attacked her again.

Heat magazine was later to claim that the row had in fact been over a man, but whatever the truth, it was a vicious, cowardly beating. Yet, with that Essex grafting mentality, the sisters were back filming within two days, appearing on *TOWIE* in dark glasses to cover their bruises.

Despite all this adversity, the ending of series three was a triumph. Tongue in cheek, Rob Leigh in the *Daily Mirror* described it as '*TOWIE* raising its game and, frankly, getting a wee bit Shakespearean in scope...' It had the usual humour. Gemma probably assumed carbon footprint was a new footwear brand as she declared that no one in Essex travels on a bus because 'it's embarrassing'. Joey Essex thought that Guy Fawkes died on the cross and that the Queen lived in the Houses of Parliament.

But as ever it was the moments where it veered from scripted naffness to genuine emotion that the viewers loved. When Lucy took to the stage to announce that she had made a terrible mistake and woken up round at Mark's house, in an act of public humiliation to win back sulking hunk Mario, it was car crash TV, but also genuinely affecting. Nor could you imagine a scriptwriter coming up with the very Essex dialogue of Lauren and Sam with its epic 'F**k off!' and 'F**king w***er!' denouement.

Meanwhile, Mark was out-Marked by the steely Sam, who with admirable detachment coolly dumped him after the row with Lauren. Arg was finally reassured by Lydia that she loved him as he was, a big man who's out of condition and with what Tweeting footballer Joey Barton unkindly termed 'Stonehenge teeth'. And Mark was going off to do something by himself away from Essex (surely not in Australia?), getting all *Brokeback Mountain* again in a farewell scene of mutual blubbing and hugging with Arg.

As the *TOWIE* credits ran, Mark looked tearful and misunderstood before shuffling off like James Dean as a rebel with a spray tan. On *I'm a Celebrity ... Get Me Out of Here!* he was to discover temptations in the pool with an Australian model called Emily, along with a bush-tucker trial with Freddie Starr eating turkey testicles, something even Arg wouldn't touch.

A year and a half before, Mark, Amy, Arg, Kirk, Lauren, Sam, Joey and the rest had been unknown. Now they were proper C-list celebs, reem players in the celebrity jungle. Three further series followed, with the original stars replaced by new young chancers like Ricky Rayment and 'Little' Chris Drake. The celebrity magazines were still enthralled in August 2012 when Arg ended up dating Gemma Collins; they appeared on the front cover of *Heat* with the subtle headline, 'The best sex I've ever had.' All in all, a right result, as they say in Essex.

2

ESSEX HUMOUR

Why has God's county spawned so many come- dians? Just a cursory roll call gives us, among others, Russell Brand, Phill Jupitus, Lee Evans, Alan Davies, Russell Kane, Rik Mayall, Griff Rhys-Jones, Phil Cornwell and Dudley Moore.

Then there's the caustic but funny wannabe taxi driver columnist Richard Littlejohn (born in Ilford and still thought of as a bit left wing in some parts of Essex), the onstage banter of Billy Bragg, the comic rhymes of Ian Dury, the saucy banter of Jamie Oliver and the 'you doughnut!' double act of *TOWIE*'s Mark and Arg, a sort of Laurel and Hardy of the Chigwell circuit.

How did this sense of humour arise? Is it from the old East End wit, the spirit of the Blitz, or the fact that Essex is so naff you have to larf?

For the comic, Essex is a deep mine of potential mate- rial. Much of it is to do with the exiled East Enders' attitude to class. The old East Londoners have never quite got the idea that less is more. There's none of the upper classes' understated attitude to wealth and mistrust of vulgarity. Essex Man has acquired money quickly and wants to flaunt it; hence the plethora of electronic gates around Billericay, the flash motors, the mock Tudor palaces, the dark brown bay windows, the fireplace shops that dominated the A13 in the 1990s, and Mark Wright's £200,000 Mercedes purchased after the success of *TOWIE*.

There's something inherently comic about notions of class in the Thames gateway. Back in 2005, Phill Jupitus, still a resident of Leigh-on-Sea, told me:

> That Thames corridor always having been industrially based, it's constantly changing and now they're putting leisure parks on it. They put in four restaurants, a multiplex cinema, two Burger Kings, a Pizza Hut and a restaurant serving genuine Mexican cuisine called Chi Chis. It's not genuine Mexican cuisine, you're off the A13 in a Nissen hut!

The Fenchurch Street line used by so many Essex boys and girls is another source of Jupitus material. He still uses it to travel into his management's offices in north London. Despite being seen on *Never Mind the Buzzcocks* every Friday night, Jupitus can travel on public transport without being hassled.

> No one ever speaks to me. It's the advantage of the British psyche. If I travel in the day people talk to me and that's fine. But on commuter trains no one dares talk to you, as they're more worried about what the other commuters

will think. So it's a really good way of travelling in, I love it.

I like doing interviews for free papers because I remember picking up things like *Midweek* at Fenchurch Street when I was working as a bank messenger. I always dreamed of the day that I'd be on the cover. I thought 'you'll have arrived when the women at the bottom of the escalators at Fenchurch Street are holding your face!'

It's typical of Jupitus's unassuming persona that he has no plans to leave Essex:

The furthest I've lived from the A13 is Bow. If my life takes the A13 route I'll die at Shoeburyness. In fact, I should be shot out of the gun at the artillery ranges. My ashes put in a cannon and shot out across Shoebury Flats. The Essex equivalent of the Viking funeral, my ashes on a burning Ford Cortina on Pitsea Marsh...

As for Essex Girl jokes, Jupitus said in *The Independent*:

I've got a very dim opinion of them. It was just part of a pervasive misogyny in the City in the 1980s. They are just repackaged blonde jokes. My mum's from Essex as well and I know for a fact that she would put her chips down before proceeding with any kind of loving.

Like most residents, Jupitus is a little schizophrenic in his relationship with comic Estuary Essex and Constable country in the north of the county, on the border with

Suffolk. 'I do like that untouched, wasteland feel of things in Essex,' he tells me. 'When you drive north of Braintree to Frinton and Clacton there's a feeling that it could be post-nuclear but it would never change, that flat dull seaward side of Essex.'

Deep down the Essex comic knows that the industrial side of his county is a little naff – and there's an uneasy sense of being an outsider when success arrives. Dr Feelgood thought of themselves as being like bank robbers driving down the A12 to London every time they left Canvey Island to do a gig. And there's a lovely moment in the film *Oil City Confidential* when Wilko describes driving through New York in a limo and thinking, 'I'm from Canvey Island, I shouldn't be here!'

Barking's Billy Bragg still encores with 'A13 Trunk Road to the Sea' (often with his old Essex mate Wiggy on guitar). There was something inherently funny in hearing Chuck Berry's 'Route 66' rewritten as an Essex road trip: 'Now if you ever have to go to Shoeburyness…' Meanwhile, Bragg's 1991 video for hit single 'Sexuality' was something of an Essex in-joke fest, with the ideas coming from Phill Jupitus, then working for Go! Discs, who makes a brief all-dancing cameo alongside Kirsty MacColl on backing vocals. Bragg appears on the video holding a sign with the word 'uality' over an Essex border sign on the A13 and is also filmed driving a Robin Reliant with furry dice above the dashboard and Billy and Shirley on the sunstrip.

In December 2011 Billy Bragg, now fifty-four, played live at The Forum. That Essex banter was still there. He couldn't have survived as a left-wing balladeer through the post-Thatcher years if it wasn't for lacing his ideology with the sharpness of a stand-up comedian. On 'Greetings to the New Brunette' Bragg sang the line 'How can you lie there and think of England when you don't even know who's in the team?' before exclaiming, 'Bobby Zamora!!?'

Billy advised us to buy his CD because 'otherwise I'll have to do the John Lewis advert next year' and also explained that you now hold up iPhones with a lighter app rather than a lighter. He dedicated the magical 'St Swithin's Day' to 'all the David Nicholls fans' (the song partly inspired Nicholls' novel *One Day*) but joked that the song wasn't on the film soundtrack 'because of the blatant wanking reference in the second verse'. He wound up his set by telling us 'the revolution is just a tea towel away' in a self-mocking reference to the Billy Bragg tea towels on sale in the foyer.

Even the harsher side of uncultured, money-obsessed Essex Man stereotype can be turned into comedy. Another Southend resident, Russell Kane, won the 2010 Edinburgh Comedy Award with Essex-inspired material. Kane is a Middlesex University graduate but still seeks inspiration from his home county. In his act he describes his cockney dad who has 'neck muscles so strong he can climb stairs with them' and who thinks all Penguin Classics readers are gay and would tell Russell he's proud of him, but he's off to his shed instead. Kane's *Fakespeare* was Shakespeare set in Essex, where King Nigellio was a banker contemplating suicide after the credit crunch, along with his mistress, Donna from 'Billericoy'.

Even the *TOWIE* stars get what Essex wit is about. There's a great moment where Amy Childs is giving Kirk Norcross a verbal lashing over his flirtations with another babe. After a long diatribe she flounces off and as she leaves Kirk quips, 'I suppose a kiss is out of the question?'

Russell Brand is a master of Essexual humour. He has managed to turn a dysfunctional childhood into comedy gold, recalling his dad 'diddling birds' in his Brentwood flat and babysitters who masturbate in his bathroom. In fact, Brand's dad Ron appears to be Essex Man personified. In *My Booky Wook* Russell tells us about Ron's get-loaded-quick schemes on a Romford market stall selling laser prints, double glazing and water filters. In his own mythology, Brand becomes a heterosexual Oscar Wilde figure among the Essex marshes.

Essex people can never take themselves as seriously as they do in, say, the United States. In 2007 Brand told the *Thurrock Gazette* of his time in a US sex addiction clinic:

> I've never felt more English in my life than when I was sat in that American cliché swap shop. They'd say, 'I hear your pain, it's good that you shared.' And I'd be thinking, Oh do f*** off. For Christ's sake, someone put *EastEnders* on the telly and get me a glass of gin and a toasted crumpet.

For many talented people from Essex, it's given them the incentive to escape. As Brand explains in *My Booky Wook*, 'In Grays I didn't possess anything people wanted. I was trying to spend a fantasy currency from an irrelevant island.' Once at the Italia Conti school, Brand quickly dates a black student called Kelle, because being from 'white man's last stand' Grays, he finds the chance of going out with someone black incredibly exciting. When Kelle confronts him about this in the ladies toilet and dumps him he ends with a Kirk Norcross-style quip: 'Kelle, no! Kelle, could you find out if Louise is free later? Also find out if she's got any ethnic blood in her!'

In *Gavin and Stacey* there's yet more comedy to be had from the unsophisticated, but at heart noble, behaviour of James Corden's Smithy. And Essex juxtaposes nicely with its Celtic counterpart of Barry's Island (as Pam calls it) in South Wales.

Essex humour also has its roots in the East End cockney – a fast innovative language with colourful rhyming slang ideal for banter. The slow drawl of an accent from, say, Lancashire, might result in a dry wit. But cockney is better suited to motormouth piss-taking and cheeky wisecracks.

East End humour was a response to often desperate times. The worst industries were situated in the East where the prevailing winds took the nasty niffs out to sea. Many ancestors of now prosperous Essex residents grew up in severe poverty. It was a land of gasworks, sugar, glue and match factories and huge explosions in Silverton when things went wrong. Life on the docks was rough and employment prospects tenuous. The Great Depression of the 1930s hit hard and the Blitz and the Luftwaffe decimated much of the area in the Second World War.

Some of the roots of that humour can be found at the spiritual home of many Essex men and women, West Ham United FC. The Chicken Run at Upton Park was renowned for its humour and shouts of 'Come on, Hammers, really pep it up and make it mediocre!' West Ham fans were among the first to sing a club song in the 1920s. There was an element of irony, of awareness of life's imperfection in the fans' adoption of 'I'm Forever Blowing Bubbles' and perhaps that was an early example of what was to become Essex wit. Tough dockers sang of fortune always hiding, dreams dying and blowing pretty bubbles in the air that were invariably popped.

In *West Ham United*, Charles Korr comments:

> East London has been the place for dreamers even if few dreams come true. One way of coping with life was to develop a sense of humour tinged with a dose of irony. That was the way to change reality without withdrawing from it. Players and journalists who came to see West Ham always remembered the humour of the crowd as its most distinctive feature. Even at the worst times, maybe especially then, someone would see the humour or absurdity of what was happening. *Bubbles* was just one example of that approach to life.

Another distinctive form of humour is the attitude to road signs. Stanford-le-Hope is frequently renamed 'Stanford-No-Hope' and somebody has risked their limbs crossing the A13 to change the name of Aveley to just plain 'Weirdsville'. Basildon has given itself a Hollywood-style sign on the A13 roundabout, only to be parodied by Benfleet.

The poverty of the East End; the cockney dialect; the spectacle of the working class trying to get cultured through in-your-face consumerism; the sheer amount of comic material available in Estuary Essex. These factors have all combined to put Essex at the centre of the comedy map.

Or maybe it's just that no one in Essex takes themselves too seriously – it's a place that ridicules pomposity. In LA they'd be in therapy. But in Essex the likes of Russell Brand can turn heroin addiction, alcoholism and worse into comedy. Top of the comedy league? Essex is having a laugh.

3

THE BONDS OF BASILDON

'It's hardly Hollywood! Basildon gets its own sign to welcome drivers to the wonders of … er … Essex,' read the *Daily Mail* headline above a picture of the roundabout with Hollywood-style letters spelling out the legend: BASILDON. *The Sun* ran the story – 'New Town's Sign Like LA Icon – It's Hollywood … near Brentwood' – over a picture of the roundabout, the white letters standing on grass before a rather apologetic cluster of poplar trees.

In March 2010 the media had huge fun with Basildon's Hollywood roundabout on the A127, which the *Mail* claimed had cost £90,000. It would be illuminated at night too, though this was delayed for several months by road works. The story was all the more amusing because the white letters were only 5 ft high, compared to the giant 45 ft letters in Hollywood.

The *Daily Mail* trawled the message boards and quoted Laindon resident Karen James: 'They may as well have just erected a massive white stiletto for all the good that sign's going to do us.' Another person commented,

'Top marks to the council for managing to come up with something to make Basildon look even more kitsch than it already is.' Richard from Rochford wrote on the *Mail*'s website, 'Good idea as it helps identify where Basildon begins so that we can avoid going to the hell-hole!'

In some ways that sign appeared to be an extension of Essex humour – the county was prepared to laugh at itself, though the letters had a serious point too. Deputy council leader Steve Horgan explained to *The Sun*: 'Some of the local press seem to think it's a bit of a laugh, but it's not, it's deadly serious. The problem is our local geography makes it possible to zip through without realising you've just gone to one of the largest employment areas in the country.'

The *Mail* described Basildon as the spiritual heartland of Essex Girl, Essex Man and White Van Man and mentioned the spoof 2007 email declaring that Basildon had been decimated by an earthquake. An urgent appeal was put out for Burberry baseball caps and shell suits.

Almost inevitably, Basildon makes an appearance on the Chavtowns website. The anonymous nominator writes:

In the cold light of day, you might consider braving the race track of Basildon's roads and taking a tour into the chavvy suburbs. It is here that you may encounter some of the ugliest social housing this side of the Bronx, with many identikit flat-roofed, rabbit hutch council houses and Soviet-style flat blocks.

Interestingly, though, even amid the Stalinist insults, the Chavtowns writer does point to some kind-heartedness and warmth among the locals.

There's much more to the history of Basildon than the chavtown cliché. From the 1900s Basildon had developed as a series of ad hoc plotlands. These plots were sold by developers – often over a drink or seven – to East Enders wanting to escape to the countryside. Some houses were made of recycled old junk, others of brick, but most were lacking basic amenities such as water, gas, electricity and roads. Concerned by the haphazard development and lack of amenities Billericay Council and Essex County Council asked the government to designate Basildon as a new town in the 1940s.

Basildon was officially named a new town in 1949 under the New Towns Act. It was to be primarily an East End overspill town for those displaced by the bombing of the Second World War. The first house was built in 1951 and a lot of idealism went into the planning of Basildon, with hopes of creating a socialist utopia for the displaced working classes, offering them good housing, parks and leisure facilities.

Basildon was later to develop a place in the national political consciousness as the key seat in general elections, backing the winning party in every general election since 1974. Mrs Thatcher knew that if working-class Basildon went Conservative in 1979 then the Tories would win the election; similarly, Tony Blair knew he had to win it back in 1997. Indeed, watching Billy Bragg at the Mean Fiddler on election night in 1997, there were huge cheers from his audience when Bragg announced early in the set that Basildon had fallen to New Labour. The general election was in the bag.

Some of the political changes in the working class filtered through to David Eldridge's excellent play *In Basildon*, performed at the Royal Court Theatre in 2012. Set around a family funeral, it managed to avoid patronising its subjects while dealing with topics such as ambitious Basildon folk buying council houses, voting for Maggie Thatcher and starting their own businesses. As a bonus it also contained numerous West Ham United references and a chorus of 'I'm Forever Blowing Bubbles'. Seeing a play about Basildon being enjoyed by theatre-goers in Sloane Square certainly emphasised the cultural resonance of Basildon.

As a piece of PR the 'Basilwood' sign achieved an admirable number of column inches, even though the *Daily Mail* continued, 'To add to the derision, the sign is in a spot beside a leisure park already nicknamed "Bas Vegas" by locals because the tacky strip of fast food restaurants, nightclubs, and cheap hotels reminds them (vaguely) of the Nevada gamblers' paradise.' Its Wikipedia entry reads: 'The Festival Leisure Park is colloquially known as "Bas Vegas", and is a well-known trouble spot, especially on Friday and Saturday nights, usually fuelled by alcohol.'

The Chavtowns website writes of a deserted town centre, the locals preferring Bas Vegas:

It is the place to come if you want to encounter boy racers doing wheelies in the car park, moody and aggressive bouncers, and mouthy Barbie-doll Essex girls walking around in their underwear on their way to Time and Envy, or whatever it's now called. Like the town itself, it's completely and utterly artificial and is a testament to the void in our society and is worth visiting purely for its anthropological interest (and the Chinese restaurant there).

Indeed Festival Leisure Park is so notorious that it has spawned its own Bas Vegas spoof website. Written by one Bas Vegas, it contains snippets of news taken from local papers that endorse the downtown Bas Vegas image. Sample stories include: 'Bouncers attack left me with broken foot' (this incident occurred while queuing for the memorably named Liquid and Envy nightclub at the Festival Leisure Park); 'Man returns home to find intruder watching TV'; 'Move to keep drunks out of town centre'; 'Man charged after off-road chase'; 'Plague of rats at Wickford station'; and 'Thieves steal fifty fish from garden'. The site also sells Bas Vegas souvenir mugs and T-shirts.

One very Essex response to the Basildon sign came from Jerry Watson, a hairdresser in Benfleet, who after a few drinks erected his own BENFLEET sign made out of hardboard and wooden rods, at a cost of £25 rather than £90,000. 'Everyone was talking about what a waste of money the new Basildon sign was. I thought, let's make one for Benfleet to take the Michael. I spent most of Wednesday sorting and cutting out the letters and the girls from the hairdressers painted them white,' Watson told the *Daily Mail*. 'We had a right laugh. We haven't got a

Bas Vegas but we've got a few decent pubs and an industrial estate. Hopefully this will put us on the map too!'

In August 2010 style expert Laurence Llewellyn-Bowen arrived in Basildon to record his TV show *House Gift*. He told the *Basildon Echo*, 'I love the sign – it's very shiny, very sexy, very elegant and very discreet. It's tailored, just like Basildon itself.' *Come Dine with Me* also visited and featured Basildon's sign of the times.

Indeed, by February 2012 the Bas Vegas locals appeared to have mellowed in their attitude. After heavy snowfall the roundabout sign was augmented by a giant snow penis, which was a very Basildonian form of acceptance.

Something else good arose from that Hollywood sign. Denise Van Outen, soon to provide the narration for *TOWIE*, was quick to defend Basildon in *The Sun*. 'I'd take Basildon over Hollywood any day,' declared Denise, who had stayed in an apartment overlooking the real Hollywood sign. She contrasted LA's insincerity and yes men with the honesty of Basildon's residents who tell it like it is:

> Basildon may be the butt of a few jokes but at least it's real. In LA everything is fake, including the noses and wrinkle-free faces. I think our Stateside counterparts could learn a lot from our town and its residents. We don't take ourselves too seriously and like a laugh – even if it is at our expense.

She also mentioned how her parents had moved out from the old East End and that, like them, most residents had a really strong work ethic. She was sure this was why Basildon had so many showbiz success stories as its people 'believe in working hard and we can be tough when it counts'.

Another interesting point she made was that in the 1980s Basildon was in fact a new town full of creativity. It spawned synth-rockers Depeche Mode and Alison Moyet and was quite a cool place before the Essex Girl jokes and white stiletto associations. Indeed, Basildon features heavily in *Just Can't Get Enough*, the book about Depeche Mode by *NME* journalist Simon Spence. It's commonly forgotten in the UK that Depeche Mode were huge in the US and sold 100 million records.

The band were never part of the London scene, they were always on the last train back to Basildon according to Spence. He interviews many of their early acquaintances, including the greengrocer at Basildon bus station where Dave Gahan worked, students at Southend College, where he qualified as a window dresser, and, this being Basildon, the magistrates who dealt with him at the juvenile court. But it's the ambience of the new town where anything is possible that Spence feels was crucial to their futuristic sound:

> Like the music of Depeche Mode, Basildon was all about innovation, modernism, and progress, and free of grime and ugliness. The future was being reborn, and these four young men were lab rats in a truly alien landscape. It was no surprise that when they first made it out of Basildon, the London music press described the group as 'half-Martian'.

Basildon might seem an unlikely setting for spiritual angst, but Spence also cites St Paul's Methodist Church in Basildon as influential on the young Mode, resulting in later songs such as 'Personal Jesus'. Presumably their comment on materialism in the excellent 'Everything Counts' was more influenced by Basildon market.

So is Basildon the home of futurist music, a new town idyll for the displaced working classes of the East End or Stalinist chavtown? It's time to find out.

Even though I grew up just a few miles from Basildon in Great Warley, I realise I've never explored the town centre. My upwardly mobile parents would clearly rather have voted Labour than be seen in an East End overspill new town. Their orbit was Brentwood, Shenfield, Billericay, Chelmsford, but never Basildon. Yes, I sometimes drove my parents' van down the A127 to visit the O'Brien sisters in Laindon, who went to school in upmarket Shenfield, but that was as close as it got.

Arriving at the station, the first thing you see is the Beehive pub. The pub is surprisingly busy on a Friday afternoon and there's a hubbub of animated conversations. There's a map of the town centre and someone has written 'cunt's' on it. I'm not sure whether to criticise their punctuation or admire their ambition in at least using an apostrophe.

I head across the Southern Way to the nearby market stalls. The market greets you with an advert for Dave's Tattoo studio. It has several other Essex signature features, such as a pie and mash shop, a greasy spoon café with Polish waitresses, a shop selling blinds and a nail and waxing salon by the loos.

Three women cheerfully use the F word a lot by the newsagents as they say, 'Daniel don't like him. Darren don't like him…' A woman shouts into her mobile 'Inbox me!'

Ah, a portrait of the Kray brothers? I'm standing before a stall selling framed pictures of *The Sopranos*, various heavyweight champions of the world, Marlon Brando as *The Godfather* and 'notorious East End gangsters' Reggie and Ronnie Kray. In front of the Kray pictures the same stall has, without irony, a collection of memorial ash caskets.

It must be a bit of a conversation stopper having a framed portrait of Reggie and Ronnie on the wall at dinner parties. Or maybe not – some people probably think the brothers knew how to get things done and would have nailed those hoodies to the floor, in the style of *Monty Python's* Doug and Dinsdale Piranha. Maybe you could have themed evenings with cups of tea, suits, Jack 'The Hat' McVitie's biscuits and everyone's dear old mum present.

In addition to the Krays portraits stall there's a used bookstall that sells vintage razzle mags. Do the citizens of Basildon really want old editions of *Mayfair*, *Club* and *Penthouse*? It seems so.

Inside the market toilets there are four posters for Katz Gentleman's Club above the urinals. 'Elegance in Essex, purr-fect for that stag night,' reads the strapline above photos of neon-lit stages and women in their underwear.

The posters are directly above the urinals so the gentlemen of Basildon are reading about Katz, while pointing Percy at the porcelain and holding their members in hand. Now that's what I call direct marketing.

Later, after a Google search when my wife is out of the room, I discover a YouTube video of a gymnastic girl called Drew at Katz. She's pole-dancing to 'Breath' by Braintree's very own superstars The Prodigy. One of the comments reads, 'It ain't that good guys. I was there last night and it's nothing like this. The dancers all look bored and like they'd rather be somewhere else, the drinks are a million pounds each and you have the feeling you are going to be thrown out any second.'

Another Basildon local confides, with a typical eye for a bargain, 'Never knew this was local to me. We always go to Secrets in St Katharine's Dock. Mind you we usually get a good discount for free entry to go in and I just tried the £5 voucher, which doesn't work, which is a shame.'

While admiring the Essex elegance of Katz in the gents I overhear an extraordinary conversation coming from the cubicles behind me. 'Sounds like you're desperate for a shit, mate!' declares a disembodied voice. 'You can't exactly say you ain't, you're doing the same, you know what I mean?' says a voice from the adjoining cubicle. 'Now look, I ain't going to have a conversation with your sort now am I, know what I mean, a bloke I've never met in the shithouse…'

Is this good old East End spirit of the Blitz friendliness? There can't be many towns where they exchange jolly banter in the cubicles of the public loos. Still, even so, I hastily retreat before the turd conversationalists emerge.

There's a bus station with the obligatory Wimpy bar and traditional fish and chip shop, and beyond this the more modern Eastgate shopping centre full of airy white space, chains like Debenhams, WH Smith and Starbucks and Hotshots barbers offering head shaves with a cut-throat razor for £8.

From the west end of the market place I walk through the pedestrianised malls towards St Martin's Square. Past the Westgate Shopping Park and busy Wetherspoons pub The Moon on the Square there's a closing-down sale at a fancy-dress shop called Party Party – most of the outfits in the window seem to involve fishnets and miniskirts.

St Martin's Square is really rather stylish. It's wide and spacious and reminds me a little of some French architecture in Montpellier. Here lies the jewel in Basildon's barnet – the Towngate Theatre is a venue offering Roy Chubby Brown, The Manfreds, The Stylistics, wrestling and a One Night in Vegas Christmas Party.

Inside the council offices the receptionist has no maps of Basildon, but can confirm the whereabouts of the Hollywood-style Basildon sign on the roundabout: 'It's down Asda way, or you could take the 151 bus if you don't mind going round the houses.' I pick up a copy of *Borough News* and the lead story is the council's attempted eviction of the Dale Farm travellers. On page five is a picture of Councillor Frank Tomlin declaring, 'We are committed to ensuring people can enjoy the town centre.' He's holding a new dispersal order that has come into force. It gives the police powers to disperse two or more people indulging in antisocial behaviour in the whole of the town centre.

I'm still friends with Frank's daughter Sarah, who now lives in Kent but is still called Shazza by her friends because of her Essex roots. Frank was an active Tory councillor in Billericay when we were both at Shenfield School in the 1970s. Sarah and her brothers gave him a fearful ribbing over former Billericay MP Harvey Proctor's antics. So you have to admire Frank's perseverance at local politics. He must be pushing eighty, but is indefatigable in his desire to stamp out antisocial behaviour in Essex.

Back to St Martin's Square, and there's a very strange artwork called the Millennium Tower. It's a sort of glass rocket to nowhere. Beyond this, across the A1321, is the police station and the Crown and County Magistrates' Courts. Despite all this law and order there's a solitary antisocial drinker yet to be dispersed staggering through the square.

Beyond the council offices and theatre is the rather elegant expanse of Gloucester Park with landscaped lakes and plenty of cycle tracks. The town was designed to separate traffic and cyclists and you see a lot of people cycling home from work along the tracks and subways. The park also contains the Olympic Sporting Village, a sports complex used by 87,000 Basildonians a month and where some Olympic athletes trained in 2012.

The rest of the town centre is full of box-like buildings, and shops such as Costa in the middle of the wide pedestrian malls. It's all a bit clone town, with shops like WH Smith, Marks & Spencer, Toni & Guy and Primark. But it does appear to be quite well loved by its residents. There's no sign of graffiti or vandalism anywhere.

Brooke House is an office tower block on stilts that adds a futuristic touch to Town Square. There's another party shop here and another nail salon, but a number of empty shops too. The *Basildon Echo* bemoans, 'Crisis of our Town Centre Shops: Furniture store is latest casualty. Leaving over thirty empty premises.'

Retreating from the emptiness on the edge of Basildon town centre I head back towards the station. A man drives up to the Beehive pub in a Mondeo with 'Hanging Around' by The Stranglers blaring out of the speakers. There are a lot of people just hanging around in the pub too, but it's a mood of unaffected enjoyment.

There's a geezer in a Spurs top at the bar explaining some business venture – 'I tell yer, me mate's got the money for it!' I take my pint of London Pride and sit on a rickety wooden table outside. Two women join me with a bottle of wine to share, before finding a less wobbly seat. I read the *Basildon Echo*'s letters page, most of which are lambasting the Dale Farm travellers. 'If I broke the planning laws I'd be evicted,' is the main theme. One thing Essex Man hates is the idea that anyone might get one over on him.

The snippets of conversations I'm catching sound like a club mix of Essex banter: 'All right darling ... You get pissed out of yer 'ead ... Always a pleasure ... I see yer old man down 'ere ... You'll be here 'til Christmas ...

Del, you coming for a Chinese?' And then someone starts singing the old Monkees theme tune: 'Here he comes walking down the street...' It's happy, rather than anti-social hour.

Behind me a group of men are having an animated conversation about razzle mags. They are clearly connoisseurs of porn. 'You gotta pay cash, he don't take cards. He's got *Playboy*, *Penthouse* and *Mayfair*, but I prefer *Razzle*. With *Razzle* it only had three or four fit birds in it, but they used to last a bit longer, you know what I mean?' Clearly Basildon puts the sex into Essex.

Leaving the earthy environs of the Beehive, I take a taxi to Bas Vegas, the infamous Festival Leisure Park. The driver agrees to show me the back of the roundabout where the Hollywood sign is, though to view it properly he says I need to approach from the Brentwood side of the A127. I mention the Benfleet spoof sign to him.

'The other year they nicked the 'A' out of the Basildon sign and put it up down here in the town centre,' he reveals with a hearty laugh. 'You get used to the sign. The celebrities like it and if I'm giving directions I always say, "Turn off at the junction where the Basildon sign is," so it's worked, hasn't it?'

We glide round a roundabout and down the A176. My driver is, like most cabbies in Essex, happy to talk. 'Course, all that Hollywood thing, it came about because of us cab drivers. We christened the festival park Bas Vegas as it was all lit up at night with the nightclubs and that and it stuck!'

I ask him if Bas Vegas is really like Las Vegas. 'Well they

did want to put a casino in but they ain't got planning permission. It's got four nightclubs that all join up into one huge nightclub. It's OK for us because it contains it all into one area. The police like it because they have a control and contain situation.'

The taxi driver goes on to describe Bas Vegas in terms once reserved for Belfast or Beirut.

'There's a lot of security. What a lot of these stupid pissheads don't understand on a Friday and Saturday night is that security have been given the power of zero tolerance. If you cause an affray you get thrown out, it's as simple as that. Whether or not you're actually causing real trouble is irrelevant. If you're starting to get a bit lairy and they think it might kick off they can throw you out of the club. And once you've been thrown out security ain't gonna fuck around, they'll phone the police. You might as well go home, mate.'

So why are the clubs all a couple of miles out of town by the A127?

'The leisure park was always there; initially it was a gym and a hotel,' he explains. 'We had a lot of trouble in nightclubs in the town centre. There was the famous case of Leah Betts [she died after taking an ecstasy tablet]. That was in the club where the snooker hall is now. After that the council decided to keep it in a contained situation rather than have people running around the town centre where you can go almost anywhere. There's nowhere to go if you try running away in Bas Vegas, the police are gonna find you.'

We arrive at what appears to be a large rectangular car

park surrounded by franchises. This is Bas Vegas. Having paid my £8.20 cab fare as we stop by the Empire cinema, I wonder if the visitor should be darting for cover after the cabbie's description. But thankfully it's still light and there are only cinemagoers and a few diners at Nando's around.

Here are the four nightclubs with logos on a concrete block. There's Envy, New York, JJs and Liquid. 'Free entry before 11,' reads a poster. 'Why pub it when you can club it for free?'

Bas Vegas contains more Americana than in the whole of the United States, including the Hollywood Bowl bowling club, Frankie & Benny's New York International Restaurant, McDonald's and the Chicago Rock Café. To this mix can be added Villagio restaurant, Fitness First, Chiquito Mexican restaurant and bar, the Sky Sports Bar, Pizza Hut, Pizza Express, TGI Friday's, the Toby Carvery and Harvester pub and grill. There's also a Travelodge offering rooms from £19, a Premier Inn and Holiday Inn. A cheap holiday in Bas Vegas off the A127? It seems so, though Bear Grylls has baulked at the opportunity so far, citing a previous engagement jumping across 100 ft ravines.

I buy a Costa coffee in Harry's Kitchen ('from California to New York') at the Hollywood Bowl, accompanied by the sound of ten pin bowling, amusement arcade bleeps and piped music. Through the Empire Cinema and past the curry restaurant there are doors outside to a fenced-off lake with a small island in the middle. Here there's a lane called Waterfront Walk that heads towards the

A127 Arterial Road. Before the clubbers arrive and the contained zone kicks in, I walk off past the Premier Inn in pursuit of the Basilwood sign on the roundabout.

On the A127 there's a hot tub clearance sale at the Summerhill Garden Centre. Nobody ever walks along the Arterial Road. The cycle track offers this solitary beleaguered pedestrian some defence against the incessant roar of speeding motors and the toxic combination of asphalt and exhaust particulates. It's a lonely walk for a mile and a half past industrial estates, litter-strewn woodland and the Upminster Panel Craft Crash Repair Centre. It feels like I'm in an Essex dystopian movie.

But the roundabout edges closer. Here are the Basildon exit signs and finally a slip road takes me to a grass pyramid topped by trees. And there it is – the fabled Basilwood sign. I clamber up the grassy knoll and take some photos. The letters are about the size of a person, fronted with shiny white material. Though this being Basildon there's a notice on the back of the letters reading, 'This sign is made of stainless steel of limited resale value.' Does the real Hollywood sign have a similar warning?

It's only a tenth of the size of the real sign in America, but in my journey around Essex it's surely a *Titanic* moment worthy of Hollywood drama. I'm marooned on an island in a sea of traffic heading down dual carriageways. If the Basildon equivalent of Kate Winslet was here it might be tempting to hold her Leonardo DiCaprio-style and declare, 'I'm flying ... I'm the king of the A127!'

4

BRENTWOOD: THE WORST ADDRESS IN ENGLAND – OR THE BEST?

Back in my teen years Brentwood was suburban and safe, just a satellite of London, to quote a Sex Pistols B-side. In reality, it was probably quite a nice place to grow up. Greenish, safe, and free of knife crime. My lack of therapy, rebirthing and autobiographical misery memoirs must prove something. And now I'm back, the return of the native in search of the only way in Brentwood.

Thanks to *The Only Way Is Essex*, Brentwood is Britain's most unlikely tourist mecca. Following the huge success of *TOWIE* the town attracts stag parties, hen nights and reality TV tourists from all over Britain. The whole world now knows of Sugar Hut and Minnies boutique and every weekend good old Brentwood is full of northerners shouting, 'Awoight, mate!'

It's bleeding famous, innit; though some would say infamous. In 2010, after *TOWIE* had stormed the celebrity world in a shower of vajazzle crystals, the *Sunday*

Telegraph featured the word Brentwood in Hollywood-style lettering accompanied by the question: 'The worst address in England?'

It was never like this when I was growing up there. Brentwood? Trendy? 'Brentwood's burning!' we used to sing in 1977, parodying 'London's Burning' by The Clash. 'Brentwood's burning with boredom now, Brentwood's burning dial 999!' Stranded between sixth form and university, with spiky hair, Oxfam jackets and straight jeans, my punk gang restlessly played black vinyl in post-pub flats above shops. Hippies skinned up joints on album covers and we waited for something, anything, to happen. Brentwood was an anagram of Bored Town pointed out the chairman of the bored.

Brentwood has a long history of being average. Daniel Defoe wrote in *A Tour Through the Whole Island of Great Britain* (1724–26): 'Brent-Wood and Ingatestone and even Chelmsford itself, have very little to be said of them, but that they are large through fare towns, full of good inns. And chiefly maintained by the excessive multitude of carriers and passengers which are constantly passing this way to London.'

The name Brentwood is a corruption of Burnt Wood, suggesting it was an area of forest cleared for settlement. My wife, an environmentalist, would probably say it was typical. I come from a region of Essex that actively celebrates deforestation. If we'd got hold of the Amazonian rainforest it would be full of commuters, beauty salons and tandooris by now.

The station hasn't changed much, apart from a

dedicated waiting room for taxis. You never seem to find any staff here. Commuters trudge up the steps to the exit; express trains to Colchester thunder through and shake the platforms.

As a teenager I'd heard a rumour that Paul Simon wrote 'Homeward Bound' while sitting at Brentwood station. It was easy to imagine him in the moribund waiting room writing lines about shades of mediocrity. But in the internet age it's possible to verify such assertions, and the truth is that Simon penned 'Homeward Bound' in either Ditton or Halebank stations in Widnes, while waiting for a train back to Brentwood, where he was living with his girlfriend. Yes, it was Brentwood that made him get all poetic.

He made his UK debut at the Railway Inn Folk Club in Brentwood in 1964 and met Kathy Chitty there, the inspiration for 'Kathy's Song' and 'America'. She was a seventeen-year-old Essex girl on the door selling tickets to men in cord jackets. They dated for two years until Paul returned to the US. Kathy now lives in Wales and maintains a diplomatic sound of silence on all Simon-related subjects. Although we can picture her as a slightly folksier version of Amy Childs.

Here's another change. The Amstrad office in Kings Road was taken over by Sky a year or so ago. There was always something amusing about Lord Sugar and Amstrad being here. If Simon had been homeward bound to Brentwood in the new millennium, he'd have walked out of the station, trudged 100 metres up Kings Road and come to the Amstrad headquarters. You wonder what Lord Sugar would have made of the wandering folk troubadour...

'Paul, shut up a minute will yer, you're doing my head in! You took a bloody trip to Widnes to play a gig and all you could do is whinge about yer bleeding girlfriend Kaffy. No sales figures, just lyrics scrawled on a British Rail timetable. I'm not having that. Shut up, I am talking! OK, you can knock out a decent tune, but you ain't doing it for me. If I asked you to build me a swimming pool you'd be knocking off every time you saw some leaves that are green turn to brown. With regret, Paul, you're fired!'

Sugar is one of the richest men in the country, the curmudgeonly star of *The Apprentice* and a mate of famous politicians. So placing one of his offices in Brentwood always seemed an act of deliberate perversity. But it was significant. Sugar, a spiritual godfather of Essex, was distancing himself from the City flash boys with their derivatives and hedge funds. Brentwood is Sugar's heartland; the Utopia of exiled East Enders who graft hard and set up nightclubs and steakhouses.

From the station I head up King's Road towards Minnies boutique. Brentwood must have more hair stylists, boutiques, wedding shops and beauty salons per head than any other town in the known universe. Vega Hair Stylists has a sign in the window reading simply, 'TOWIE Haircare'. My short journey to Minnies takes in Beginnings and Matchmaker wedding shops, The Hair Company, John Richards hairdressers, Isabella, French

Quarter, Paula Beauty, Comfort and Joy boutique, Racquel, Angela Mills and Hub Hairdressing.

Then there's the multi-storey car park, a sort of temple to the internal combustion engine and where I used to park my mum's minivan. Once I drove off leaving a newly purchased copy of Elvis Costello's 'This Year's Model' on the roof and never saw it again – a memory of wasted dosh that still traumatises me. Everyone took driving lessons at seventeen. It still feels like I've let the Essex car culture down a little by living a motor-free life in north London.

A couple of hundred yards past the multi-storey is Minnies, in Roper's Yard off Hart Street. It's set in an enclave of beauty shops; next door is Sui Generis, with a board advertising botox, dental filling and teeth whitening for £250.

There are racks of dresses and tops down each side of the shop and a desk at the far end where manager Lynn Amato is sitting behind a pile of black Minnies diaries, embossed with the shop's logo: a golden silhouette of a reclining woman. Lynn's blonde, probably in her forties, and happy to talk.

Is it true that people come from all over the country to visit Minnies?

'Oh yes, we've had Geordies, a load of girls from Lancashire, everywhere really. We've had people drive from Wales for five hours just to come. They buy their outfits here before going to Sugar Hut. Of a weekend we have to stop people coming in because it's too crowded in the shop. We've had Australians in too, because it's on over there. We send our stuff out from the website to that weird place in Wales ... And our new diaries are selling well, have a look at these...'

I'm reminded that shopping in Brentwood is a gentler experience than in London; here people are happy to talk and, as is frequently demonstrated in *TOWIE*, gossip about who's seeing whom. Or what dodgy hack has been pestering them in the shop. Handing over a tenner, I purchase a diary for £8.99 and Lynn handwrites a receipt.

'Why don't you come back at 4.30 as Billie will be in and she can sign it? Sam will be in tomorrow. They Tweet when they're coming in.'

Have there been any funny incidents with the *TOWIE* fans? 'We get funny phone calls. People saying "Shu' up!" or people putting the phone down on us. Sometimes they say, "Are you reem?" If they could see us they might not ask that! What do you mean "no"?'

I assure Lynn it was a slip of the tongue and that she and her sales team are utterly reem.

And where do the *TOWIE* tourists stay? 'They're banged out at the Travelodge and the Premier Inn,' says Lynn. 'Tourism has shot up, they closed the tourist office but they've had to reopen it now!'

'Have you got those pink dresses?' asks Julie, a customer wearing a white coat with black spots ('my Dalmatian coat'). She tells me she's from Yorkshire, but now works at Brentwood Theatre. 'I've never had so many people come to stay with me since *TOWIE*. I've got my mate from Lancashire coming down with her two daughters tonight. You should look at Lucy's new boutique in Ongar Road, and Amy's salon. We're all a bit over Sugar Hut, but we still go there, don't we?'

Fortified by this revelation of a new *TOWIE* outlet, I set off down the high street. Very close to Minnies is Sugar Hut. In my youth it was the White Hart, an old coaching inn selling steak and chips. Now the courtyard is guarded by large black doors, securely bolted against the non-reem residents of Essex. A poster advertises various Sugar Hut nights. In front of the doors is the obligatory chandelier.

Mason's restaurant at Sugar Hut is open though. It's still providing upmarket steak and chips (instead of the glory days of Berni Inns it's now '28-day matured steak'). There are bling chandeliers over the gold and black bar, plus a parquet floor and a golden Hindu God on the wall greeting guests as they walk in.

Further down the high street, in the Oxfam shop, Brentwood's MP Eric Pickles is having a meeting with some Oxfam bigwigs. In his warm Yorkshire accent he congratulates a young man gaining work experience behind the till and tells the Oxfam crew how he's proud the coalition has kept its pledge on overseas aid. As the group of politicos chat, I hear a woman saying, 'This *TOWIE* thing is getting out of hand, people are ashamed to say they're from Essex now.'

Halfway up the high street there's the Thomas à Becket Chapel, founded by the St Osyth monks in 1221. The stone walls and arched doorways of the ruined tower are fairly intact, but gated off from the public, possibly for fear of them being used as a public loo. The wall foundations are not fenced off, which makes the ruin a pleasingly organic part of the modern town. A board reveals a little of the origins of the town: Brentwood grew up as a response to knife crime. After the murder of Thomas Becket in Canterbury, pilgrims on their way to Canterbury found Brentwood a convenient stopping point at the crossroads of the Kent and Colchester to London roads. By the late twelfth century it was a small town with tenements.

Another enticing piece of information comes in the form of the revelation that Brentwood was the birthplace of the Peasants' Revolt of 1381. Rebellious Essex men reacted to an over-zealous poll tax collector by giving him a good slap. The revolt spread to Kent, Hertfordshire, Suffolk and Norfolk. Perhaps angered by high taxes on beauty salons, Kentish geezer Wat Tyler and his Essex mates proceeded to London with the medieval equivalent of West Ham's Inter City Firm. One of the places they trashed became known as Jack Straw's Castle, an old manor house in Highbury Barn. They probably smashed up the delis too.

Little bits of history permeate the modern veneer of Brentwood. There's an old-style Essex weather-boarded alleyway leading to some Indian restaurants and the less delightful multi-storey car park. A prancing, clapping, cavorting couple have a laugh with the security guard by the Chapel High shopping centre. 'I'm winding her up, in't I? Embarrassing her!' says the Brentwood geezer with a hop and clap.

Brentwood High Street has several *Whatever Happened to the Likely Lads* moments, where you find the icons of your youth trashed by a metaphorical ball and chain. The old Chariot chippy where they served excellent saveloy and chips is now Café Rouge. As with all towns, the chains gang have moved in – the Slug and Lettuce, McDonald's, Starbucks, Costa Coffee.

But the newsagents is still there. A billboard outside advertises the good old *Brentwood Gazette*. Inside the *Gazette* there's a page-fifteen feature on the opening of Amy Childs's salon ('Amy's new salon will make others "well jel": *TOWIE* redhead offering four shades of spray tan') and a picture of Amy with her staff in smart purple uniforms.

Like most local papers, the *Brentwood Gazette* would never knowingly undersell a story. It used to find endless angles on a 'terror footpath'. When our dog barked to scare off burglars he was billed as 'hero dog Patch'. Its political campaigns were usually on big issues like getting the high street toilets refurbished. Though strangely it seems a little embarrassed by *TOWIE*. While Amy has to make do with page fifteen, on page two is the story 'Residents prepare for food recycling'.

This is the same *Brentwood Gazette* where Richard Madeley, of Richard and Judy fame, found his first job. He went to my old school in Shenfield. With his embarrassing questions about sex in front of a flustered Judy as he discusses the menopause or stockings versus tights on daytime TV, Madeley's repressed laddism has always hinted at the Essex geezer beneath the suit and green room make-up. Yet his well-reviewed autobiography *Fathers and Sons*, detailing his beatings at the hand of his father, revealed something darker behind the mock Tudor frontages of middle-class Brentwood in the 1960s.

Further down the high street is the bus stop where I'd wait for the 247 London Transport bus to Colliers Row. The pub there is now a Kentucky Fried Chicken. At least Fenton Sports is still there. This used to be run by Ted Fenton, the old West Ham manager, back in the days when former managers had no access to Setanta punditry as a career option. And by the bus stop is a place called Tides, full of silver wrought-metal dressing tables and purple Union Jack cushions.

Shopping has always been important in Brentwood. An old 1980s promotional leaflet from Brentwood Council that I found at my parents' house reads: 'It is a town of shopping facilities with modern paving, attractive lighting, a CCTV security system and an abundant variety of shops, both multiples and individuals.' Clearly the blurb works, for here I am, checking out the most excellent modern paving and CCTV system.

The high street terminates at Wilson's Corner, named after the defunct Wilson's department store. Wilson's has been replaced by a variety of beauty salons and hairdressers. I turn left at the crossroads and head down Ongar Road desperately seeking Lucy and her new boutique. I discover that The Castle, an old pub once frequented by bikers, punks and hippies, is now Eclipse nightclub.

Opposite the Victoria Arms pub is Lucy's Boutique, set up by *TOWIE*'s Lucy Mecklenburgh. In the window are several dresses and a pink 'I Love Mario' cloth bag. Four women are standing chatting around the silver reception desk. To my surprise, Lucy is there herself, and apparently happy to work in the shop, having had a fashion background before *TOWIE*. She's trying to sell cheaper items too to appeal to the budgets of her young fan base.

She's wearing a white jumper and black trousers and, in reality as well as on TV, has a Kate-Middleton-with-glottal-stops type of Essex appeal. Lucy tells me about the visitors since her boutique opened a week earlier, although it's hard not to get distracted by thinking what a big mistake that young Mark made by dumping her. Or not to think, 'Wow, I'm talking to Lucy from *TOWIE* and does she really think Mark Wright is a tosser and shouldn't Mario just lighten up a bit and all she did was wake up in her clothes round at Mark's gaff but still, what a great honest speech to make on national TV, though will it all end in tears like my missus thinks?'

'We've had Scousers, people from Scotland, Geordies,' explains Lucy. 'They stay at the big three, the Premier Inn, Holiday Inn and the Posthouse. They come in on Friday and Saturday to get glammed up and then we see them on Sunday coming in all hungover. They like the handbags, scarves and dresses and then go to Amy's for her fake tan.'

Does she see Amy Childs's salon as a rival? 'We're all friends. Kayleigh here's from Amy's Salon, look she's got the uniform.' Kayleigh, standing a few feet away, reveals her purple uniform and badge.

I mention that in my Brentwood youth it was seen

as quite a boring place and that the Castle pub (now Equinox) a few doors from her shop was full of hippies. She seems a little nonplussed by this concept.

'Hippies in the Castle? Really? I read some survey where Brentwood was voted the most boring town. There's a few complaining about Sugar Hut but we needed it. It's been helpful. We're just a tiny town in Essex and now it's packed out.'

High on my proximity to *TOWIE*ville, I move on to Amy's Salon at Wilson's Corner.

For me, Wilson's Corner will always be associated with the burger bar of the 1970s. Visiting the burger man was the culmination of a big night out for the sort of youths whom Ian Dury memorably described in his song 'Blockheads'. They drove black-and-orange cars and wore 'shoes like dead pigs' noses'. They'd drive up in their done-up Cortinas with sun strips across the windscreen emblazoned with names like Darren and Sharon. They'd arrive for a post-pub burger, and if feeling sophisticated, purchase a pineapple cheeseburger. One of the men managed to drive straight through the plate-glass window of the store while showing off. His girlfriends' names no doubt had to be rapidly removed from his sunstrip.

The burger man has gone now. He's probably a millionaire in a gated estate, leaving just the lonely war memorial and a busy crossroads sans pineapple-themed refreshment. Now there are sports cars with personalised number plates where once there were done-up Cortinas with sunstrips. That's progress, I guess.

Amy Childs's salon is completely white inside, reminding me of the interior of that spaceship in the film *2001*. 'I'm sorry Dave, I can't do that pejazzle.'

Kayleigh is there by the counter in her bright purple uniform and name badge. She has tinted blonde hair and a friendly Amy-style accent. 'Weekends are crazy,' she says. 'The phone's not stopped. You can't get off of it. It's the glam, the tan. There's no recession here. Tell me about it! They come from Manchester, Liverpool, Leeds, Scotland, we've got someone coming from Dubai next week. They like the full session before they go out. They like their stripped lashes, spray tans like the Oompa-Loompa, nails. Oh and vajazzles are popular, they're from £15 to £30. How long do they last? I'm not sure really, about two nights?'

I mention Amy's new TV show, *It's All About Amy*. 'Did you see it last night?' asks Kayleigh. I tell her that I enjoyed the section where Amy took her dog to training classes and refused to pick up its poo. 'I couldn't pick up dog poo either,' laughs Kayleigh. 'It's illegal isn't it? Is it illegal? I'd need ten pairs of gloves!'

It's hard not to feel a little giggly. I'm a middle-aged man, married with two children. Never before have I spent a Friday afternoon discussing vajazzles and dog poo in Essex.

From Amy's Salon I decide to visit Brentwood School. My dad and Nigel and Gavin, my pals at West Ham games, went there.

Down Ingrave Road and opposite the spot-lit Cathedral Church of St Mary and St Helen is where you find Brentwood School. This is the alma mater of, among others, quintessential Essex beardie Noel Edmonds, Sir Robin Day, Frank Lampard Jr and Jack Straw (the Labour politician not the revolting peasant).

Douglas Adams went there too and, in a testament to a public school education, learned that the meaning of the universe is forty-two, a fact later repeated in *The Hitchhiker's Guide to the Galaxy*. Another famous old-Brentwood boy is the comedian and presenter Griff Rhys Jones. He wrote about his old school in his excellent memoir *Semi-Detached*, revealing how new pupils were given a *Blue Book* with numerous school rules, such as the need to call prefects 'preaposters'.

Perhaps the *Blue Book* didn't extend to apostrophes though. Feeling a flush of forgotten inter-school rivalry, I score a victory for my own Shenfield School by noting that the sign on Brentwood's big posh gates reads: 'All visitors must report to the porters (sic) reception via the Bayman Gate in Middleton Hall Lane.'

The front entrance of the school is certainly imposing, looking like a chunk of Oxford or Chancery deposited in suburban Essex. It's all red brick, giant clock towers, coats of arms, cloisters and chapels. Mind you, fee-paying parents should be aware that it stands on a murder site.

As a penance for burning someone to death, Sir Anthony Browne started a school. As you do. This was in 1557 and the school was built on the site where nineteen-year-old William Hunter had a hot date with history, being burned alive. There's still a memorial to Hunter in Shenfield Road. As a Justice of the Peace, Brown had sentenced Hunter to death for refusing to accept the transubstantiation of bread and wine into the body and blood of Jesus Christ. The *Daily Mail* probably thought burning was too good for him. This was in the reign of Queen Mary. When Queen Elizabeth I came to the throne Browne clearly thought of putting a clever spin on the affair by founding the school as penance for Hunter's martyrdom.

Griff Rhys Jones revealed how Brentwood's bizarre school song still celebrates its foundations, even if it does sound like something from *Mississippi Burning*:

> They bound a lad to a green elm tree
> and they burned him there for the folks to see
> and in shame for his brothers and sisters all
> they built them a school with a new red wall.

A group of girls in navy tracksuits jog past me and into the school. Girls at Brentwood School? Surely enough to make Sir Anthony Browne tie himself to the martyr's elm and indulge in self-immolation.

The school is conscientiously fenced off from the rest of the town. You wonder what the kids do for illicit entertainment. As it's Brentwood they probably sneak out for furtive Oompa-Loompa tans.

Past the school is the Artichoke pub, which in my day was full of boring old hippies, 'Hotel California' on the jukebox, blokes selling raffle tickets and an Orient supporter. Now it's a Toby Carvery and Inn.

A little further past the school there's a major cross-roads by Shenfield Common. Endless Ford Kas wait at traffic lights and pelican crossings. But the Common itself, opposite Brentwood County High School, has a great old village pond and the remnants of a stone water pump.

Shenfield Common Woods is a place to 'hook-up' for young people according to the Knowhere Guide website. Mind you, the teen diarists and Ali G wannabes also list 'Sittin in St Thomas's graveyard at lunchtime eatin ur lunch frm Stav's dwn the arcade and watchin da boyz go by!' as a required activity.

Another youth asks, 'Who hasn't snogged in the grave-yard?' While someone else warns, 'The graveyard is where you want to go if you want a nice old fashioned arse-kicking by the Harold Hillians.' There's enough material for a Morrissey concept album in this. Still, it's time to return to Minnies and get my diary signed. There's no sign of Billie Faiers yet, but Sam and Billie's blonde (is there any other hair colour in Essex?) mum Sue Wells is there. She's forty-two years old but looks younger.

Sue and Lynn introduce me to some customers by the racks. Natalie and Ria are from Kent, and tell me, 'Yes, we want that Essex vibe and we'd like to meet Mick and get him to buy us a drink.'

Louisa from Sunderland is with five friends, one of whom emphasises she is from Chesterfield, celebrat-ing her twenty-first birthday. 'It's not that different to Newcastle or Sunderland, people just want a good night out, and there's just the same amount of leopard print. We met Mick in Mason's, he's so lovely! We're on the guest list for Sugar Hut tonight...'

Mick Norcross is emerging as an unlikely sex object. The fact is confirmed by Mick coming tenth in *Heat*'s Weird Crush 2011 poll, with the magazine describing him as 'Everyone's fave rich dad off *TOWIE*'. Those Mackem girls know who has the cash down south.

So what does Sue think of everyone from *TOWIE* starting up a shop? Is there a different work ethic in Essex?

'Essex people are grafters,' says Sue. 'There's hard workers and slackers everywhere, but we moved out and maybe there is something in that East End background about working hard.'

'If you don't work, you don't eat!' chips in a sales assistant. Which sums up the Essex work ethic rather nicely. Though in Essex some work is more legit than others.

What a day it's been in Brentwood. Three *TOWIE* icons taken in, so it's time for a drink. Eschewing Minnies and the attractions of the graveyard, I turn and pace back towards the town centre, seeking a pint. It pays to look back in Ongar Road, opposite Lucy's Boutique. The good old Victoria Arms, where my dad would drink his two pints, is still there and still serving Greene King's Abbot and IPA ales.

There's a pleasing hubbub of conversation in the place as I take a seat at a table with my pint of Abbot. A self-improving couple at a nearby table discuss whether to do a four-week patisserie, yoga, Pilates or swimming course. When I visit the gents an elderly man makes phlegmy sounds at the urinal.

'Excuse my disgusting noises,' he says. I tell him his

disgusting noises are fine. It's coming back now. In Essex people talk to you in pub loos.

A group of building types in trainers and jeans, including a man in a Brentwood Lofts sweatshirt, stands near the bar, busy in banter. 'Yer 'avin a larf ... nah, elitist people say they like to spend ten grand in a year ... he's a brilliant odd job man ... yeah. He's Oddjob! ... nah, mate, I'm a Manc ... yeah, there's a lot of ex-teachers in here!'

'Valerie' is playing on the jukebox. A geezer wonders through the door. 'Hello, Paul, cheers, Dan, I got some nice chicken wings for you...' Is this another Brentwood industry. A brisk trade in black-market chicken wings?

I'm struck by how friendly the place is. And I've just heard someone mention 'that Amy Childs' with a knowing chuckle. Maybe it's Essex in the DNA but it's good to be in a town where no one laughs at your accent and you can wear a West Ham hat without ridicule.

Get Essex folk away from their trains and they talk. Anyone deposited from space into this boozer would surely swear they must be in the friendly north of England. Everyone seems to know each other in the Vic.

In the far corner a group of grey-haired but young-hearted friends discuss the death of a drinking man. 'I just happened to be in the pub at his funeral they put a plaque in the garden ... used to see him in the Swan ... he had £1,700 in the bank ... he was always pissed...' 'Yes, very often pissed,' agrees a woman in their party. 'Bobby knew him well ... He didn't deserve to be barred, a lot of people done much worse...'

The builders continue to banter. 'Jed's taking the piss

... All you do is sit at a computer all day ... You haven't done any building work all year ... All you do is project management ... You sacked all your team today!'

Meanwhile, the silver pint-surfers on the table have moved on to one of those pub trivia moments: 'You must remember Jack Hargreaves, you know, the TV presenter in the 1960s and 1970s?'

It's tempting to say that yes, I do.

Fortified by Abbot ale, it's time to head out into the rain and traffic. A pick-up truck passes me bearing the impressive legend of another bespoke Essex industry: Warren and Son Golf Course Alterations.

Back along the high street most of the retail shops have closed, but not the hairdressers. Brentwood, the town where the barbers never sleep. The queues have started to form outside Sugar Hut and there are the girls from Sunderland and Kent and everywhere else all dressed up in their reem gear from Minnies.

I'd go in if I didn't feel so old and unreem – though the success of Mick as a middle-aged sex symbol gives me a little hope – and if there was any chance of getting past the bouncers. The dress code is a complex formula of 'Smart, Casual and Trendy' that even Professor Brian Cox might struggle to unravel. Fridays is 'Strictly no baseball caps, hooded tops of any kind, polo shirts, ripped clothes, shorts, trainers of any kind (shoes or smart boots only – NO Timberland-style boots, Converse or Vans).' Though on Saturdays 'box-fresh deck/boat shoes are acceptable'.

Later my friend Jacqui tells me of her visit. 'We only got as far as the back car park where I took a grainy photo of the building and now have it as my screen saver. We didn't go in because I think we were twice as old as everybody else there and I was wearing a skirt and top and therefore somewhat over-dressed!'

Opposite Brentwood station I buy a portion of chips from the Flying Fish kebab and chip shop. The smiling young woman serving me is orange, wearing tight jeans and more make-up than all the combined cast of *TOWIE*. A drunken man thanks her profusely for his fare. Essex towns should always have a chip shop, where they call a gherkin a wally. It's no coincidence that when Bill Bailey chose to parody Billy Bragg he chose to do so in a song called 'Unisex Chipshop', with a great line about running naked in the woods around Rainham (except, as Phill Jupitus pointed out, there are no woods around Rainham). The chips are good, not too hot and a crumbly white texture inside. I eat them outside the station while observing the commuters return.

An astonishing fleet of eighteen taxis waits on the sliproad outside the station. A commuter train from Liverpool Street pulls in and a mass of humanity emerges. Suddenly the quiet streets of shining black tarmac and shadowy sodium lights are full of brisk London walks, everyone rushing to get somewhere. The taxis glide into action as if moving a small army and in five minutes the place is deserted again.

At the station there's only around a dozen people heading back towards London. Brentwood feels like the centre of the commuting universe. My new best friend is the automated announcer: 'Will customers on platform one please stand clear of the platform edge as a through train is approaching...'

I'm sitting in the railway station. Like Paul Simon I've been 'Homeward Bound' to no-longer-boring Brentwood. What would he make of the place today? Would he still long for Essex after a one-night stand? Probably not. Post-*TOWIE* he'd be more likely to be seeking a one-night stand in Sugar Hut.

• • •

The only way in Brentwood is not necessarily Sugar Hut, Minnies, Lucy's Boutique and the Amy Childs Salon. One of the reasons for its popularity as a dormitory town is that it contains many fine parks, often the grounds of old stately homes, such as South Weald and Thorndon Park. Though for this Brentwood Man the best hidden countryside spot is Miss Willmott's garden at Warley Place, next to my dad's old farm tenancy in Great Warley.

Some weeks after my initial visit I return with my daughters Lola and Nell and my sister Kaz, a Romfordian. We take a taxi from Brentwood station. The driver is talkative and a Man United fan who followed them away all over Europe a couple of years ago. 'Rome's a nice place in the daytime, but you don't want to go out at night if you know what I mean, they'll draw up on a moped and stick a knife in you ... And don't ever go away to Turkey.'

He has inside information on *TOWIE*. 'See the Premier

Inn over there, it's booked out until the end of May. You know what? Over the last four bank holidays it took £1.2 million!'

We ask him if he'd ever go. 'Not likely, mate. Twenty pound to get in ... Five pounds for a glass of wine!' Ah, the taxi drivers in Essex, they know the price of everything and the value of everything.

The taxi passes what was once Warley Mental Hospital, but is now posh flats called The Galleries, offering 'stylish contemporary interiors that make a statement'. We drive past the old Headley Arms, where in my teenage years numerous Cortinas were parked outside, Led Zeppelin's 'Rock 'n' Roll' played over the jukebox and the girls had nicotine and rum-and-black breath. Gratuitous tonsil hockey was played by many an underage drinker at midnight on Christmas and New Year's Eve. Now it's a curry restaurant called Headley Spice.

We get out at Great Warley village green. On one side of the main road to Brentwood are the daffodil-strewn fields of Miss Willmott's famous garden. On the other side is a fabulous view across the lowlands towards the Thames and the Kent hills. It passed me by as a kid. Sometimes you're so busy trying to escape, you miss what's there.

A sign announces that this is 'Great Warley: a conservation area'. It would once have been a charming village set well away from London. Today it's a little spoilt by the perpetual flow of traffic at the village green junction.

The war memorial stands in the centre of the small village green and the blacksmith is still on Warley Road, although the post office has now been converted into a private dwelling. Here's Two Door Cottage where Mr and Mrs East used to live and Chestnut Tree Cottage, which has a wooden carving of, well, a chestnut tree on its side.

When I was last here at election time there was a tribal 'Conservatives' poster on the hedge of The Wallets, a real Tudor beamed house nestling in the heartland of the mock Tudor mansion.

It would be strangely apt if the village pub, the Thatcher's Arms, had been renamed in a fit of Tory fervour after Maggie Thatcher had kicked Michael Foot's stick away in the 1980s. But no, it's always been the Thatcher's Arms, and never has a name been more apposite than during the 1980s when Essex Man was billed as 'Maggie's mauler'.

The Thatcher's Arms is busy at lunchtime, with several cars parked outside, including an open-top BMW. At the tables two women share coffees, a man with a white beard smokes a pipe and several others nurse lunchtime pints. It's really not a bad boozer.

It's nicer inside than I remember from my underage visits to the public bar; all the bars are now knocked together and there are dark wooden panels, hunting pictures, and a framed plan of Warley Place in its 1900s heyday.

By the bar is a framed pair of jodhpurs from A. P. McCoy with '1,500 wins' written on them, which a man at the bar tells me he purchased at an auction. There's a customer in a darts shirt marked Bristow talking to a man who's had a sniff of the barmaid's apron and is saying it's been years since he's seen Bristow play. Someone else is saying, 'I tell you, when I sell that house I'll be fucking rich!'

The food is good hearty Essex fare. My daughters enjoy scampi and cod with chips, Kaz has the tagliatelle and my omelette and chunky chips goes down agreeably with a pint of Flying Scotsman.

Entry to Warley Place is through a black gate next to the Thatcher's Arms. There's a hut with leaflets and a donation box run by the Essex Wildlife Trust as today is an open day. There are even a couple of Warley Place novels on sale, written by one of the Essex Wildlife Trust's volunteers and inspired by the romance of the grand old gardens. A booklet explains how the Monday volunteers, many of them well past retirement age, worked tirelessly to save the gardens.

Collapsed cellars, a ruined conservatory, hidden reservoirs, stone paths, cold frames and boating lakes emerging from the undergrowth. If Warley Place were in Cornwall or Scotland it would surely be the subject of a *Lost Gardens of Heligan*-style TV series.

As a child I remember scrambling up a huge earth bank in Dark Lane and discovering the Narnia-like ruins of an old house in the woods. It was, in fact, the remains of one of England's finest gardens created by the formidable Ellen Willmott, one of the top gardeners of her day. It was also a bit of a health and safety nightmare with concealed pits, decaying cellar roofs and deep ponds. 'Dad, you could have been killed!' say Lola and Nell.

Forty-odd years after my childhood glimpse of an Indiana Jones-esque ruin, the gardens have been renovated by the Essex Wildlife Trust. Ellen Willmott moved into Warley Place with her parents in 1875 and spent a lifetime developing a sumptuous garden. Numerous plants are named after her. The Eryngium giganteum, which she used to furtively scatter in her friends' borders, is still called 'Miss Willmott's Ghost'. Plants that she bred often feature the words 'willmotti' and 'warleyensis'. Around the 1900s she employed more than a hundred gardeners. She was a big mover in the Royal Horticultural Society and was awarded the society's Medal of Honour in 1907. She died penniless in 1934 at the age of seventy-six, having spent all her dosh on her obsession with gardening. Despite her reduced means in later life she remained an influential figure in the horticultural world until the end.

After Ellen's death Warley Place was sold to property developer A. J. Carter, who intended to build houses on it. Her decaying house was demolished in 1939 as it was felt to be a danger to local children illicitly playing in it.

The Second World War interrupted property developments and after the war the area was designated part of London's Green Belt. Paul Carter, the grandson of A. J. Carter, still owns the land and leases it to the Essex Wildlife Trust.

The Warley Place walk begins along the old main road to Brentwood that pilgrims used when travelling from Walsingham to Canterbury. Past the crocus field is South Pond, Great Warley's watering hole in medieval times, into the woods and on to the ruins of the Willmotts' old house. Flowering daffodils are everywhere and the ha-ha has just been fully excavated.

The roofless shell of the grand old conservatory is still standing, an evocative sight in the dappled green sunlight, while around it are hazardous drops into the old base-ments. You can see the tiled floors of the kitchen and the alcoves of the old wine cellars. Mosaic stone paths have been unearthed and the walled garden is still relatively intact, housing a palm tree, a ginko tree and magnolias, comfrey and anemones.

The wooded trail continues past wild garlic and the remains of Willmott's cold frames, greenhouses, a half-moon-shaped pond and a deep reservoir. Down the hill, the boating ponds are empty but the brickwork is still there, complete with a mooring rail. A huge earth bank, now supported by steel trusses, descends to my dad's old farm workers' cottages in Dark Lane. You sense the huge effort Miss Willmott went to in taming and controlling nature – a very Victorian philosophy.

There's a carp pond with water and a birdhide. We sit inside and in the children's sightings book, full of blue tits, Nell writes that she has seen a sheep, a pig and crocodile, while Lola pens cryptic messages from Harry Potter and Lord Voldemort.

Past seven huge Spanish chestnuts (reputedly planted by the diarist John Evelyn in the seventeenth century) there's a viewpoint by a meadow full of daffodils. Here you can gaze across the fields of my dad's old farm towards the M25 and then, in the distance, the towers of the City of London. It's hard not to feel the history of encroachment at Warley Place, of both time and the city.

The tour ends with a bridge over a gorge that Willmott created to showcase her Alpine plants. Water used to flow through it and into the South Pond. The huge rocks in the gorge were lugged all the way from Yorkshire.

Willmott never married and as she grew older she became increasingly eccentric, if not all stations to Barking. Her CV includes being arrested for shoplifting (the charges were eventually dropped), carrying a revolver in her handbag when she walked home alone from Brentwood station and booby-trapping her daffodil fields as a deterrent to bulb thieves.

Miss Willmott's garden was certainly the project of a *nouveau riche* eccentric with prosperous parents (her father was a successful solicitor). Like any *TOWIE* star of today Ellen wanted an ostentatious display of wealth. In a way she was very Essex. Her gaff was perhaps equivalent to Mick Norcross's country pile. She received a whacking £1,000 a year from her godmother and she inherited a fortune from her godmother and parents.

Instead of giving her son a BMW for his birthday, as Mick did, the childless and unmarried Ellen spent her dosh on expensive plants, creating huge garden features and buying extra land in France and Italy. At the age of twenty-four she was ordering a company to move huge rocks from Yorkshire for her Alpine ravine. She wasn't great on workers' rights, and was said to sack any gardener if he allowed a weed to show. But the scale and ambition of her life's work is still inspiring. Inevitably her money eventually ran out, but she gardened right on to the end.

Ellen's pristine garden was overtaken by undergrowth, decay and Japanese knotweed, until those dedicated volunteers started unearthing it in the 1980s. It's now one of Essex's undiscovered treasures. And the sense of decay makes it even better: within sight of the M25 and down the road from Sugar Hut lies a place to reflect, wander down mysterious overgrown, shadowy paths and move back in time to an era of grand projects in the shrubbery.

5

LOOK BACK IN ONGAR: WHEN ARMAGEDDON CAME TO ESSEX

In a post-apocalyptic world Essex could have emerged as the supreme power in Western Europe – its white stilettoes tottering over a ravaged planet.

When I was at school in the 1970s, there were rumours of a nuclear bunker somewhere in Essex. We all assumed this to be an apocryphal piece of Cold War disinformation. Now we know it was real, thanks to the modern-day tourist attraction that is the Secret Nuclear Bunker. It was really there all the time. The world would have been reconstructed around – hang on a minute – Kelvedon Hatch? That's a small town halfway between Ongar and Brentwood.

Maybe Joey Essex from *TOWIE* wasn't so far from the truth when he claimed that there was a Prime Minister of Essex. The place where the British Prime Minister and military and scientific elite would have sheltered was in a bunker beneath a suburban bungalow off the A128. Just as Colchester was once the capital of Britain in early Roman times, so Kelvedon Hatch would rise again for

Essex to claim its rightful heritage. Not that there would be much left to govern, of course.

Presumably the Cold War warriors and Dr Strangelove types would have made big efforts to recruit a selection of prime Essex Men and Girls to the bunker. The location of is no coincidence. What better county to kickstart civilisation and promote capitalism over Eastern European state communism? Essex – there was no alternative.

In the Cold War world of *Mad Max*, or possibly *Barmy Barry* in the UK remake, 1980s Essex would have had all the excess mechanics, boy racers and car culture to easily dominate the market in customised new barbarian motors and furry dice. Tiptree jam and marmalade might have become a world staple and Russian cabbage been consigned to the dustbin of history.

Repopulating the world would have been no problem had the parents of Mark Wright been recruited to that bunker. Had young Mark been raised in the bunker, the *TOWIE* lothario and 007 wannabe would have been the perfect candidate to go out and repeople the region from Chigwell to Colchester, then on to Russia and even the Australian jungle, all in the name of post-war reconstruction.

That Essex entrepreneurial attitude could have restarted a post-nuclear economy with a worldwide chain of nightclubs and boutiques. In the alternative post-push-the-button scenario Mick Norcross might well have ended up as Mrs Thatcher's enterprise tsar. Joey Essex could have become a world statesman. If Ronald Reagan could do it…

'We're going to see a nuclear bunker, girls,' I tell my daughters as we plan a dad's day out. It beats our local Pirate's Playhouse anyway.

These days the Secret Nuclear Bunker has proper brown tourist signs in Chipping Ongar and at Wilson's Corner in Brentwood to indicate its newfound non-secrecy.

Initially, on a day trip with my kids, we look back in Ongar. It's a pleasant surprise, full of old Essex weather-boarded buildings, bulging medieval timbers and an ancient church and castle. Although, being Essex, it does have a couple of beauty salons too.

We find the beautiful old church of St Martin's. This early Norman church has brick and flint walls and a white weather-boarded tower with a weather vane perched on top. It's utterly charming. Near the church are old timber-beamed cottages with wobbly beams and floor levels.

The Rev. Susan Cooper is inside the church and happy to see some visitors. She points out the fourteenth-century roof timbers standing on stone corbels and an original Norman stained-glass window by the altar.

'I can't believe Ongar isn't on the tourist trail,' says the Reverend Cooper. 'When I came here I thought it would be like Dagenham, but it's a beautiful place.'

She shows my daughter Nell the mysterious tiny hatch in the north wall of the sanctuary. This was for an anchorite cell, attached to the church. Here a hermit could live without even an iPod or mobile. If he got really bored he could open the small window to catch a bit of the service.

There's a stained-glass window commemorating the work of missionary David Livingstone – famed for meeting Stanley in Africa – who it turns out spent fifteen months training in Ongar.

Ongar's done pretty well for churches as it also boasts the oldest wooden church in the world at Greensted. It's a mile or so from the high street via the Essex Way footpath. We used to do school trips to Greensted and none of us could ever see what the fuss was about a few old timbers. I'm more impressed seeing it today. There's a white weather-boarded tower, brickwork and lovely old black timbers.

Dendrochronological research has dated the oldest timbers in the nave of the church to around 1053, before the Norman Conquest. Another interesting feature of the split oak trunks is the Leper's Squint, a small hole which some theories suggest is where lepers could receive a blessing without entering the church, though it might in fact be a holy water stoup.

Greensted Church also has the stone grave of an unknown crusader. He is said to have arrived at the church badly wounded and died there – or he could have just been involved in a bundle round the back of Sugar Hut. There's further history to note in the fact that the Tolpuddle Martyrs were granted farm tenancies in the area in 1837, having been kicked off their Dorset land, and one of them, James Brine, was married at Greensted.

Back in Ongar, we go into Grumpy George's Old Fashioned Sweet Shop and discover low ceilings and more ancient supporting timbers. The building might be antique, but the young assistants have more modern preoccupations: 'Do you do eyelash extensions?' asks one. 'No, but my mate does,' answers her friend.

We explore Ongar Castle, just off the main road, built in the tenth century by Richard de Lucy to compensate for having a girl's name. There's still a well-defined moat, although the castle mound is fenced off. And on the far side of the castle the moat has been refilled with water, and several house gardens terminate with their own bit of moat.

The footpath from the castle emerges at the Ecclesiastical Church where a plaque marks the room in which David Livingstone studied in 1838, and a palm tree and blue walls in the morning sun make it seem a little like Livingstone's Africa. Livingstone was a timid bloke who once forgot his sermon and ran out of the church in shame, though he did like a pint in the Royal Oak. He then went on to discover, for Europeans at least, the source of the Nile and the Victoria Falls.

But it's a different type of exploration of uncharted areas we need to do. The Secret Nuclear Bunker, I presume?

From Ongar we catch the 501 bus to Kelvedon Hatch. There's no stop near the bunker so we have to get off at Kelvedon. In the afternoon it appears to be a town bereft of inhabitants. We walk up the A128 through the town. There's a deserted pub and that's about it. No shops, no children; it could be an episode of *The Survivors*. Finally we find a man gardening by his bungalow.

'Excuse me, do you know where the secret nuclear bunker is?' I ask.

'It's down that way on the left, mate, but it's a long old walk,' he says of the not-so-secret bunker, with the bemused look of someone who has never before seen a man and two children attempting to access a nuclear bunker via public transport. It doesn't look like he expects us to return.

The pavement soon disappears. It feels like a nuclear strike has already hit Essex. The verges, hedges and ditches of the A128 are full of shattered plastic mineral water and Coca-Cola bottles and rusting lager cans. Hatchbacks and Range Rovers pass at great speed, forcing us to clamber for safety on earth banks.

Eventually we come across a brown bunker sign pointing down a long winding track across a ploughed field. There's just a grassy hill in the distance with a mysterious mast perched on its top.

'This feels like a real adventure, girls,' I say hopefully. It's a trek into the unknown regions of both history and Essex. The track descends into a gulley where there's a sentry box and a paintballing shed. Ah, paintballing, another Essex perennial. Surely Smithy from *Gavin and Stacey* would have played paintball here.

We walk on past a stream and wood, post-apocalyptic paintballers scaling ropes in the trees, and eventually find a car park and a path to a suburban bungalow on the side of the hill.

Eerily there are no human staff on duty, just hand-held audio guides in a rack. We pick up our audio guides, enter to the left of the bungalow and find it's a huge steel corridor. On the wall are bunker plans. Geiger counters to measure radioactive contamination hang on the coat racks.

The entrance corridor is square and featureless and designed to defend the government from civilians if they tried to storm the bunker to escape the radiation, or perhaps query their MPs' expenses. There's an 'Armageddon Time' soundtrack on the public address system of four-minute warning wailing sirens.

'Will Captain Palmer please head to the operations room,' announces an eerie voice on the tannoy.

We move through huge blast doors that are the weight of four cars each and descend further into the depths. Soon we're 100 feet underground and encased in 10 feet of reinforced concrete. The signage reveals that the bunker was built in 1953 and decommissioned in 1993 as it cost £3 million a year to run. The owner of the bunker is farmer Mike Parrish. In 1952 the government approached Parrish's grandfather and, under the threat of compulsory purchase, took twenty-five acres of land.

Parrish told *All The Rage* magazine:

> They built the bunker and I farmed over the top as part of the cover until 1992, when we were able to purchase the top back under the Chrichel Down Rules. The bunker itself did not fall under these rules and in 1994 we went to sealed public tender to buy it. Our bid was the best and the rest, as they say, is history.

It took Parrish seven months of drilling day and night to create the second exit required by the fire brigade.

He's had two requests from *TOWIE* to use the bunker, but tells me, 'I turned them down as they wanted it for nothing!'

We descend further. There's no natural light and only circular vents in the ceiling to circulate the air. We enter the communications area where 1950s switchboards give way to ancient telex machines.

'This is cool! Everything's grey. These are so old. What are these?' says my daughter Lola, banging the keys of a telex machine.

A uniformed female dummy sits in the incoming messages booth. The bog-roll-like print-outs list innocuous towns like Aberystwyth. Here the 300 self-appointed survivors of a nuclear holocaust would search for signs of life in other bunkers around the blighted landscape.

Panic pervades our party. Static crackles in the scientists' centre where the fallout patterns would have been monitored. Red phones stand in a box on the wall.

'I want to leave, it's scary!' says Nell.

It feels a bit like the end of *Planet of the Apes*. I'm sure we're going to emerge and just see the top of the ruined Telecom Tower emerging above the rubble of London and a flattened Sugar Hut in Brentwood High Street, and I'll be shouting, 'The idiots, they did it, they actually did it!'

In the BBC Studio a blue-suited dummy of Margaret Thatcher stands with headphones on, ready to talk to the shell of a nation. How long would they have hidden down here? And, this being Essex, would they eventually have got in some strobe lights and a disco ball?

Lights flash on machines and everywhere there are

great big clunking boxes with dials on them. It all feels like 1970s *Doctor Who*. The dummies look like Autons and there are gas masks on the walls. It would be no surprise to find Brigadier Lethbridge-Stewart and his chaps from UNIT here, trying to maintain discipline and lay on a cup of instant coffee in an impossible situation. Jon Pertwee's Doctor would be shaking his head at humanity's folly and then asking Jo Grant to make him a cup of tea.

We move up a flight of stairs to the 'floor', where there's a map of Britain complete with pointers for military planning. The children watch a TV playing *Protect and Survive*. It's the best CND recruitment video ever. Everyone must stay in their improvised house shelter for fourteen days with water and tinned food. The sections on placing your toilet waste in a plastic bag and storing it in a large bucket fascinate Lola and Nell. 'If someone dies wrap the body in plastic or blankets and move it to a separate room,' says the keep-calm-and-carry-on voiceover.

We see the giant grey tanks and pipes of the plant room where the life support systems supplied water and pumped filtered air around the bunker. Then it's up another flight of stairs to the sick bay where a dummy lies with a bloody eye. 'Look, there's a coffin!' says Nell.

It's the most surreal family day out. We see the bunks where staff would have 'hot-bedded' in the dormitory and a large room full of ancient computers that would have been the devolved central government. Although now it's staffed by dummies with no legs and flapping white sleeves. A sign says 'Justice' on the walls. And the controller of this bunker truly would have had the power of life and death. After the nuclear winter those Essex taxi drivers really could have put their theories of retributive justice to the test.

We find our house on the giant laminated map of London on the wall. And in the gents piped music plays 'You Can't Hurry Love'. Weird. The children try on gas masks and army uniforms in a dressing-up area.

And then it's up to the canteen where the smell of institutionalised food from stainless steel ovens evokes just how awful the post-nuclear bunker would have felt. A sign declares that the food may contain nuts, which seems rather a trivial thing to worry about after the invisible death cloud arrives. I'm tempted to ask if they do irradiated food.

Finally we find two staff alive behind the counter, although everything has to be paid for in the honesty box. We admire the nuclear bunker mugs, postcards, pencils and rubber toys beneath the grey tomb-like beams.

'Are these dead?' asks an elderly retainer picking up our coffee mugs and cans. 'No, but everyone outside is!' I quip.

We take our final exit, walking down a long arched tunnel that finally emerges at a small camouflaged opening in the side of the hill. Daylight at last. And thankfully there's no sign of fallout. Essex survived! Paintball prospered. The Western way of life triumphed and the Russians discovered they really rather liked the decadent customs of Brentwood and Ongar. It was Essex what won the Cold War.

6

BILLERICAY DICKIES

Billericay was described by Julie Burchill as 'a foot-baller's idea of the countryside'. Back in the late 1970s, Burchill and her then-husband Tony Parsons were 'hip young gunslingers' championing punk in the *New Musical Express*. Not only were they married, they lived in Billericay – the most unhip commuter town imaginable.

It would be nice to think that relocating to Essex was a deliberately ironic move from two writers who made careers out of iconoclastic statements. Although it's more likely they were seduced by cheaper house prices and the easy commute to Liverpool Street.

The Burchill/Parsons sojourn in Billericay is one of many examples of Billericay attaining a fame that far outweighs its status. Back in 1977 my old school mate Paul 'Gaffer' Garrett and I would get together in our university vacations and ponder the implications of Ian Dury's song 'Billericay Dickie'. 'People in America must think it's somewhere like Chicago or Philadelphia,' declared Paul, in wonderment, before we'd adjourn to The Castle and despair of Brentwood's still-large hippie contingent.

Actually US fame was rather appropriate – a meeting of the Pilgrim Fathers was said to have taken place in Billericay. Four Billericay residents were on the *Mayflower* (they all died at Cape Cod) and others followed. The town of Billerica in Massachusetts was set up in 1655 to commemorate the Essex influence (with cars and shopping malls presumably).

As for the name Billericay, the town was considered part of Great Burstead in the *Domesday Book*. The first mention of 'Byllyrica' was recorded in 1291. It's believed to be derived from Medieval Latin, *beller-ca*, which translates as dyehouse or tanhouse. Yes, even back then the residents were into tanning.

Ian Dury's song catapulted Billericay to worldwide iconic status:

> Good evening, I'm from Essex,
> In case you couldn't tell!
> My given name is Dickie, I come from Billericay
> And I'm doing very well!

It remains a classic pop song, music hall in tone and full of wonderful rhyming couplets. The song's lyrics immortalised the sexual prowess of a very Essex character – the East End/Essex wide boy chirpy chancer, who has a fine line in patter and is working his way through a roll call of chickies in the back of his Cortina. Biographer Will Birch suggests in his book *Ian Dury* that it was written about Dury's one-time drummer Terry Day, who actually hailed from Dagenham and had a gift with the ladies. Dagenham Dickie wouldn't have scanned so well though.

Sexual conquests tend to be greeted with humour in earthy Essex and it's all there in Dury's rhyming slang about 'her rum and her Ribena'. There's Joyce and Vicky, a love affair with Nina, Janet from near the Isle of Thanet (actually in Kent, which gives the song a bit of inter-county authenticity), Sandy (who didn't half go dandy), a nice bit of posh from Burnham on Crouch and a 'charming shag' from Shoeburyness.

Like his ancestors among the market stallholders of Canning Town and Romford, Dickie is perhaps prone to exaggerating his wares. Dickie is a brickie, a manual labourer who hopes to raise his station and other parts through an inflated opinion of his sexual magnetism. Dury has been disdainful towards the character and the song is in part laughing at Dickie; however, Dury – despite a withered arm and leg from contracting polio – was a notorious womaniser himself. He was in his late thirties when stardom arrived, yet he apparently seduced women as if he were a naïve twenty-year-old on his first tour. Clearly there was an element of wish fulfilment in 'Billericay Dickie' for Dury. A middle-class kid from Upminster who'd spent his childhood in an institution wanted to be like the brash bird bandits he encountered in the Essex hinterlands.

'Billericay Dickie' was an unreconstructed sexist and an Essex stereotype, but one that everyone recognised because of its basis in truth. Suddenly Billericay was transformed from dormitory town to a comic variety-club turn – a saucy postcard town from the Thames Delta.

There really is something a bit music hall about Billericay. Comedian Lee Evans went to school there, possibly wearing his 'octopus shoes', and still lives in Billericay, and the town's innate sense of comedy contributed to the huge success of the BBC's *Gavin and Stacey*. Gavin is from Billericay and Stacey from Barry in Wales. Much of the humour stems from the collision of Essex and Welsh mores. The Billericay scenes are actually filmed in Wales, but there's a clear warmth to the well-observed Essex values on display.

Gavin's mum Pam, played superbly by Alison Steadman, is blonde and brassy, likes a knees-up and mispronounces her soon-to-be daughter-in-law's home as 'Barry's Town', but she is a warm, loveable character. His dad Mick is the sort of decent bloke you'll find throughout Essex, someone who gets the job done and tolerates, even loves, his wife's idiosyncrasies. Gavin is a Billericay Dickie with noughties sensitivity, forever wondering how to keep Stacey happy, while the real star is Smithy, played by James Corden. The West Ham-supporting Smithy is brash, a fat lad who eats too many chips and curries, but is also caring, a good mate, and prepared to face up to fatherhood and his obligations to Nessa when it matters. He's how Essex Man would like to see himself.

Billericay has more cultural baggage than Smithy on a trip to Barry. To 'Billericay Dickie' and *Gavin and Stacey* can be added some typically right-wing MPs such as

Teresa Gorman and Harvey Proctor, who was famously done over by the *News of the World* when it exposed his spanking sessions with rent boys.

Proctor's demise got a mention in Simon Heffer's original Essex Man profile:

The county has sent more than its fair share of exceptional hardliners to Westminster: Teddy Taylor, Tim Janman, Teresa Gorman, Norman Tebbit and, of course, Keith Harvey Proctor. All these MPs offered themselves to the electorate on platforms of unashamedly robust Thatcherism, laced in some cases with a degree of xenophobia to appeal to the exclusivity of the tribe.

The simple values of the old cockney electorate found an echo, though it was not without its ironies. Perhaps the touching sincerity of the Essex creed has never been better seen than when one of Proctor's supporters, besides himself with incredulity, responded to the MP's downfall with the observation: ''Ow can a bloke who wants the wogs out be a pooftah?'

Proctor went on to run a shirt shop, sparking numerous dodgy 'shirtlifting' jokes in the Essex tundra.

So where does all this leave Billericay today? Well, like most parts of Essex it has the capacity to produce the unexpected. We drive out to Essex in May to search for the famed Norsey Wood bluebells.

Most of the houses in Norsey Road have two or three cars outside, usually a BMW or Freelander 4x4. Two black stretch limos drive past, on their way back from a funeral. The electric gates and pillars proliferate as we proceed further into the country.

As my wife Nicola drives past the large gaffs of wannabe footballers, looking for the famed bluebell woods, she's perhaps going too slowly for the driver behind. He veers off at the next left giving us a one-fingered salute out of the window. Well, this is Essex, where the car is king.

Eventually we find the turning for the woods. You don't expect to find ancient coppiced woodland in the heart of Billericay, but here it is, as featured on BBC2's *Natural World*. Thankfully it's now protected and run by Basildon Council. We park up and set off on one of the guided trails with our border terrier Vulcan. By the car park there's a warden's office, a whiteboard for bird sightings, leaflets on the woods and coppicing and a set of loos. As we walk along the woodland paths the bluebells are stunning, all over the undulating leafy forest floor and giving the whole place a Narnia-meets-Ian-Dury feel.

We picnic on the fallen trunks of a coppiced hornbeam amid a swathe of bluebells. Nicola spots wood anemones, townhall clock, yellow archangel, wild garlic (ransoms) and sweet woodruff, all overseen by a robin whose territory we are obviously invading to judge by his tweeting.

There's plenty to see in the woods as you pass female dog walkers in purple boots: a not very clearly defined bronze-age tumulus (found to contain two cremation urns in 1865), a hazel plantation, ponds and trenches dug in both world wars by the London Defence Volunteers. Vulcan goes off-lead and makes joyous circular runs up and down the surprisingly wet valley system, which makes the wood feel more like lush Devon than flat old Essex.

We get hopelessly lost in the valleys, but eventually return to the start, where the likeable warden says he's only ever had to rescue one person at post number five. Who would have believed you could get lost in Billericay?

A white van draws up in the car park and a group of youths in green luminous jackets get out. On the back of their jackets it reads 'Community Payback'. If Billericay Dickie had an errant son he might well have been set to work tiptoeing through the bluebells. Nicola asks the man in charge what they are doing with their saws and if they've volunteered to do some coppicing. 'None of 'em here are volunteers!' replies the man. 'We're sawing some timber up. Most of 'em enjoy it though, they're a good bunch of blokes an' that, they have a laugh.'

Norsey Woods is a weird outpost of the Iron Age in Essex and a romantic spot with its May carpet of flowers, though later we discover that 500 men were slaughtered in the woods during the Peasants' Revolt. We wonder if Billericay Dickie might have found it an ideal spot to take Joyce and Vicky or indeed rendezvous with Janet from the Isle of Thanet.

It's easy to forget that Billericay is surrounded by fields and woods. A mile or so down the road is Stock, where the writer Lavinia Greenlaw moved as a teenager. In her novel *Mary George of Allnorthover* and her punk memoir *The Importance of Music to Girls*, she wrote many poetic descriptions of the Essex fields in both frost and arid summers. Though, this being Essex, she also worked at a hairdresser's and wrote about youths in souped-up motors driving much too fast around multi-storey car parks and careering down country lanes, always with the cassette player turned up to maximum volume on the way to parties and punk gigs.

Fortified by nature, we leave Norsey Woods and explore urban Billericay. As we walk towards the high street, strolling behind a buggy-pushing mum in unwise black leggings, a huge holler pierces the air: 'JAAAAY! WHAT YOU DOING!' The toddler has run backwards as mum is trying to cross at the lights. There's no Islington cooing here, parental commands are demanding and, frankly, deafening.

After a couple of decent pubs, the Railway and the Crown opposite, the shops begin with Masons 'high-class family butcher' (in Essex class is never understated). These towns are starting to look familiar. Billericay has all the signature shops of its neighbour Brentwood. There appears to be some form of legislation that requires all Essex towns to have a nail salon (here it's 'Natural Nails – American-style professional nail care for ladies and gentlemen').

Similarly, a kosher Essex town has to have myriad hairdressers. In Billericay there's Revere Hairdressing, Hair by Alaattin, Essensuals 'next-generation Toni & Guy' (does this mean *Star Trek* Barnets?), Graham Webb international hairdressers (cut and blow-dry £28), Headline Hairdressing, Billericay Barber Shop, Red Hairdressing and Beauty Spa and Hotshots Hairdressers (barbers with a difference).

Add to this mix a number of beauty spas such as Bronzed and Polished, a chippy, several Indians, half a dozen pubs, a jeweller called Sparklers and a Wimpy bar (yes, the Wimpy bar has survived in Essex's lost world of fast food) and you have the ideal Essex dormitory town.

Even the chains become quintessentially Essex. At the tables outside Costa Coffee there's a sixty-ish bloke telling his Pam-like blonde wife and Gavin-like son, 'You'd have to give the old accelerator a pump like that ... twenty-five quid it was – you could buy a car on Tuesday, tart it up, sell it on a Thursday and make thirty quid! It was a lot of money in them days.'

But Billericay also has notions of class. Course it does, mate, there's a Waitrose, and several lovely old Essex weather-boarded houses by the venerable Chequers pub. It wants to be Hertfordshire, but with nail salons. Though there's trouble at Waitrose at school-leaving time. By the stash of whisky bottles there's a female member of staff talking to two shirt-sleeved policemen.

'It's hot out, innit?'

'Tell me about it!' says the PC. 'We've had quite a few reports of attempted theft, people acting suspiciously…'

It's like an episode of *The Wire*, but with more glottal stops.

Fortified by some legitimately purchased Waitrose organic bread and fresh pasta, I head past The Village Bar and Grill ('buy one cocktail get one free') where you could imagine Gavin's parents, Pam and Mick, enjoying some tagliatelle, and on past The Old White Hart. In Red hairdressing and beauty spa I discover a poster that's very *The Only Way Is Essex*. It's offering a 'Brazilian blow-dry, £60 Tues and Wed, £90 Thurs and Fri, £120 Sat and Sun'.

I'm not sure if this is referring to Brazilian blow-dry hair straightening or a shaved pubic region combined with a blow-dry, and don't really want to ask. But I hope it's a Brazilian and a blow-dry, not a blow-dry of a Brazilian. But just how much do the women of Billericay have to spend on Brazilian blow-dries?

Inside Red I ask Amy, the beauty manager, if *TOWIE* has boosted trade. 'Not particularly. I don't do vajazzles, that's more up Brentwood way,' she says, as if Brentwood is a different world to Billericay. 'They're all from Brentwood and it's more touristy there, people come just for *TOWIE*. We do nails and tans mainly, but people in the salon do like *The Only Way Is Essex*, definitely.'

I return to the pavement outside and become lost in thoughts of Brazilians.

'FUCKING TWAT!!!' There's a male voice loudly hollering abuse as I look at Red's window display. Oh dear. Have I been rumbled as a pervert from London hanging out at beauty spas and taking an unusual interest in blow-dries?

No, thankfully it's just a spot of road rage. A geezer in a Ford at the roundabout has drawn up next to another car and is giving him some Essex-style abuse. With a squeal of tyres he accelerates down the road to Basildon.

After my family return to London, I rendezvous, not with Ian Dury's Janet, but with my old pal Chris, a Scouser marooned among Billericay's Dickies. His wife comes from Essex and a career in the City has resulted in Chris and his family moving out from central London and into the 'burbs of Essex. Chris is waiting in The Railway, wearing a polo shirt and ordering a pint of IPA.

'How would I describe Billericay? I always describe the place as "everything I need, but nothing I actually want",' he declares. 'You wouldn't live here if you could afford Shenfield or Brentwood. People come here because of what it's not. It's not Wickford, it's not Basildon...'

So how does Billericay differ from, say, Basildon?

'Basildon, it's so bad it reminds me of Bootle!' laughs Chris. 'I did jury service there and the first thing you see is the Crown court, the county court and jobcentre all in one square. A lot of people there say, "I like it here, so I'm never going to leave." There's a kind of wilful ignorance. In Basildon you're on the doorstep of the most affluent city in the world and you still complain about asylum seekers. I can forgive Bootle, because it really is poor there...'

'Oh and there's the iron curtain of the A127!' adds Chris, downing his pint and apologising for drinking at City speed. 'Travel on the Fenchurch Street line and they're seven years younger on average the other side ... Oh, and write about Pikeys. Everyone's obsessed with them – there's a camp at Crays Hill off the A127. They all live in fear, like in *Snatch*.'

Winston Churchill might not have spotted it, but Chris has a point about the Essex iron curtain. South of the Southend Arterial Road, the A127, lie the badlands of

Basildon, Grays and Thurrock. North is the more affluent Billericay and proof you've made it.

Meanwhile, the Irish travellers community at Dale Farm in Crays Hill made national headlines in 2011 when Basildon Council evicted the travellers for not having planning permission for their plots. They had lived on the site of an old scrapyard for ten years and many children faced being made homeless. The United Nations Committee on the Elimination of Racial Discrimination got involved, calling for the evictions (or 'site clearance' as the council preferred to call it) to be postponed.

Basildon Council leader Tony Ball was adamant, telling the press, 'I am clear that the residents of the borough overwhelmingly support what we are doing. And I believe what we are doing is right. It is the opposite of racism. It's applying the law evenly and consistently.'

By the time we move on to the Crown and some excellent Adnams bitter, Chris has more to say about old-style East End views on Essex.

'The cabbies here are great. They all hate Ken Livingstone and Gordon Brown and they'll openly say, "I pay fuck-all tax." But sadly people are also very open in their racism. People feel very confident in expressing their views. They'll say things like "It's all right, there's no blacks here…" There's a casual racism, though they're decent people in every other way. I say London's always been a melting pot and try to at least get them thinking about it. My kid came home and there's only one black kid in his class and he said, "He's not from England, is he?" I said, "He is!" My son had picked this up from the other children, even at five.'

Chris confesses to finding Essex a strange place after living in central London.

'They're conservative with a small "c" here. The woman who cuts my hair said, "I've never been abroad; I like it here. So I don't ever want to go." No thought of giving it a go. There's a kind of wilful ignorance. There's a kind of Essex mafia where I work; they never discuss a novel or a film. They're very meat and two veg and set in their ways.'

So how does he find driving in Billericay?

'Cars are a status thing too. They say you've made it. That's why people drive so aggressively. There's no "after you" here. It's a working-class-made-good thing. They think they've risen out of the mire. They'd all live in detached houses if they could. They don't like their neighbours much.'

The Chequers is our next high street pub, a delightful old boozer with a weather-boarded exterior and cosy bars. We discuss house prices, local obsessions with schools and the campaign to save Buffers coffee bar at the station.

Chris has much to air about his mixed relationship with Essex, though not without some wit too. Ironically, he's now bringing up his children in Essex, a target of local mirth amid the regional stereotypes: 'My children are the cockney kids of a Scouser. Someone here said, "You can nick cars and they can sell 'em!"'

It's time to leave for the train back to Liverpool Street.

At the station I manage to purchase some crisps from the vending machine and admire an advert offering me a chance to 'Be a part of it. Essex Location City Style'. It's for boutique two-bedroom apartments, just thirty-one minutes from the City and twenty-one minutes from Stratford. 'Enjoy late City nights, dining by the Thames, going out in the West End or watching the theatre. All within reach of 8 Stock Road,' declares the optimistic copywriter. I try not to think of Simon Heffer's description of vomiting on trains home from Liverpool Street.

The train arrives, departs and then halts between Billericay and Shenfield. The driver announces there has been a fatality in the Ilford area.

'What sort of stupid wanker tops themselves on a Friday night when we're all trying to go out?' asks a Dickie who's boarded at Billericay. After forty minutes the train judders into Shenfield, as three girls in designer clothes bemoan the sabotaging of their clubbing and say they've met Mark from *TOWIE* and all that Essex lot are 'suffering from ADD'.

Bereft of announcements, this commuter despairs and heads outside to try and find a bus. Maybe I'll never escape Essex. But I've been to Billericay and I'm the right side of the iron curtain of the A127. And I'm doing very well.

7

CHIGWELL: THE LARGEST MIRROR IN ESSEX

The barmaid in the King William IV has huge fake eyelashes and is wearing a black leather apron. She looks a little like Amy Childs and has the same Essex friendliness. Though she's a bit baffled when confronted with six silver lager taps, I spot a solitary hand pump and ask if they have any real ale.

'Is that bitter?' she asks. No, they don't have any, she affirms, so it's a Peroni for the gentleman and a white wine for the lady.

I'm here with my wife Nicola because the King William is one of the venues on the unofficial *TOWIE* coach tour of Essex. I ask the barmaid if it's true that *The Only Way Is Essex* people come to this very pub.

'Yeah, we had the two Laurens in here the other day. Did you see it last night? It weren't as good as the first two series. Not as cringey...'

The pub has a wooden floor, white bar, simple pale wooden tables and spotlights. It's tastefully decorated and has several much-older-than-*TOWIE* groups enjoying lunch.

This is Chigwell, at the heart of Essex's 'Golden Triangle' along with Loughton and Buckhurst Hill, where mock Tudor houses change hands for millions. West Ham footballers live here. Paolo Di Canio used to sometimes take the tube from Chigwell to training.

It's also famed as the setting for the BBC comedy *Birds of a Feather*, which ran from 1989 to 1998. Pauline Quirke and Linda Robson played Tracey and Sharon, the wives of two jailed armed robbers. Tracey's expensive gaff in Chigwell had been bought with the proceeds of husband Darryl's heists. Though in fairness, Darryl also had a more Essex-friendly legitimate business building conservatories. He claimed to be just a bank robber 'on the side'.

In Chigwell, Essex meets London and imposes itself with more columns than you can shake a personalised number plate at. When I interviewed *Sunday Sport* publisher David Sullivan, now chairman of West Ham, at his Chigwell home in the 1990s, there were deep carpets, Doric columns and statues of jockeys on the lawn. Chigwell is where Essex Man goes when he gets seriously loaded.

Back in the King William, we take a seat in two of the armchairs and order some Romana white onion soup with a cheese croute and winter bruschetta with asparagus, Gorgonzola, prosciutto, balsamic onions and Stirata Romana bread.

'Look out for eyelashes in the soup,' quips Nicola. It's a creamy onion soup that's pretty good, even if it comes without bread. 'How's your bruschetta?' I ask. 'It's magnificent!' says my hungry wife.

The barmaid asks us if everything's OK with our meals

and we answer yes, everything's fine. Nicola asks if the staff get to taste the meals and Amy says they've tried everything on the new menu.

We hope to celebrate the 200th anniversary of Charles Dickens by also visiting The Olde King's Head, built in 1547, the pub on which the author based the Maypole Inn from *Barnaby Rudge*. In one of his letters, Charles described it as 'the greatest place in the world ... Such a delicious old inn opposite the church ... such beautiful forest scenery ... such an out of the way rural place!'

'Do you know where the King's Head is?' I ask 'Amy' the leather-aproned waitress. 'Charles Dickens used to drink there.'

'Oh reaaaaally?' she answers in her high-pitched Essex accent. The (possibly unkind) thought occurs that maybe she doesn't know who Charles Dickens is. Perhaps she thinks he's some sort of Essex luminary in the latest issue of *Heat*, a sort of literary Mark Wright.

'Nah, I've never heard of the King's Head.' Her Polish colleague intervenes. 'Oh, they mean Sheesh!' exclaims Amy. 'It's a Turkish restaurant. Do you have a car? No, well walk down that way for ten minutes.'

We walk past a series of modern houses with names like El-Noor, all fronted with columns and ostentatious white urns for plants behind electric gates.

'He had both his hands off the wheel!' exclaims Nicola leaping towards me, as a driver passes, busy changing his mobile from one hand to another.

Opposite the white weather-boarded tower of St Mary's Church and Chigwell School – the public school that educated William Penn, founder of Pennsylvania – we find The Olde King's Head. There's a sign for the King's Head pub still on display, but also a modern swirl on another sign by the gate saying Sheesh.

The outside of this magnificent building is still delightful, with overhanging upper storeys, black-and-white beams and a Dickensian frisson. It looks relatively unchanged in this leafy village setting, if you don't count the motors.

Only it seems to be shut. We explore several locked doors and eventually make a final bid to enter by the car park. By the electric gates there's a side entrance. 'Ah, I see you don't exist unless you have a car in Essex,' I mutter.

We stroll across the car park and are greeted by a statue of an Ottoman warrior on a horse. Well, it is Essex. And a statue of bison. Plus two concrete lions by the entrance.

The conservatory has now become the main entrance of Sheesh. Probably so you can better admire the black 4x4 motors in the car park. There's a red MG sports car parked next to the outdoor chairs. This is where the waiters keep menus and condiments in the open boot.

'Good afternoon, have you been here before?' asks a black-shirted Turkish waiter, rushing to greet us. When we say we haven't, he insists on giving us a guided tour.

The first thing you notice is that everything is black and white. And that there are bling chandeliers every-where and faux gothic mirrors.

'Charles Dickens used to drink here,' says Nicola.

'Really, I didn't know that.'

The waiter invites us to view the large dining room,

again full of chandeliers. 'And here we have the largest mirror in Essex,' he announces with a proprietary air, gesturing towards a huge mirror that covers the whole of the far wall. Nicola laughs.

'No, really, I'm serious, it is the largest mirror in Essex!' he says.

Is there a competition for the largest mirror in Essex? Maybe so. Is the restaurant with the second-largest mirror in Essex plotting an extension?

The staff confirm that the building is owned by Lord Sugar, who rents it to Sheesh. Something has indeed turned up at the King's Head, and it's the grizzly old Amstrad supremo. Dickens channelled by Alan Sugar and *The Only Way Is Essex*? Only in Chigwell.

The stairs are covered in a zebra-skinned carpet. It's hard not to giggle as we ascend them.

'It's fabulous!' says Nicola. 'It's lovely! I love that over the top Idi Amin style of decoration.'

'But you're the poshest person they've had in here and you like it?' I whisper, incredulously.

'Maybe it's just because I like animals and want to stroke it.'

'They say that Charles Dickens liked this pub when it was the King's Head,' says Nicola again to the waiter, as he guides us past the piano to the Love Lounge private dining area.

'Did he have a drink here?'

'I think he came in here more often than that...'

I reflect that at the end of *Barnaby Rudge* the Gordon rioters trashed the fixtures and fittings of the Maypole

Inn. In the modern era some might say that *TOWIE*-style does a much more effective job. What would John Willet of the Maypole, possibly the prototype for Al Murray's Pub Landlord, make of it? He'd be staring at the fire in bemusement with his cronies Solomon Daisy and Phil Parkes (the gamekeeper not the ex-West Ham goalie).

We are ushered up to the VIP area on the balcony, where the waiter tells us 'the average spend is £1,000'. 'So do *The Only Way Is Essex* people come here?' I ask.

'He's here now! Mark Wright's in the conservatory.'

Wherever you go in Chigwell, *TOWIE* is not far behind. Feeling a little light-headed after all this Tudor-meets-Dubai chic, we are ushered to our seats. We've decided to have our second mini-meal of the day.

'Why do you think they're being so friendly?' I ask Nicola.

I'm wearing scuffed DM shoes, black Craghopper trousers, a Ben Sherman shirt and Braintree hemp jacket. Nicola has wild hair, a washed-out pinkish Arsenal T-shirt, no heels and a designer jacket that she got from a charity shop.

'Is it that we're so scruffy they assume we must be posh? Or is it completely obvious we must be journalist types?'

Everything is black. The bar is black and there's a Nanny Pat lookalike in a black armchair. Our table and the floor are both covered in gleaming 'mockodile' material.

The table has those huge wine glasses you see on *The Only Way Is Essex*. There's no real ale, of course, so we have another Peroni and a large Pinot Grigio. We can indeed glimpse Mark Wright sitting in the conservatory. If he were alive today Dickens might use Mark as a modern-day Thomas Steerforth, tempting Essex lovelies away from lives of purity and innocence. The party of Essex wives lunching behind us burst into a chorus of 'Happy birthday to Jean'.

Our food arrives on black plates and is actually very good. There's a feta cheese salad, three excellent cheese and spinach rolls and a splendid variety of hummus-style dips served with chunky pitta bread.

'Are you the strippergram then?' asks birthday girl Jean, as a retired friend ambles over. We can hear snippets such as 'She's done quite well, she's an attractive woman...'

There's a blonde Lydia Bright lookalike in stonewashed jeans and an expensive top outside. A young Joey Essex wannabe and his girlfriend in leopard print and stilettos arrive. They appear to have come straight from school and order Coke and chips. It's Monday and the place isn't short of custom. There's a few mums arriving now with their sons in Chigwell School uniforms.

Visiting the gents, the urinals are – yes – black and so too are the loos, while the mirror has a glittering smashed-glass diamante effect.

After coffee we ask for the bill (£39 once service is added, how do these *TOWIE* people afford to lunch every day?) and the waiter ushers us upstairs again and stands us before a portrait.

'Can you tell me which king this is?'

It looks like Charles I, but with a different face. Suddenly a man in paint-spattered work clothes stands next to the portrait. We read the label below the portrait: 'King Colin XIII, who reigned during the construction of this restaurant.' We congratulate King Colin on his elevation to royalty and his massive mirror and suggest he wears the wig more often.

'Now you can say you have met a king,' says the waiter.

We leave the restaurant, walking past the happy groups in chairs outside, past the patio heaters, the Ottoman warrior on his horse. The electric gates whirr open and a huge black SUV with a personalised number plate reading 'VEG' pulls up. The driver stops to lean out of the window and chat to another driver in a Smart car branded with the logo of a fish restaurant on the side.

One reason Chigwell is so popular is its proximity to Epping Forest. We've enjoyed the area on many a day trip from London, exploring its dreamy paths and ancient tracks. It's an amazing place when the leaves are falling and the lack of signage means it's easy to imagine yourself miles from the nearest city.

A favourite spot of mine is Loughton Camp, an Iron Age hill fort in the middle of the forest. There are still huge circular earthworks and pits where flints were mined and worked. You can hold a flint flake made by an Essex Man 2,500 years ago.

Loughton Camp is also the place where dandy high-wayman Dick Turpin was said to have hidden after committing highway robbery on the A13. There's an unsubstantiated legend linking the camp with Boudicca and her big bundle with the Romans, while a more modern legend, Rod Stewart, still has a house on the edge of the forest.

We walk back towards the Chigwell High Road and

detour down a footpath. It runs alongside a house with grounds protected by a concrete fence, a wire fence behind, barbed wire on top and CCTV.

'That person really doesn't want to be disturbed. Must be a footballer. Look, you can see a swimming pool through this gap,' declares Nicola, standing on tiptoe and peering through a small chink into this Chigwellian fortress.

The footpath emerges in Meadow Way, a road of little mock Tudor palaces. 'Look, there's a gym in this person's extension!' says Nicola.

Every house has at least one large motor at the front, behind locked gates, even though street parking is free. 'None of them know how to garden, the ideal seems to be concrete,' muses Nicola. 'Neither wildlife friendly nor pleasing to the eye.'

A skip reads 'ESSEX WASTE' in the front of one of the gardens.

At the bottom of the solidly suburban Meadow Way the road emerges in attractive hilly freshly ploughed fields. A few miles away is the farm where Sally Gunnell grew up, learning to hurdle over bales and eventually winning a gold medal at the Barcelona Olympics in 1992. This prompted a tabloid to come up with the risqué headline: 'Proof that Essex girls do come first.'

'It's the posh part of Essex, but it wasn't a posh farm,' Gunnell, who now lives in Sussex, tells me today. 'It was a good working farm with plenty of mud, just six miles from the new Olympic Village.'

Around Chigwell station the High Road has a predictable quotient of Essexy shops. Tanners has a tanning machine in the window and advertises eyelash extensions at £10. A woman in a pink tracksuit stands outside In-Jeanious boutique. There's Debra, where Gemma from *TOWIE* has her hair done, Village Deli, Balanced Life therapy centre, AJS Blinds, Squash boutique with a leopard-print window display, and a Volvo showroom.

At the tube station we find pretty flowers growing in the yellow sand containers. Someone has taken a lot of care of Chigwell station. It's on the London Underground – the Central Line – but spiritually Essex.

There's a woman with her daughter chatting loudly into her mobile: 'I'm on my way to Westfield. Saturday was a nightmare, it was mobbed. I'm not an online person, Shell, I've got a couple of things to change. It's absolutely massive! They've got a nice champagne bar there though. Did you 'ave a late one then?'

It would be quite easy to write a sequel to *Birds of a Feather* just ear-wigging at Chigwell station. We're still a little dazed by the excesses of Sheesh, the motors, the pillars, the lunchtime alcohol of Essex. I'm thinking of Dickens. He would have certainly relished observing the *TOWIE* characters and venues and writing about them.

And Dickens did like a bit of end-of-pier sensationalism – so maybe he'd have enjoyed the zebra carpets, electric gates and not very 'umble Range Rovers in the car park of Sheesh, Alan Sugar's done-up old boozer. What larks, Mark Wright, what larks!

8

HARLOW, I LOVE YOU

Harlow is the town that inspired David Cameron to declare, 'The only way is Essex!' in the House of Commons. The PM was responding to a loaded question from Harlow's campaigning Conservative MP Robert Halfon in March 2012. Halfon asked:

> Is the Prime Minister aware that Harlow has the highest rate of business growth in the whole of the United Kingdom thanks to a Conservative council that is open for business, and a government that has invested in an enterprise zone, increased apprentices and cut taxes. Will the PM come to Harlow so we can show Britain how to lead the economic recovery?

The Prime Minister replied, 'In danger of being accused of watching too much television I think you could summarise the question by saying, "The only way is Essex!"' Flanking Cameron, Nick Clegg smirks at this point, while George Osborne looks as if he prefers *Made in Chelsea*. Cameron continued:

And I know he speaks up for his county. What I would say, I congratulate Harlow on the fantastic achievements that they have. The government wants to play its part, not least by the enterprise zone in west Essex that's covering Harlow, and we hope it will create 5,000 new jobs.

Following Cameron's *TOWIE* reference, *The Sun* immediately turned to an unlikely economic guru in Amy Childs, who commented, 'I've always been proud of Essex and hearing David Cameron talk about Harlow being helped by the *TOWIE* effect is mental.'

Robert Halfon, who describes *TOWIE* as 'a great programme, absolutely hilarious', was so pleased with the PM's reply that he placed the video on his Essex-friendly *Rob's Blog*.

'I don't know if David Cameron watches *TOWIE*, but he might, as my question wasn't prompted at all, he didn't know what I was going to ask him,' Halfon tells me from his hands-free mobile, while driving from Harlow to the House of Commons. 'But I was really proud that Cameron said that. We had the highest business growth in the whole of the UK and I wanted to shout about it, because Harlow gets a bad press outside, but it's an incredibly entrepreneurial place. It's also conservative with a small "c". There is a huge work ethic. Harlow is a town based on aspiration, people come here to make their lives better. It's very strong on small businesses, you only have to go to a fair and see people selling jewellery or business cards.'

Harlow is part of East End Essex, stranded on the

Hertfordshire border. It has cheaper-than-average houses and is better positioned for commuting and flying than many Essex towns, being one fast-train stop from both Stansted Airport and Tottenham Hale.

One side of the station borders the river Stort, full of narrow boats under overhanging trees – only it's fenced off, spiritually and literally, and the exit takes you determinedly towards the new town. Down the line are quiet Hertfordshire towns, Sawbridgeworth with its antique shops set in old maltings, and the rustic charm of the river walks around Roydon.

But Harlow has more in common with Basildon. It's a new town, designed in 1947 to tempt east and north London overspill residents away from urban decay, with lots of roundabouts to speed workers to their factories. It scored a number of firsts: the Lawn was the first residential tower block in Britain in 1951, and it also had the first pedestrianised centre. Harlow's creator was Sir Frederick Gibberd, a man with a magnificent handlebar moustache who lived in the town he built, unlike the creators of other new towns.

Like Basildon, Harlow has a disproportionate hold on the political consciousness. Ed Miliband was careful to visit on the very same day that David Cameron and Nick Clegg were addressing workers at a tractor plant in Basildon in May 2012. Both were seeking to appeal to aspirational Essex voters, or to use the technical term, second and third generation exiled East Enders who want to make a bit of dosh.

Though Miliband rather perpetuated his policy wonker

image by not being able to tell Lucy Manning from *ITV News* who his favourite *TOWIE* character was: 'I must confess I'm not as avid a watcher as I should be ... But what I say is, Essex always has stood for aspiration. For people aspiring to get on here in Essex ... they feel like they are running up against a brick wall.'

I ask Robert Halfon about the synchronised Cameron, Clegg and Miliband visits to Essex. 'Essex is the voice of Britain,' declares the MP. 'Whoever wins Essex wins the country because it's the voice of the working man. We're the weather vane of political opinion!'

Halfon is an expert at campaigning on Harlow-friendly, not particularly Conservative issues, such as increased apprenticeships (he was the first MP to employ a paid apprentice in the House of Commons), lower fuel prices for white van businesses, and Conservatives becoming involved in trade unions. His website reveals that he is 'a huge curry fan' and a supporter of Harlow Town and Chelsea FC, who were once managed by Harlow's Glenn Hoddle. Brought up in north London, Halfon's cousin owned John Walton clothes shop in Harlow.

His expenses policy is very down-to-earth Essex. His website states: 'I do NOT claim for a second home, as I have only one home in Harlow. I do NOT employ a relative. I do NOT claim for a newspaper allowance. I do NOT claim for first-class train travel. I do NOT claim a large food allowance.'

'I lived in Harlow during the expenses scandal and people were outraged,' says Halfon. 'The good thing about Essex is you don't get the politics of envy. It's a bit like America. Nobody minds if you're rich, but they want you to have earned it fairly.' Halfon's lived on a new estate in Harlow for ten years, having moved from nearby Roydon. He suffered two election defeats before winning by a narrow margin in 2010 and, despite the fact he's a professionally optimistic politician, seems to genuinely like his constituency. He went to Highgate School and then Exeter University, but says living in Essex has changed some of his political values.

'I love it. I'm so proud to be MP. I wouldn't live anywhere else. Lots of people use Harlow facilities and then moan and groan about the place, which annoys me but we've got a university now and the best FE college in Britain and the best sports complex in southern England. There are amazing things going on here.'

Harlow achieved further national prominence through Channel 4's *Educating Essex*, a compulsive documentary on the heroic efforts of headteacher Mr Goddard, his deputy Mr Drew and their fellow teachers to educate the demanding teenagers of Passmores Academy in Harlow. Deputy Head Stephen Drew became a national cult figure, coping with truancy, rudeness, insecurity and a teenage pregnancy by offering his pupils a mixture of tough love, tucking in shirts and doing up ties.

Educating Essex was not without moments of Essex earthiness. The *Evening Standard* reported:

In one scene Mr Goddard hides behind his door as Mr Drew enters the room, only to reach his arm around the door and welcome his deputy with a two-fingered gesture, drawing a 'You are such a wanker!' response from Mr Drew. Defending his behaviour, Mr Goddard said: 'Mates muck around.'

Particularly in Essex, it seems.

Robert Halfon was so impressed by this 'fantastic school' that he persuaded Education Secretary Michael Gove to visit Passmores.

So what is this town like that has inspired questions in the House and a TV series? Arriving at the station, you initially wonder where the town is – you're confronted by an office block and bus stop. Sir Frederick Gibberd couldn't have been a train user, as the station is a half-hour walk from the town centre.

There are buses, but after receiving convoluted instructions from the lady in the coffee bar, I opt for the walk. Before leaving, I'm intrigued to discover you can get a tan at the station. Tan Express offers a 'new revolutionary spraybooth' for commuters wanting to top up their orange factor. It's both entrepreneurial and reem. You don't get that in Hertfordshire.

My trek into town takes me down the New York-sounding Fifth Avenue. On one side of the Avenue is new housing for sale and on the other is a horse showground set in the fields and woods of Harlow Town Park, one of the 'green wedges' included in the design of the new town. Illuminated signs on the main roads display one of the town's priorities, the number of spaces in the town's three multi-storey car parks.

Near a concrete Sainsbury's store there's a subway and

grass-lined cycling track, which takes me across a couple of streets into Birdcage Walk. This has the first shops of my journey, Coral bookies, Kebabery, Fancy Fry fish and chips and Café Elite. They stand beneath box-like offices with yellow walls and 'To Let' signs in the window.

Birdcage Walk leads into Market Square. There's a sign on a building reading the 'Harlow dvi e Centre', which is actually the Harlow Advice Centre with two letters missing. In the square, a trader hollers, 'Come on, two boxes of strawberries for £1.50!' Yates's Wine Lodge is on the corner and in the middle of the square is a sculpture by Ralph Brown of two meat porters with a side of beef. One of the quirkier aspects of Harlow is fairly lowbrow shops surrounded by highbrow sculpture. There's a Goth shouting, 'Ah, it's raining, me hair's gonna get fucked!' while standing by the sculpture 'Portal Figure' by F. E. M. Williams. And there's a Barbara Hepworth: a high sculpture with a council crest on it that resembles the monolith from *2001* crossed with Cleopatra's Needle. Harlow has more than a hundred pieces of public sculpture and in 2009 the council voted to brand Harlow as 'Harlow Sculpture Town – The World's First Sculpture Town'.

This is something of which Robert Halfon MP is very proud.

'You get loads of snobbery from idiots who don't know better or who've never been here. Not many people know we're sculpture capital of England with Henry Moore sculptures all over the place. How many other new towns have that? We have amazing green spaces and Harlow Mill by the canal is just beautiful.'

By the civic centre, flanked by Pizza Hut and Nando's, stand the Water Gardens, listed by English Heritage. They're basically two oblong ponds with fountains in them and sculptures of a pig and a bird in the water. A Henry Moore totem pole-like structure stands at one end and 'Eve' by Rodin, whoever he plays for, is at the other. Health and safety signs declare 'WATER FEATURE' and 'CAUTION WATER'. From the Water Gardens there's a pleasing sense of distance as you look outwards from the town towards the woods of the Nettleswell Planation, though it's rather spoilt by the car park in the foreground next to the busy Third Avenue.

All these avenues remind me of Paul Simon lyrics – could it be the Seventh Avenue in 'The Boxer' is actually a reference to Harlow? Simon did lodge in Brentwood, after all.

And what's this? It's Mr Drew from *Educating Essex* going into a toyshop with his wife and children. He then moves on to Asda and I follow him in but, not wanting to shout out, 'Mr Drew, I think you're brilliant!' for fear of a detention outside his office, I retreat back to Esquires Coffee House, which is full of students from Passmores Academy.

Interestingly, Mr Drew is soon to take up an appointment as headteacher of Brentwood County High School. This prompted the *Brentwood Gazette* to run the headline 'Reality TV star is new head'. For a moment it appeared Amy Childs might be moving into education.

There's an interesting church made of brick and concrete and also the Harlow Playhouse, which is facing away from the town centre. Its entrance is pointed firmly towards the cars coming off the avenues. Forthcoming shows include Derek Acorah, Jimmy Tarbuck, *D-Day Darlings*, *Wrestle Force*, *Ultimate Bowie* and *Hormonal Housewives*.

Outside Riley's Snooker Hall there are four hoodies smoking and having a very Essex conversation: 'Know anyone who wants to buy a chassis? The only thing missing is the engine.'

Dodging traffic over a busy roundabout I track down the Square, Harlow's quite trendy music venue, which is strangely cut off from the rest of the shopping centre. Coming acts include Julian Cope and Dodgy.

Harlow had a thriving music scene of left-leaning bands in the 1980s. Norman Watt-Roy, bass player with Ian Dury and Wilko Johnson, is a former resident. Local band the Newtown Neurotics played at the Square, as did Porky the Poet, later to be Phill Jupitus, at a 1984 Miners benefit gig introduced by Billy Bragg. Other local artists included Paul Howard and ranting poet Attila the Stockbroker, who was living in Harlow at the time. Despite relocating to Brighton, Attila celebrated his thirty years of performing by returning to the Square for a gig in 2010.

My old schoolfriend Nick used to visit Harlow for Young Socialist meetings. The place is in a perpetual struggle for its political soul, never quite knowing if it's Old Labour, New Labour or Tory and forever marginal.

Harlow is definitely architectural Marmite. 'The biggest problem with Harlow is people want to preserve it in aspic,' says John Young, who moved to Harlow in 1967 and spent fifteen years as a Labour councillor, retiring in 2002. 'The sixties new town pioneers have now become nimbies!' Young had many planning battles with Lady Patricia Gibberd, the widow of Sir Frederick Gibberd, prior to her death – she was known as 'the titled heckler' to some councillors.

Young is proud to have been on the committee that redeveloped the Water Gardens, moving them twenty yards south. 'They were previously underused and sited between two footpaths from the car park. The town hall developed concrete cancer, with the metal rods rusting inside the concrete, which gave us the chance to build the civic centre. The Pat Gibberd lobby went ape and had the Water Gardens listed. But we got listed building consent and moved them and the place is much more used now. The original concept was a formal garden *a la* Versailles with a grand lawn and the mansion behind, but the mansion was never built. But when the town hall was demolished (it's now an Asda) and the civic centre was built, it became the mansion. In good weather it's lovely.'

Another of Young's achievements was managing to save an iconic Henry Moore sculpture of a family group that had been vandalised. 'The baby's head was snapped off and it went away for renovation. We managed to have it placed in the foyer of the civic centre, even though the Pat Gibberd lobby wanted a purpose-built pavilion for it to remain outside. But it was made of stone that didn't stand the weather.'

Harlow has problems with the town centre 'becoming a desert in the evening', says Young, and another problem is the fact it was built to be self-contained when now many people commute. 'The M11 buggered the Harlow town plan, as it was meant to be on the other side of the town by the railway so the industrial areas face that way. Parking is another issue. When Harlow was built the town planners thought there would be one car for every three houses, whereas now some houses have three cars. There's five at the house opposite me. Like everywhere else the place is being choked with motor cars.'

Nonetheless, he remains proud of his home. Young, a physicist, points out that ten years ago Harlow had 'the biggest research community outside Cambridge and Oxford' and that, though some of the houses may not look great from the outside, 'inside they're brilliant'. He also tells me that all the pubs are named after butterflies and moths, which is a poetic touch. 'Harlow is maturing, it's more like a normal town now,' he says.

The only other pub in the town centre apart from Yates's appears to be the William Alymer, run by Wetherspoons. It's set in what looks like a converted office fitted out with Sky TV monitors. The barmaid's friendly though, as she serves me a remarkably cheap pint of Ruddles. She's very *TOWIE*, saying things like 'Thanks, babe ... I'm so hungry don't even let me look at that ... my sister ain't got no money ... shu' up!' Upstairs by the gents it's good to see some civic pride. On the wall is a framed picture of Harlow's creator, Sir Frederick Gibberd, and also the Lawn tower block.

Taking a bus back to the rail station involves queuing by a pretty ugly dull grey multi-storey car park. Harlow is a strange place – full of green wedges, cheap houses, sculptures, some of the uglier or more classic aspects of post-war town planning depending on your viewpoint, and all surrounded by lush Hertfordshire villages. What everyone agrees on though is that the people of Harlow want to better themselves.

Robert Halfon has a typical Harlow anecdote about the Tesco I've just walked past. 'Harlow people are straight talking. If they think you're crap they'll tell you. But there's also lots of *Carry On* humour. I was outside Tesco leafleting and a lady said, "I saw your leaflet and you look very 'andsome, but you look bloody awful in real life!" She wasn't saying it maliciously, just to make me laugh. They don't like people who are pompous. They're very genuine in Harlow, not up their own backside like in some of the Home Counties.'

9

MADE IN DAGENHAM

As a child in upmarket Brentwood, Dagenham was somewhere you went by mistake after driving through outer Hornchurch. My dad, who grew up in Upminster, would lovingly drive his Ford Zodiac to all sorts of exotic locations such as Tilbury and even Frinton, but never to Dagenham. He had made it to Brentwood School, the masons and self-employment and he wasn't looking back to a land of council houses and a car factory.

Technically, Dagenham is part of the London borough of Barking and Dagenham. But spiritually it's always felt 100 per cent Essex. And maybe the place has been misjudged. Dagenham has bred an inordinate amount of talent; and the common theme is nearly always a desire to escape.

In 2011 Billy Bragg, born in nearby Barking, explained what made him a singer to *The Guardian*:

A desire not to go and work in the Ford factory in Dagenham. That's what everyone where I lived was being educated to do. To get out of it, it seemed I needed to be a boxer, a footballer or a rock star. I didn't want to get punched on the head, and I'm not that good at football so I went for the music.

Sixties legend Sandie Shaw worked for six weeks as a punch-card operator at Ford, and at the end of 2010 revealed to *Desert Island Discs* that escape propelled her entire career. Dudley Moore was another who left to achieve stardom. Partnering the great Peter Cook, Moore managed to combine cleverness and filth in some memorably obscene recordings such as *Derek and Clive Live* before becoming an unlikely Hollywood star in *Arthur*.

England manager Sir Alf Ramsey, the man who won England the 1966 World Cup, came from Dagenham, although it didn't sound like he did. Sir Alf famously had elocution lessons, which resulted in him sounding like a bizarre combination of Parker from *Thunderbirds* and Bertie Wooster, and all with a Captain Mainwaring-esque air of pomposity. Throughout the Swinging Sixties he maintained his upwardly mobile received pronunciation, indicating a deep insecurity about his working-class origins.

Ramsey's captain, Bobby Moore, was raised in Waverley Gardens off the lorry-strewn River Road in Barking and hat-trick hero Geoff Hurst was also a Barking lad. While former England gaffer Terry Venables was born on Valence Road and, through a variety of business schemes such as selling thingmywigs, setting up Scribes West bar and buying Spurs, demonstrated the eye for a deal beloved of a self-made Essex Man.

Tottenham legend Jimmy Greaves grew up in Daggers and during my childhood, according to local gossip, moved down the road to a house near Upminster Common. After recovering from alcoholism – West Ham suffered in his final season – he used his Essex wit to create a new career as the cheeky half of Saint and Greavesie on ITV's *On The Ball*. The walrus-moustached Greavesie also became a beloved *Sun* columnist.

Yet another footballer, Arsenal and England's Tony Adams, grew up at 6 Foxlands Road, the son of an asphalter, playing for the youth side Dagenham United alongside former West Ham skipper Steve Potts. Chelsea's John Terry is another son of Dagenham and so is Leicester City's Paul Konchesky.

Dagenham has also featured in song more than most towns. The Stranglers wrote 'Dagenham Dave' about the eponymous Dave, a Mancunian scaffolder who once worked at the Ford plant. Dave followed the band everywhere and eventually committed suicide jumping off Tower Bridge. Morrissey also penned a song called 'Dagenham Dave', this time with more homoerotic tones.

More recently, the suburb has given us rapper Devlin and, oh my gosh, *The X-Factor* star (she came third) and *I'm a Celebrity* winner Stacey Solomon, a single mum from Willoughby Close. After winning *I'm a Celebrity*, Solomon said she'd rather be back in Dagenham with a Malibu and pineapple cocktail. Her humility, big personality and garrulous humour made her an instant hit with the viewers. Even 'Mr Nasty' Simon Cowell described her as 'one of the most genuinely nice people we've had on this show'.

When Solomon first appeared on *The X-Factor* the show created a spoof episode of *Location Location Location* in Stacey's Dagenham, 'a delightful little town situated in the south-east of England'. It was full of charm and famous for its 'sumptuous baths, churches next door to other churches and, of course, its grass'. It cited the 'dazzling array of quality outlets' as Stacey visited the corner shop, filmed the Moby Dick where she had her Sunday roast and showcased the tallest tower block in Dagenham. Just in case we didn't get the joke, the spoof ended with the trailer: 'Next week: Luton's best sheds.'

Daggers deserves another look. Inspired by *Made in Dagenham*, it's time to visit the Ford Motor Works. Nigel Cole's film tells the forgotten story – though it's a bit *Carry On Striking* at times – of the Ford strike for equal pay for women in 1967. It's astonishing that it was so recently that this basic right had to be fought for. Sally Hawkins gives a fine performance as Rita O'Grady, a cipher for all the women who fought against the Labour government, Ford bosses and some of their male colleagues.

It's also the only film to ever mention Warley, where the strikers had meetings with the Ford management. When I was growing up I thought it was simply called 'WarleyFords', as that's what the bus stop was called. On the way to Warley in the film, the untrustworthy union officials stop at a Berni Inn, then a symbol of sophistication.

Despite many a trip to Dagenham Heathway when my sister lived there, this was my first visit to the mysterious area of white by the Thames in the *London A–Z*. It looks a bit like *terra nullius*, the Latin term meaning land belonging to no one. Do you fall off the edge of Essex if you venture there?

The Ford Works lies at the southern end of Dagenham Heathway. Built in 1929, it was once the biggest car works in Europe, making nearly eleven million cars, trucks and tractors up to the year 2000. Essex and the Cortina had a symbiotic relationship – the only thing the Ford Works didn't supply was the furry dice and sunstrip. Although it no longer makes cars, Ford still has a press shop and transport operation here – and the Dagenham Diesel Centre, powered by the three wind turbines.

Once I've recovered from the shock of hearing classical music playing at Dagenham Heathway tube station, I turn past the nail salon and pie and mash shop and head towards the wind turbines that rotate steadily beneath the slate sky.

Certain shops give the area an archetypal Essex feel. There's Val's Hair and Beauty, Luxury Nails, Bairstow Eves, a Bonmarché in an ugly red brick shopping centre and a bearded smoker outside the Lord Denman boozer. But the demographic is changing, as demonstrated by the Afro-Caribbean Food Store selling salt fish and Tez Halal butchers. The library doubles as a council one-stop service. Several blokes in baseball hats, white trainers and tracksuit bottoms loll on chairs waiting for their numbered ticket to come up.

The Heathway's full of identikit post-war current and former council homes striving for individuality through cottage cladding, mock Tudor frontages, porches, extensions, new doors and, in several cases, palm trees planted incongruously in the front garden. It terminates at a crossroads populated by three Bangladeshi Indian restaurants, Kevin's Corner (selling washing machines) and RTV Satellite, set in a mock Tudor block and covered in a vast array of satellite dishes.

The Heathway becomes a more constricted industrial gulch called Chequers Lane. To my right is a new Homebase warehouse, plus Halfords and KFC. On my left is the Jobcentreplus, as if to emphasise that here lie your only options for work, and then the large red-brick Ford works with a sign reading Ford Stamping Operations, which sounds a little violent to me. There are two palm trees by the Ford entrance. There's little evidence of activity apart from two men in luminous jackets having a fag break outside.

Ahead lies the flyover of the A13 Thames Gateway section (the Thames Gateway housing development has been metaphorically bricked up, cut by the government) and a park of rust-coloured containers stacked five-high.

Chequers Lane takes the post-apocalyptic pedestrian to the unstaffed Dagenham Docks station. A concrete stairwell leads up to a bridge over the railway line that is defended by barbed wire. 'Danger of death' warns a sign by the tracks. The vista here is huge pylons, rail tracks, motorway, the black pool of Dagenham Breach and a wind turbine on Barking Power Station.

It doesn't feel like London. The wind picks up and you start to smell the river. There are no other pedestrians.

It's all very *28 Days Later*. This would be a great place to dispose of bodies, do dodgy deals or set up a ruck between the ICF and Millwall's F Troop.

On the other side of the tracks the road widens, there's a bus stop with no one waiting and wide pavements lead past the square blocks of the power station and Chequers Lane Sustainable Industrial Park.

Then the cement lorries and Hovis trucks start to rumble by. Here there are fenced-off warehouses and a Hovis depot full of bread-carrying yellow lorries. A blue cyclists' sign points down Choats Lane with the words 'Thames View'. Opposite Kuehne + Nagel Drinks Logistics (is there anything logistical about drinking?) brave cyclists and pedestrians are instructed to turn down Hindmans Way.

Hindmans Way is narrower and is an unofficial dumping ground for every piece of detritus in Dagenham. Rusting temporary fences conceal tyres, bits of sofas, mattresses, beds, carpets in bin bags, cans, plastic bags and paper coffee cups.

It's very blue collar and Bruce Springsteen. Here men do geezerish things like drive trucks fast down empty roads and throw their lunch in the hedge. Would Bruce have taken his girl down to 'The River' via the mud of Hindmans Way? Probably not if he ever wanted to see her again.

The pavement ends and becomes mud surrounded by concrete markers. As ever-more-heavy lorries trundle past it starts to feel dangerous and, seeking safety from death under large wheels, I find my DMs trudging through soft, oozing grey mud. My phone battery runs out, adding to the sense of doom as the road passes a set of gasometers. 'Danger of flooding' reads a road sign. A black pool has mysterious broken pipes rising out of it. Reeds flank the road to marshland.

Then the lane terminates with a solid black fence at a T-junction and signs for TDG and Cemex. There's a sentry post with a hut and a red-and-white pole barrier. The operative eyes me with bemusement.

And suddenly, by some disused tram tracks, there's the riverbank and a curved pier stretching out into the choppy waters of the Thames. There's a silo and a lorry at the end of it. I stand on the pier to escape the danger of demise by speeding cement lorry.

So here I am at last, sitting on the dock of Dagenham's bay like Otis Redding, watching the ships go by, wasting my time. That song was about unemployment and no doubt Otis would have been forced to get himself down to the Jobcentreplus by the motor works had he lived in Dagenham.

The waters of the Thames meet a bank of reeds, mud, fishing trays, floats and blue plastic bags. Across the river lies Thamesmead (featured in *A Clockwork Orange*) and two strange funnel-like industrial structures. I'm standing on the evocatively named No. 7 Jetty. A trendy Dockland Quarter it is not.

The dusk draws in and there's an urge to escape before I fall off the edge of the known world. I pace past Prax Petroleum, braving oozing cementy earth, along the wide pavements past more Hovis lorries, and into Dagenham Docks station. Three young salesman in suits get off the train and head for the industrial park with a look of apprehension. I dash onto the train and discover people and digital signage and that Fenchurch Street is only twenty minutes away. It's all so different to the other-worldiness of the Essex industrial marshes.

• • •

A few weeks later I return to sample another aspect of Dagenham life: Dagenham and Redbridge FC. It's an easy walk from Dagenham East tube to the stadium in Victoria Road. You can tell much about an area from its football fans. There's a friendly atmosphere around the pay-on-the-day turnstile and when I drop my programme a steward instantly alerts me. It's more like a bunch of mates than a football crowd.

As the teams emerge I hear a rhythmic drum beat. There's something in the Essex psyche that embraces the imperfection of life. Why else would a fan at Dagenham and Redbridge – at the time bottom of League One – be banging a huge drum as if he's at the Noucamp or the San Siro?

Dagenham might only get crowds of less than 3,000 (or 4,000 when the club offered 99p admission) but it's welcoming, stewards stop to chat and the fans in the North Stand create an atmosphere that outclasses the Arsenal Library. What's striking compared to a Premiership game is that the crowd is much younger – the drummer looks about nineteen – and there's more laughter and camaraderie.

The match against Yeovil begins with more rhythmic drumbeats of tribal Essex Man. Beside me there's a fat bloke in Dagenham shorts and a Vincelot replica shirt and a youth with gold-and-black bling headphones around his neck.

The chants are either a staccato 'DAGNAM!' or an elongated 'Dagg-er-nam! Dagg-er-nam! Dagg-er-nam!'

'Come on the 'Nam!' shouts one fan, evoking an unlikely image of grizzled war veterans on the Heathway.

Yeovil's Williams slices a one-on-one dismally wide and is greeted with chortling mirth and a double chant of 'You're not very good! You're not very good! You're not very good! IN FACT YOU'RE SHIT! And you know you are ... You're shit and you know you are...'

Only veteran keeper Tony Roberts keeps the Daggers in the game. Against the run of play, the home side score through Vincelot.

'ZIGGER DAGGER ZIGGER DAGGER OI! OI! OI!' chants a bearded man with guttural gusto, in a variation of the old 1970s chant of 'Zigger Zagger Zigger Zagger Oi! Oi! Oi!'

Yeovil equalise almost immediately through the tricky Oli Johnson, a player on loan from Norwich. A cry of 'Sort it out!' comes from the terraces – Essex vernacular for retrieving the situation by any means necessary.

There's a big cheer from the Dagenham fans when the half-time score reveals that West Ham are losing 3–0.

In the second half there's more enjoyment when a Yeovil striker heads hopelessly wide of an empty goal. 'How wide d'you want the goal?' is now the chant.

Then things go mental as Jonny Nurse turns his man to fire into the bottom corner. He runs to the side of the ground and embraces the Dagenham fans, earning a yellow card.

The crowd senses a home win and there's a sense of delirium. The appearance of sub Bas Savage sparks a quirky chorus:

> There's only one Bas Savage!
> He used to be shite but now he's all right!
> Walking in a Savage wonderland!

Yeovil go close and the fans sing, to the tune of 'Go West', 'Hands up if you thought you'd scored!'

The Daggers' Femi Ilesanmi earns a Vieira-style chant of 'He lives in Becontree!'

BOOM BOOM BOOM! The drum beats on. 'DAGNAM!'

The tension is too much for the fans: 'Let's pretend we've got Tourette's!' comes a chant, followed by a torrent of industrial language, F words and C words. And then a rousing chorus of 'DAGNAM TILL I DIE! I'M DAGNAM TILL I DIE!'

Rarely can Dagenham have evoked such cries of undying devotion. Is anyone really Dagenham till they die? There has to be an undercurrent of irony to all this, an awareness that reality doesn't match the dream. Otherwise why don't Terry Venables, Tony Adams, John Terry and the rest still live close to the dreaming wind turbines of Daggers?

The evening sun casts a benevolent light on the Victoria Road pitch. It's all rather enjoyable. David Cameron's Big Society is right here on these terraces, if only he'd look. And it's chanting, 'Who the fuck are Barnet?'

The whistle blows and the fans surge towards the Bury Road end, banging their drum and stopping to turn to the sparse gathering of Yeovil fans and sing to the tune of 'I Wanna Go Home', with yet more self-deprecating humour: 'We've won at home! We've won at home! How shit must you be? We've won at home!'

It's a great chant, mocking, yet taking humour from life's imperfections. If you are Dagenham till you die then at least you might die laughing.

10

GLAD TO BE GRAYS

Russell Brand says that in Grays you had to be good at either football or fighting to survive, and he was good at neither. This doesn't seem to apply to the twenty-year-old in a suit on the C2C branch line to Grays. He is having a loud phone conversation with his mother about the trial for ABH he's been involved in that morning. 'At one point the CPS had to point out that there was a victim in all of this … What Scott said helped. I was bricking it, but the judge said that he was clear that Mr Smith was defending his friend. OK, if he hadn't had as much to drink he may not have lashed out in the way he did but his main motive was defence.'

What's striking is the calm, analytical way he is discussing the case, almost as if he was with Alan Hansen or Lee Dixon on *Match of the Day*. You almost expect him to start making a point about interpretation of foul play and consistency among judges. 'He was umming and aahing over what he was going to give me. At the end of the day what I didn't want was a twelve-month suspended sentence. A £250 fine and fifty-six hours of community service and a year to do it in, that's fuck all. I'm delighted with the result.'

Grays in is the borough of Thurrock. The word Thurrock does not have the most romantic of connotations: the council's website reveals that in Saxon or Old English, 'Turroc' meant either 'the bottom part of a boat where the bilge water lies' or 'a dung heap in a field'. In July 2012 *The Guardian* asked, 'Is Thurrock really the most miserable place in Britain?' in response to the news that Thurrock had come bottom of the government's new wellbeing survey.

Grays station is surprisingly close to the Thames. There's a level crossing back over the railway lines and the grey waters of the river are immediately visible at Grays Town Wharf. I cross over the tracks and move past Dhillon's Traditional Fish and Chips and the Pullman pub. There's a charming old church here, St Paul and St Peter's, with Victorian graves, reminding you that this was once a village by the Thames. Some effort has been made to inspire the youth of Grays towards better things. There's Thurrock Learning Campus, a pseudo-weather-boarded building, on the left and the Beehive Volunteer Centre on the right.

Past another two pubs, the White Hart and the Theobalds Arms, is the Grays Town Wharf. The bank-side shows signs of Docklands-style redevelopment. New flats with balconies overlook the river. There's a muddy river inlet here, railed off and with riverside benches. Black and yellow slashes surround 'Flood Gates Keep Clear' signs on two black metal barriers. In the mud lies driftwood, two sunken shopping trollies, a car tyre and a bike frame. Broken groynes lie stranded in the muddy riverbank.

Upriver is the bright white Queen Elizabeth II Bridge over the Dartford Tunnel. Looking seawards, there are grain silos, warehouses, cranes and a large ship at the L-shaped wharf before the river meanders round to Tilbury Docks. It's possibly Essex's version of *Get Carter* country.

Walking seawards by the Thames, there's a grey concrete sea wall and then Thurrock Yacht Club. Small boats bob in the river and larger yachts are in front of the clubhouse, their rigging causing a metallic tinkling in the wind. The wooden wreck of the *Gull* lightship adds a pleasing Dickensian vibe to the riverfront here.

Further along the seawall, in front of three grim tower blocks, is Grays Beach Riverside Park. Someone has used their sense of humour in creating this name. There is a patch of green grass, yes, and then more muddy Thames foreshore, a forbidding sewage outfall pipe with a 'Danger: Keep Off' sign on top of it and another muddy stream inlet with a whole bike and a shopping trolley. But no sign of golden sand or, indeed, a beach. Did Russell Brand woo his former California Girl Katy Perry by promising her a trip to Grays Beach? No wonder they split up.

I retrace my steps back towards the town centre, passing a dog walker and a young couple ferociously snogging in the drizzle by the river. There's a group of hoodie lads by the Learning Campus.

'See you later, geez, message me on Facebook!' shouts one. His mate gives him the finger and smiles. Clearly they're learning something.

Russell Brand wrote in his memoir *My Booky Wook* that the psychogeography of Grays meant very little to him in 'grey desolate suburban Essex ... It was just very banal'. Crossing back over the railway line and negotiating the town centre, you see how a picaresque metrosexual male in tight trousers and winklepickers might not have fitted in to the general ambience of Grays.

Across the railway line the shopping area begins with a wonderful piece of Essex nomenclature, a shop called CURTAINS BABE. The sign is in upper case. Does it mean the shop sells curtains suitable for your babe, or is it run by a babe with a penchant for curtains? Or does it mean it's curtains, babe, it's all over? Or was it simply named after someone shouted out 'Curtains Babe!' at the brainstorming session on deciding a name? Whatever the scenario, it's got lots of curtains on offer.

At the crossroads there's another Essex staple, the black exterior of KT Nails Spa Beauty with plenty of fairy lights and nail technicians inside. Market stalls in the street are selling the sort of thing that goes down well in Thurrock, such as black rugs with tigers on them.

'Ten nice breasts for a fiver!' What, is this some relation of Russell Brand's? No, it's a man at a meat caravan with a microphone offering chicken. The company appears to be based in Birmingham and the same caravan also appears in Basildon. The Thames Estuary is a meat magnet for butchers from all over the land.

The main street leads to the war memorial and an imposing red-brick building that appears to be a rather nice town hall. Except it's not. All roads lead to the focal point of Grays – the Magistrates' Court.

Grays has at least four other fish and chip shops, a pie and mash and the Essex/Australian habit of abbreviating titles, hence we find Trop Shop, an emporium full of fish tanks. Several shops offer ready cash such as The Money Shop, Herbert Brown ('we buy gold for cash') and Cash Generator. Outside Cash Generator the balding manager is berating one of his polo-shirted staff: 'That geezer with the guitar sixty yards down the street ... you lost yourself money there.' Inside Cash Generator, the buy-and sell-store, there's a huge variety of items on offer that have previously been sold to the shop for cash. Electric kettles, music systems, chunky silver TVs that were state of the art ten years ago, DVDs, guitars, CDs, DVDs. It's capitalism at it's most simplistic, buying and selling in the ideal shop for Essex Man.

The very name of Grays is all about money. The parish of Grays Thurrock was named after the French Norman knight Henry De Gray. He purchased the parish of Thurrock as a nice little cash generator with the permission of King Richard the Lionheart in 1195.

Inside Grays Shopping Centre there's another Essex perennial, a Wimpy restaurant with a 'beat the crunch' breakfast. At the Break Bar (Starbucks might have colonised the UK but it's passed on Grays) a sixteen-year-old serves me warmish coffee with a hearty 'cheers'. On the next table four women are discussing how to escape when trapped on a cruise liner such as the crashed *Concordia*, apparently with detailed knowledge of the layout of such ships. Their friend comes over and declares, 'You're like a bunch of bleeding old fisherwives.'

There's not too much of interest inside Grays Shopping Centre. It's clearly suffered from its proximity to Lakeside shopping centre, a gigantic temple of consumerism one stop down the train line at Chafford Hundred.

To reach Lakeside from Chafford Hundred station (which incidentally has pink seats) the pedestrian climbs on to a covered bridge straddling eight lanes of traffic. It's as if the visitor is hermetically sealed from the exterior world of pylons and motorway cuttings. At the multi-storey car park visitors walk down from level six to level three and find House of Fraser and the other delights of Lakeside. It has all the usual chains, a Range Rover on the court to promote a win-a-car raffle, and a pie and mash shop. On Fridays Lakeside is full of teenage girls in white ankle socks and short skirts. Russell Brand writes that he used to go shoplifting in Lakeside, but strangely there's no blue plaque.

Back in Grays, you notice that there are more black and Asian faces than in other parts of Essex. It's poorer and therefore cheaper, with plenty of social housing and properties for sale at around £170k. It's not been an easy transition. In 2010 the *Thurrock Gazette* ran a piece on how the notorious nightclub Entourage had had its licence revoked after a brawl between clubbers and the police. It reopened as The Redeemed Christian Church of God House of Praise. Pastor Nivi Olujobi told the *Gazette*, 'A church has got to be better than a nightclub.'

Or maybe not in Grays. On the *Thurrock Gazette*'s website you can read the racial abuse against 'Africans' that ensued in the emailed readers' comments after the original piece.

This story matches some of the tales remembered by my pal Big Joe, who grew up nearby – 'I'm a Stanford-no-Hope man. Rainham was always the West End as far as I was concerned.'

'I believe I'm right in thinking that Thurrock was one of the only boroughs in the country not to license a night-club, apocryphally because the policing costs would be too much,' Big Joe tells me. 'When I lived there, between Raquel's of Basildon and The Circus Tavern in Purfleet it was a music-free zone – unless, of course, you happen to remember the night Radio 1 were stupid enough to visit Blackshot's Baths in the late 1970s. I suspect that might have been what did for Dave Lee Travis. I met his manager over a decade later, who went white when I reminded him of the incident. The banner headline on the cutting I saved read "Animals", you can probably guess the rest. The general consensus being Radio 1 was never going to pitch up in the borough again.'

Culture in Grays lies in Orsett Road, where a National Theatre-style brutalist building houses the Thameside Theatre, as well as the library and museum. A digital display above the doors is sending the message *Fur Coat and No Knickers*. Is that the dress code? Ah, no, it's the Mike Harding play at the Thameside Theatre. The forthcoming shows reflect old and new Grays: *An Audience with Jack The Ripper*, Tony Stockwell the psychic medium, and *Chat Masala*, a curry and chat show night with Hardeep Singh Kohli.

Thurrock Museum is rather good. As the only visitor I find plenty of space to look at displays on the history of life by the Thames. Grays is an urban outpost surrounded by fields full of history.

The displays cover the West Thurrock amphora burial, the Bronze Age barrow at East Tilbury, Roman kilns at Mucking and seventeenth-century meat bones found in Grays High Street, possibly sold by that bloke with the microphone offering chicken breasts for a fiver. There's plenty on Elizabeth I at Tilbury, the naval training ships that used to be moored off Grays and Thames sailing barges. Plus a 1960s poster for Hughie Green and *Opportunity Knocks* at the Regal, Grays, though no mention of the fact that Lee Evans went to Thurrock art college.

Chalk mines were once important in Thurrock. You can still see the chalk in the cuttings on the train line. The one positive thing Russell Brand has to say about Grays is his love of the old chalk pit that lay next to his childhood home, which had an air of C. S. Lewis and Enid Blyton to it. One of the old chalk mines is now Chafford Gorge, quite possibly Essex's answer to Cheddar Gorge.

The diversity section is an interesting antidote to some of the BNP-type views in the area. Thurrock was heavily influenced by the Bata shoe factory, built by the Czech company in 1932 complete with model housing for its workers. Other foreign influences included Anglo-American Oil, Procter and Gamble, Lafarge Cement,

Dutch engineers sent to drain the marshes, Irish settlers who helped build Tilbury Docks in the 1880s and Scottish farmers who took advantage of low rents in the nineteenth century.

From the museum, I walk back to the station in time to see a man in a black hood vault the level-crossing barriers because he can't wait for the train to pass.

I think better of trying a pub as my pal Gavin tells me a bloke wanted to start a fight with him the last time he visited a beer garden in Grays, where he was quietly supping a pint of Crouch Vale Brewers Gold – 'I just got long, menacing stares and loud coughs, presumably because I was a stranger, wore glasses, or he didn't like my footwear.'

He does add, though, that the locals were friendly at Grays Athletic Football Club. 'A couple of years ago I went to their FA Cup game against Carlisle United. After about twenty-five minutes the floodlights packed up and the tannoy announcer said, "Is there an electrician in the crowd who might be able to get the lights working?" There wasn't, and the game was abandoned with Grays 1-0 up. The poor Carlisle fans had to come all the way back to Grays a couple of weeks later, but they did win!'

It's a strange place, Grays, separated from Dagenham by Rainham Marshes and then Purfleet, and merging into Tilbury Docks in the other direction. A piece of inner-city London with tower blocks, stuck on a loop of the Thames but surrounded by marshland, farms and a northwards journey towards the aspirational destination and gated homes of Brentwood.

Yet it's not without some grim charm, once you see the sun set on Grays Beach. Maybe Russell Brand will retire to a riverside penthouse there one day.

A little further round the curve of the Thames lies Tilbury. My next trip is to a meeting about the Big Ocean Project, the proposed redevelopment of the derelict Tilbury Docks station into a museum of migration and the sea with a café and riverside viewing area. The station is 'Britain's Ellis Island', claims Big Ocean, comparing it to the entry point to New York for immigrants to the USA.

The meeting is being organised by KDC London, run by my old friend Dave Kampfner and his wife Nishani. Dave is a former photographer who saved the SS *Robin*, the world's oldest complete steamship, built at Thames Ironworks in 1890. During the SS *Robin*'s refurbishment it was moored at Tilbury, and Dave and Nish developed an affection for the area during this time.

'There's so much history here,' Kampfner says of the disused station. 'The *Windrush* arrived here in 1948 with the first immigrants from Jamaica. It was a holding station for the Dunkirk rescue fleet. The ten-pound Poms left for Australia from here. George Orwell writes about leaving from Tilbury in *Down and Out in Paris and London*. Gandhi arrived in Tilbury. And Cliff Richard arrived here as Harry Webb…'

'I'd keep that quiet if I were you,' I joke.

From Tilbury Town station it's a bleak industrial walk down Ferry Lane to the London Cruise Terminal, where the disused station lies. The Ship on Dock Road, the pub

that *The Sun* billed as 'the hardest pub in Britain' thanks
to the large number of fighting sailors, is now a pound
shop. When The Ship gained its title in the 1980s, rumour
sugggests that several other pubs wanted to come down
and fight the locals to prove they were tougher. Tilbury's
version of the Berlin Wall guards parks of lorries and
piles of containers, while juggernauts roar past every few
seconds. The tops of dockside cranes are visible but the
river Thames is blocked from view. It's all very *Sweeney*.

The London Cruise Terminal is still the departure
point for some fifty cruise liners a year. It's the first
section of the Thames where the river is deep enough for
large ships and in pre-flight days this was where immigrants arrived and emigrants departed from Britain.
From the Tilbury Riverside station new arrivals could
travel directly to London. Comfy seats and brochure
racks line the Cruise Terminal, but through a door at the
back is the old covered station forecourt, most recently
used as a car park.

It's an impressive but sad place, as ghost stations are
when contrasted with the old pictures of uniformed staff
and newsstands. Sir Edwin Cooper built the current
station in 1930. The station closed in 1990, but seeing
it today you realise how rapidly buildings decay. The
central clock is rusting away, the ticket office is full of
debris and water, yellow paint is peeling from the walls
and 'Buffet' signs are fading away. Yet it's a large airy
space and with a customer base of cruise passengers and
locals wanting to see the Thames it could surely be viable
as a riverside museum and café.

Ken from a Tilbury heritage charity tells me that this was the first place he saw when he arrived in Britain from Kenya. The harbourmaster of the Port of Tilbury, says he remembers being a P&O cadet ushering ten-pound Poms onto their boats from this spot.

A projector shows photos of the station and docks in their glorious prime. 'Tilbury Scrubbers, nothing's changed there then!' jokes one stakeholder, standing before a picture of the aforementioned Tilbury Scrubbers, the women who cleaned the gangplanks and decks of ships. Also on display are pictures of Gandhi arriving at the station, paddle steamers going to Southend, Clacton and Margate, and the grand Tilbury Hotel that was destroyed by a fire bomb in the Second World War.

There's a presentation and a sit-down discussion at the Cruise Terminal. 'There's people in Tilbury who don't know there's a river down there! We've got to open the river up,' says one Thurrock councillor. 'People come to sit in a small car park by the Cruise Terminal because that's currently the only place you can see the Thames.'

The consensus is that it's an excellent idea to regenerate the site, and the front at Tilbury is compared unfavourably to Gravesend on the opposite bank of the Thames. The Big Ocean Project might get people using the ferry to Gravesend again. 'I know people who haven't been to Gravesend for twenty-five years! And we want to get the Gravesend people coming here too.'

Another suggestion is that the area might become attractive to tourists who also want to visit the nearby World's End pub, mentioned by Pepys in his diaries, and

Tilbury Fort, while Coalhouse Fort can also be reached by a riverside footpath. Dave and Nish introduce me to Kevin Diver, the manager of Tilbury Fort, which is an English Heritage site. As the meeting ends, he kindly offers to take me on an after-hours tour of the fort.

We drive past the World's End and the sea wall to the fort. Across a marshy field lie the smoking chimneys of Tilbury Power Station. Kevin unlocks a small door in the imposing Water Gate, built in 1682 when the present fort was completed by Charles II. The stone facade features a pair of cannons, the royal coat of arms and an inscription, 'Carolus Rex', commemorating the King.

Once inside the fort it becomes apparent what a massive, impregnable place it was. We're in a huge parade ground standing in front of the guard room and chapel, with the officers' houses at one end, the foundations of the old barracks, magazines covered by protective mounds of earth and emplacements from where gunners would have defended the river from attacking battleships. It's the best-preserved low-profiled artillery fort in the country – something completely unexpected in container land by the Thames.

Kevin takes me up the ramparts to the defensive walls, where cannons stand in their embrasures alongside more modern artillery weapons. From this elevated position you can see that the fort is built in a kind of star shape, known as the bastion system. This meant the enemy could always be fired on from whatever angle they attacked. From the chapel terrace there's a view across the Thames to the fine old waterfront buildings of Gravesend.

There's more security here than at most houses in Chigwell. Two giant moats protect the rampart, full of flat, still water, making an inland attack practically impossible. A wooden bridge with drawbridges leads to a defensive island known as a ravelin. The geometry of the angular shapes is strangely beautiful, set against the marshes, but this was a serious military concern, protecting London and the whole nation.

As you'd expect, the fort is full of history, even though it's not seen action since the Dutch invasion of 1667. An earlier fort stood on the site and it was here, faced with the Spanish Armada in 1588, that Queen Elizabeth I gave her famous speech to her troops: 'I know I have but the body of a weak and feeble woman; but I have the heart and stomach of a King, and of a King of England too.' She then went on to say, in the tradition of many a later Tilbury woman, that any invading Spaniard would get a slap: 'And think foul scorn that Parma, or Spain, or any Prince of Europe, should dare to invade the borders of my realm: to which rather than any dishonour should grow by me, I myself will take up arms!'

There's a cell in the guardhouse where drunken soldiers were left to recover. Diver shows me the plaque commemorating the 268 Jacobite prisoners who were held here in cruel conditions after the uprising of Bonnie Prince Charlie in 1746. Some were executed, others died of disease, but, as a framed record on the wall reveals, many were sent to be slaves on sugar plantations in the Caribbean.

On a lighter note, Diver tells me about a famous

cricket match between the soldiers of Essex and Kent. 'Kent were said to have fielded an ineligible player and an argument broke out. The upshot of it was that the Kent players broke into the magazine and grabbed some muskets: one sergeant got shot and someone got bayoneted.'

We leave through the monumental Water Gate with big ships and the power station on the skyline and I reflect on what an unexpected day it's been, visiting the old Riverside station and the Fort. Tilbury seems a good metaphor for Essex as a whole. A bit rough, but amid all the heavy industry and the docks lie unexpected discoveries, dreams, hopes, adventures and history. And one day the citizens of Tilbury mighty even see their river heritage again from the viewing platform of the renovated Riverside station.

11

ROMFORD'S MARKET FORCES

Approaching Romford on the 248 bus from Upminster you realise that it's the ideal Essex town – it's completely ringed by A roads. What a great statement – we want roads, everywhere, with loads of shops in the middle.

The bus drives slowly through a series of diversions and traffic jams, past a rather apologetic section of the river Rom and stops at Romford station, scene of some legendary political infighting in 2005.

One of the most surreal headlines of election night was the BBC's wonderful breaking news story: 'Fight in Romford.' It wasn't just Tory leader Michael Howard who was given a bloody nose in that election. Conservative campaigner Robert Benham told the *Romford Recorder* he was attacked outside Romford station by a Labour supporter. Harsh words had been exchanged between Labour and Tory campaigners before the big bundle erupted. And then it went all, 'Oi, are you looking at my ballot box?'

'The next thing I remember was waking up on the floor

with police round me,' revealed Benham. Eyewitness
Davina Lawrence saw the fight while working at
Fibrecare Dry Cleaners. She told the *Recorder*: 'I heard
lots of shouting and you could see that it was going to
end in a punch-up. I've never seen anything like it. I was
disgusted and wondered if they were connected to the
BNP to be honest.'

At the time you wondered if the next Romford count
should take place in a local nightclub with lager and Red
Bull provided.

Essex meets London here in Romford – the buses are
red instead of green. It's mainly friendly, yet also gritty
and urban. This market town is very much a place of
shopping, drinking and fighting.

Next to the station is a dingy alleyway running alongside the railway arches called The Battis. My friend Katie
Dawson, a former Green Party councillor and Romford
resident turned Islingtonian, reveals that The Battis was
the stuff of childhood nightmares, a sort of *Lord of the
Rings* netherworld that was terrorised by Romford Orcs.

'My mum and dad were quite relaxed and easy-going
but when I was a teenager the one thing they said to me
was "we don't care where you go, but whatever you do,
don't go up The Battis!"'

With no little trepidation I step past the shop backs
and into The Battis. A sign warns 'CCTV in operation'.
On the left are huge cavernous railway arches, sealed off
with wire netting. On the right is a 1980s football-pen-
style high wire fence. It's a narrow corridor that might as
well say, 'Please mug me, bruv.'

When I later remark to Katie that with all those arches it looks a little like the Colosseum in Rome, her instant riposte is, 'And you've got about as much chance of surviving there!'

Mercifully I make it through and even pass a couple of people carrying shopping bags. Round the back of the new Sainsbury's The Battis reaches the river Rom. It's sealed off by more wire mesh, though someone has, with some dexterity, managed to chuck a shopping trolley over the top and it lies broken and half submerged in the water. The Rom is only a couple of feet wide and then disappears under the supermarket. The town doesn't seem particularly proud of its eponymous river.

After returning to South Street through The Battis, I notice the offices of A1 Taxis, now nationally famous. Romford gained more post-*The Only Way Is Essex* notoriety through the Channel 4 documentary *Welcome to Romford* about A1 Cars. It filmed various sozzled journeys home in the back of Sharif's cab, with one camera on the driver and one on the passengers. Memorable moments included a blonde Essex Girl pugilist. Her boyfriend explained, 'She caught me kissing another girl outside Yates's and she punched me in the face. I had to buy her flowers.'

In the back of A1 cabs could be found internet daters on the razzle; one-night stands ('Do you wanna see me again, Jim?'); the bloke who thought he'd been run over but wasn't sure; and an arrest of one passenger for messing about with a traffic cone. Plus three drunken blokes on a night out, one of whom philosophised, 'Do you know what the best thing is about Romford? It's got the greatest amount of tarts in London. And we're going home empty-handed...' When one man had nearly scored, his friend commented, 'Big boobs and a nice arse ... but she makes the Elephant Man look like a fuckin' sex machine, mate.'

Cab driver Sharif was part of the Asian influx into Essex, but had been rapidly assimilated into matehood. He'd been in the country eleven years and had developed a pleasingly phlegmatic approach to his job, along with some natural Essex wit and a flirtatious line of banter with the formidable Kelly behind the call-out desk.

Welcome to Romford was all rather enjoyable in a 3 a.m. 'desperate for a pee can you stop at the next roundabout, mate' kind of way. If Travis Bickle from *Taxi Driver* had worked in Romford he might have learned to lighten up a little and enjoy the cabaret.

Jessie J is the latest pop star to emerge from Romford, following the success of electronic duo Underworld, who composed part of the brilliant score for the London Olympics Opening Ceremony. Jessie J's heart problem ensured she avoided the drink culture. She told the *Daily Mirror*: 'I was in and out of hospital most of my childhood. But it was a blessing in disguise. It meant I could never abuse my body the way my friends did at sixteen – drink myself into a frenzy or smoke weed when everyone else was trying it.'

Interestingly, her massive hit *Price Tag* must have proved quite radical in her home town's market, an anti-materialist assertion that it's not about the money, or indeed the price tag, in the one place where it certainly is about the money.

In the 1980s and 1990s Romford was famous for the nightclub Hollywood Romford, frequented by West Ham legends like Frank McAvennie and Julian Dicks. It was a quintessentially Essex juxtaposition, the words Hollywood and Romford placed together with no apparent sense of irony.

Footballers come here to score. There's always been an undercurrent of sex running through the earthy streets of Romford. Indeed, all the latent sexuality in that A1 Taxis documentary reminds me of a brilliant anecdote from an *Independent* reader posted after my article on the twentieth anniversary of Essex Man. Under the moniker of 'Sick of Stupidity', this Essex tourist wrote the following:

My only experience of Essex was a few years ago, when a friend invited me to his family's Christmas Day dinner on the outskirts of Romford (I think). His family were typical Essex folk, in that they were very 'down-to-earth', unpretentious people, and generous and hospitable to a fault, and it was a very pleasant dinner. After the meal, we retired to the living room, and it was then that things suddenly took a turn for the surreal...

My friend's teenage sister had invited her boyfriend over for the after-dinner drinks, and decided to entertain him – and the rest of the assembled family and guests – by putting on a little show. She disappeared upstairs and came down moments later dressed in a very revealing Santa Claus outfit. She then proceeded to perform an extremely raunchy and suggestive dance number, in the middle of the living room, to the accompaniment of an equally raunchy and suggestive pop-song on the hi-fi (I think it was Madonna or similar).

Her boyfriend obviously enjoyed the show, if the hypnotised expression on his face and the impressive bulge in his trousers were any guide. Interestingly, the other guests – all local Essex people – did not seem the least bit shocked by any of this, but laughed and applauded, while her mother and grandmother beamed with pride, as if to say, 'That's our girl! Always knows how to turn on the fellas...'

I just sat there, speechless and blushing with embarrassment. Was this sort of uninhibited sexual display by teenage daughters considered nothing more than wholesome family entertainment in Essex?

Of course, being gay myself, her raunchy gyrations had no effect on me whatsoever; it was the visible arousal of her boyfriend – who was quite a tall, strapping, handsome hunk of a lad, I must say – that was turning me on. And I was secretly hoping that he would reciprocate with a raunchy dance number of his own. Sadly, it was not to be; when her dance had finished, she promptly dragged her – thoroughly primed – boyfriend upstairs, where they proceeded to copulate very noisily for the next two hours (lucky girl...).

And each muffled groan, ecstatic squeal and ceiling-shaking climax only elicited more beaming smiles of pride from her mother and grandmother, and exchanges of knowing winks and chuckles between the other guests. Welcome to Essex! I thought – 'down-to-earth' indeed!

It's a short walk from the station to Romford Market
Square. 'NO FAKES' reads a sign above one of the stalls
in Romford Market. It's a moniker that neatly sums
up Romford. The idea you would even suspect fakery
is very Essex in this old East End enclave stuck out on
the tundra of Essex. There's a pie and mash shop and a
Tubby White's stall selling jellied eels. (Why are seafood
stalls always run by men called Tubby?)

'50p yer Collins!' hollers a woman on a fruit stall.
Across the market an old geezer rasps, 'Paarnd a bowl yer
joocy oranges ... Yorksher rhubarb! Yorksher rhubarb!'

Suddenly I realise where I subconsciously attained
my '50p yer 'Ammers fanzine!' selling technique from,
when I used to sell *Fortune's Always Hiding* outside West
Ham's ground.

Romford has a market square dating back to 1247
and a couple of listed pubs in The Golden Lion and The
Lamb, along with the more rock'n'roll The Bitter End,
and, of course, a nail salon.

Lunch is in a greasy spoon where the chip portions
are large and the tea bags stay in the mug. It's opposite
the legendary Yates's, where my sister Kaz, a Romford
resident, says you can see many micro-skirts and stilettos
every Friday night.

Walking down South Street it's impossible not to think
of Ian Dury's line from the song 'Razzle in my Pocket',
about going out on the nick in his yellow jersey and
stealing a razzle mag from a newsagents in the South
Street shopping arcade.

The arcade, now covered, brings a Proustian rush of

nostalgia. This was a big trip out on the 247 bus from Great Warley when I was a kid. Unlimited shops and cheap wide-collared shorts and Oxford bags at Mr Byrite's. My dad used to say, 'You won't get anywhere messing about shopping,' and perhaps he was right.

There's a West Ham shop selling endless WHU-branded casual jackets, teddy bears and babygros. Waterstones has a tempting book on the history of Upminster and lots of DVDs on the Second World War in Essex and the East End.

It's heaving on a Wednesday market day at 3 p.m. and definitively Essex. Compared to up west, as they say on *EastEnders*, there's decidedly more leopard-print, eye make-up, chiselled cheekbones and pink handbags.

Karren Brady would love it here. Entrepreneurship is in the Essex soul. In the centre of the arcade stand numerous temporary stalls and hawkers pushing their products like wannabe *Apprentice* candidates. There are young people in red T-shirts offering LoveFilm vouchers, a stall hawking samples from Subway sandwiches, Sky offers, and a jewellery stall called Magnolia that is embossed with 'Prague, Sydney, Tel Aviv, Toronto'. Does the Prague stall read 'Sydney, Tel Aviv, Toronto, Romford'?

Seeking some local colour I accept a leaflet on Crystal double-glazing from a man in a brown and beige two-tone leather jacket standing by a selection of stained dark brown casement windows. A mistake: one thing they know how to do in Essex is sell.

'Would you like 40 per cent discount voucher too sir and a free estimate no obligation your wife makes all the decision sir well between you and me that's always the case in the home have you seen our beat the VAT offer you see it's now 43 per cent off not 40 per cent energy saving recommended seven point locking system we just need your name to prove that I've spoken to you other-wise they won't believe me and your home number and we do need a mobile which is the best number to call you on you'll receive a courtesy call within a day…'

Pleading a rendezvous, I scarper for the safety of Claire's Accessories. (The courtesy call duly arrives the next day and they may continue for the next millennium.)

So many shops, so many stalls. It's hard not to love the buzz of Romford Market, where commerce is theatre and you will never be short of juicy oranges and high-performance windows.

After the mesmerising consumerism of the arcade it's time to pay £2.50 for some higher culture at the Havering Museum, situated just off the market.

It's a small museum consisting of two large rooms. The first display features Sir Nikolaus Pevsner eulogis-ing about the marshland villages of Essex in his Pevsner Architectural Guides before contrasting them with 'the brash commercialism of Romford'. Could Romford be rather proud of its wheeler-dealing?

'You're taking notes, are you? We must be good!' declares a garrulous female member of staff. 'Are you coming to my ghost talk tomorrow at 5.30? Did you know we've got twenty ghosts in Romford? Do you live round here?'

'No, I live in north London. Actually, we've got people

coming over for dinner tomorrow but I'll tell my sister, she might want to go...'

'Well, we've got another one scheduled for October, if you leave your email at reception they can put you on the mailing list, just say Eleanor sent you. We've got poltergeists in the Market Square too.'

'Are you sure it's not just the customers from Yates's Wine Lodge chucking things about?' I quip.

Eleanor ignores this, but appears to be very good at her job. Indeed, selling it seems is in the soul of every Romfordian.

'You might like some of the sport displays. You might be in some of the pictures! Do you know you can take ghosts home with you? Course, my husband was a sceptic but when we developed some of the pictures he said, "Ellen, come upstairs and look at this," and there was three orbs on the computer screen. And they'd come and go too. How did they get in the software? Course he won't admit it, but he saw them.'

'Well, it certainly makes you think...'

Eleanor continues with a long stream of consciousness about the paranormal.

'Course the son wouldn't go upstairs, he just said, "Mum, there's someone up there ..." We've got a paranormal investigator speaking ... There's ghosts in lots of the pubs ... The Golden Lion is fourteenth century ... Military ghosts, ghosts from the RAF aerodrome at Hornchurch ... I must be going, got to pick up my grandchildren...'

Phew. Eleanor is a market trader of dead souls. And

she is so effective that I'm convinced that really I should be going to her next ghost evening.

The museum captures Romford well, for there's plenty on beer and fighting. There are pictures of the Rainham to Erith ferry featuring fiercely moustached Essex Men standing by the pub, and much on the history of the old Romford Brewery, now replaced by a cinema and restaurant complex. Havering Museum is on the site of the old brewery gate. Another wall display features an illustration of 'Prize fighting at the Dell'. No Christmas at the Dell was complete without wrestling between the men of Romford and Hornchurch. So nothing's changed there then.

It's nice to see a photo of Ian Dury performing at the Hammersmith Odeon on the wall. The self-proclaimed *Lord Upminster* used to watch Teddy Boy films at Romford's Ritz cinema in the 1950s. There ain't 'alf been some clever bastards and now Dury is one of them. A man who peppered his records with rude words would surely be amused to view himself beneath a portrait of William Derham FRS, Rector of Upminster.

There's also a display on Peter the Painter: Peter Blundell, a man who came from wealth, but spent his life living beneath the Upminster Bridge on the A127 and painting pictures of ships on corrugated iron. His inclusion adds to the quirky charm of Havering Museum.

'Make sure you get his email…' declares Eleanor as I make for the exit. 'Bet you're glad you came now!' she jokes, a whirlpool of paranormal-ish energy whizzing off to meet her grandkids.

I walk back down South Street towards the station,

standing behind four scruffy twenty-somethings. One man carries a groaning Tesco bag and is complaining about money: 'Where I've worked they've banned over-time, I'm £300 a week down,' he sighs.

'She earns more than Richard and me put together...' says his companion.

I lose them by Utter Nutter clothes shop, but then find myself behind them once more and the girl continues: 'I don't talk to my mum ... My mum beat me up ... He bought a three-piece suite right, off his own bat, nothing to do with me ... She called me a slag and tramp and I said I must be taking after you mum and she went into one...'

It's a place of in-your-face emotion here. Fighting by the station, selling by the paarnd, sex in sitting rooms, poltergeists in the square, micro-skirts by Yates's Wine Lodge, drunken rides with A1 cabs. Someone should make a film of all this. And call it *Hollywood Romford*.

12

THE ONLY WAY IS UPMINSTER

Upminster – it's the end of the District Line. London fades and Essex begins. Once a pleasant village (it still has an out-of-place-looking windmill) it became a prosperous garden suburb in the early twentieth century, after the grounds of Gaynes Manor were sold for housing development. It's way more upmarket than Dagenham, from which it is separated geographically and spiritually by the Beam River and Hornchurch Marshes.

I'm searching for the house in Courtney Gardens where my great-grandfather Alfred May spent the latter days of his life. In 1927 he was living there with his son Sidney, my grandfather, and Sidney's new wife Hilda. It was while they were all in this house that my father was born.

From Upminster tube station I turn into the nearby Deyncourt Gardens and then left into Courtney Gardens. Old Alfred May had made it when he moved here. It's all resolutely suburban, with monkey puzzle trees, paved front gardens and men vacuuming Ford cars. You wonder if this was what inspired the Upminster-born Ian Dury to pen the lyrics of 'Mash It Up Harry' on his final album *Mr Love Pants*. They depict a character who has got his little mortgage, lounge, telly, garden and shed to defend, but wants a bit of Wembley to enliven his suburban life.

My father's family were typical of the old East Londoners who moved out to the Thames Estuary. Alfred May's old house in Upminster is a 1920s semi with a leafy front garden, a bay window and an arched alcove over the door. And for Alf it would have been the triumph of his life. No fear of suburbia for him. Like many an East Ender before him, he would have felt that Essex represented the good life.

Alfred was born in Commercial Road in 1862, the son of a saddler, Alfred May Sr, close to the bustle of Limehouse Basin. In Victorian times it would have been a rough dockers' area. His home was close to gasworks, glue, rope and chemical factories, numerous pubs and brothels and the opium dens of Chinatown. Alfred Sr's father Richard was a waterman and lighterman on the Thames who was born in Lambeth. Through Ancestry UK I discovered Alfred Sr's death certificate. This revealed he died from tuberculosis at the age of just thirty-three in 1872, leaving a wife and five children. Harsh times, indeed. His son, young Alfred, my dad's grandfather, would have been just ten, but recovered from this major life blow to forge a good career in the Post Office.

Alfred Jr's mother remarried twice after being widowed and Alfred himself became a travelling sorter and then gained higher rank within the Post Office. He listed himself as a 'civil servant' on his marriage

certificate. Alfred married Mary Ann Hobbs at Bow
Common Church in 1885. Mary was the daughter of a
coachman, Thomas Hobbs, who was illiterate and made
his mark on the register instead of signing it.

Alfred fathered seven children while living with his
wife in East Ham, all listed on the 1901 census, including my grandfather Sidney, born in 1898. By the time the
eighteen-year-old Sidney had enlisted in 1916 during the
First World War, they had moved to Forest Gate, near
Ilford. Inexorably, the family was moving away from
the East and out towards the green fields and cleaner air
of Essex.

Another of Alfred Jr's sons, my dad's uncle Alfred (OK,
they weren't very original in their choice of given names)
rose in the civil service too, becoming assistant paymas-
ter general and being awarded the OBE. Quite a triumph
for a working-class family. My father and his relatives
spoke of 'Uncle Alf' with reverence. He had even been to
a garden party at Buckingham Palace.

At some point in the 1920s Alfred Jr really made it
and set up home in the executive housing of Courtney
Gardens, Upminster.

My paternal roots were a new discovery to me. My
father never mentioned his humble East End origins and
you suspected the family kept it quiet once they had
achieved respectability.

My dad's father, Sidney, became a Lieutenant in the
First World War, before being wounded and sent home,
though he was psychologically affected for the rest of
his life. Sidney was an active freemason and ran an

insurance company. His business partner lived next door. In Upminster they had something to defend. My grandfather gave the impression of being a wealthy man, says a relative who remembers him at my parents' wedding.

It's strangely moving to look at my great-grandfather's suburban home and think what it must have meant to him. His story is that of many of the Londoners who moved out to the Thames Estuary.

There's a celebrity angle to Upminster too. The next destination on my itinerary is Waldegrave Gardens, the childhood home of Ian Dury, and also my mate Gavin, whose mum knew Ian's mum. Ian Dury even recorded an album entitled *Lord Upminster*.

No. 12 Waldegrave Gardens was where the young Dury lived until his body was ravaged by polio, contracted in a public swimming baths in Southend. The effects of polio, including a withered left arm and leg, resulted in Ian being institutionalised and sent to boarding school.

Ian's old house is massively removed from his diamond geezer pearly king persona. It's painted cream and the sort of place Richard Briers would consider rather grand. It's another 1920s semi-detached home with a hint of mock Tudor. Behind a neatly trimmed privet hedge four cars are parked in the front driveway, one of which is a BMW. There's a large garage and windows to five rooms, including the attic room where Ian had his studio for a time.

The next-door neighbours have monkey puzzle trees around their front garden. Two doors away there are five cars on the drive. It's leafy and safe and an easy walk to the station. Commuterland incarnate. As it did for so many of us, cosy suburbia gave the young Dury something to kick against. Will Birch's biography *Ian Dury* fully conveys the mix of monstrous and loveable behaviour that made Dury such a very complex lyrical genius. For this fan at least, his appropriation of a cockney geezer identity that was never quite accurate makes him all the more human.

What's also striking is how much of a mockney Dury was. His dad was a bus driver and then a chauffeur, as he sang on the moving 'My Old Man', but his mother's family were bohemian intellectuals. He was brought up in Cranham and Upminster as a well-spoken boy and he later went to boarding school in High Wycombe.

Dury said he put on the cockney geezer act partly to survive the years he spent in a horrendous institution for kids with polio. It would also have given the bullied, insecure and disabled Dury an easy identity. When I was a student at the University of Lancaster northerners readily identified me as a cockney when they heard my Brentwood accent, and it was easy to play up to the caricature in the street credibility-seeking days of the late 1970s. Dury laid it on very cock-er-ney, but not without a lot of acute observation and a dollop of truth. As he once said when accused of being a mockney rebel: 'We're not posh, we're arts and crafts!'

Ian would also have been attracted to the language he heard from East End exiles around Essex because he was a poet and saw the richness of the cockney dialogue and rhyming slang. He chronicled music hall characters in songs like 'Billericay Dickie' and 'Plaistow Patricia' and created a poetic, Ealing Comedy-style world among the Essex hinterlands. You wonder what he might have been inspired to write by the characters in *TOWIE*.

Heading back down Station Road it all seems very familiar. Does nothing change in Upminster? It still has the Essex Yeoman pub by the station, where my dad and I would share a welcome pint after returning home from a West Ham game under the lights. That litany of District Line stations still has a magic feel to it: Upminster Bridge, Hornchurch, Elm Park, Dagenham East, Dagenham Heathway, Becontree, Upney, Barking, East Ham and, finally, the home of football (and 1-0 home defeats) at Upton Park. We'd drive home from the tube past Upminster Common, headlights on silver birches, the shutting of the farm gate, logs still burning in the fireplace, the breakfast table set by my mum.

Upminster does retro well. There's a proper old Wimpy bar and a newsagents still called Smokers Paradise. And here's the clincher, Roomes Department Store is still there. The very store where my mate Gav once saw West Ham's World Cup winner Martin Peters out shopping.

Gav adds: 'I saw Hursty there too, plus Bobby Ferguson in the park (my mum got his autograph cos I was too shy). Jimmy Greaves also lived in Upminster as a younger man – he gave my granddad's car a push.'

It's good to see a department store that isn't a chain – the Roome family has run it for five generations. Roomes has a definite air of *Are You Being Served?*

about it, complete with white-bloused Miss Brahms and Mr Lucas-style assistants with Essex accents saying, 'The sun's come out for yer … invoice it with them last ones…' And here comes Young Mr Roome…

Roomes was established in 1888 at Green Street, Upton Park. It closed in 1935 when the owners realised that commuters were moving out to Essex. The Upminster shop was built in 1927 and still has its stylish art deco exterior.

You can find everything here amid its black and white interiors, from Fred Perry shirts to toys (I'm sure my late Uncle David bought me a *Doctor Who* 45rpm record here back in the 1960s) and bedding. And on the top floor there's a sleepy café serving various chip concoctions and sludgy coffee.

Who knows what items Ian Dury might have nicked here as a youngster before going on to South Street, Romford? You can keep Selfridges. It's good to know there's still Roomes at the top of the District Line.

Leaving the store, my journey continues past Upminster Park where Ian Dury claimed to have lost his virginity, though his biographer Will Birch thinks this was adolescent exaggeration. It doesn't look that romantic on this grey, blustery afternoon.

There's a disturbance across the road. As I walk up Corbet's Tey Road there's a young Herbert rolling away from the Crumpled Horn pub and pushing his red-haired girlfriend. One of Ian Dury's 'Blockheads' perhaps? At first I wonder if it's the sort of joshing you might see between Smithy and his sister in *Gavin and Stacey*. But it's something more sinister.

'If you push her again I'm calling the police! You should be ashamed of yourself, she's a woman!' shouts a brave and angry middle-aged woman in the street. The best and worst of Essex in one scene. He shouts something abusive back – and he's a big bloke – she dials for the law and the Herbert slopes off with his poor female companion.

The police arrive and take a couple of statements from passers-by and shop owners, but it's too late to find the culprit. You have to admire that Upminster woman who saw cowardly injustice and took action.

It reminds me that there was always an undercurrent of violence beneath the commuter facade when I was growing up in Essex. Getting threatened for eyeing up someone's bird in that pub by the bus stop in Brentwood High Street, violent abuse after reversing too close to someone's motor, my dad threatening to knock someone's effing block off in a row over a parking space at Warley Fords, St Martin's School lads turning up outside our school with bicycle chains.

The thought occurs that if there was an English David Lynch he would surely be making *Twin Peaks*-style films in the Essex commuter belt – all is not as it seems behind the privet hedges and Ford motors.

I walk on to 21 Little Gaynes Gardens to view the house where my father grew up with his parents. It wasn't a happy childhood. In all the years we lived two miles down the road my dad never once took me to see this house.

Like most men of his generation, he didn't like talking

about his emotions. But he revealed he had been 'knocked about' in his early years. His father Sidney had suffered shellshock in the First World War, a euphemism for post-traumatic stress disorder, so could well have been difficult to live with, while his mother Hilda adhered to the 'spare the rod, spoil the child' philosophy of the time. Yet his brother David appeared to have a loving relationship with his parents. How bad was his treatment? I'll never know now, though my father lacked confidence throughout his life and placed much of his emotional security in accumulating financial security, or, as we call it in Essex, a wad full of dosh.

What's striking is how middle class my dad's old house is. He often gave the impression of having started out from nothing to set up his own business, but this is a tree-lined cul-de-sac with garages, stained-glass windows and is utterly respectable. Yet once bombs fell on it.

It was here that my father experienced the terror and thrill of the Second World War. After the death of my parents, I found my father's diary from 1939, written when he was twelve and thirteen. Here in Upminster, in middle-class, resolutely suburban Little Gaynes Gardens, he recorded the dogfights above his head with all the relish that I would later use to record football scores.

The nearby Hornchurch Aerodrome was a target for the Luftwaffe. It's hard to imagine the bombs falling on this mock-Tudor, sleepy place, but on 26 August 1940 my dad records, 'Two warnings. Heard whistling bombs. One in South View Drive and Cedar Avenue.'

On 29 August 1940 he saw a Spitfire make a forced

landing in a field near to Cranham Hall. 'Near gunfire twice. Bombs near once. Saw clouds of dust. Aerodrome undamaged. Saw Spitfire that made forced landing.'

My dad's diary includes a short evacuation to Yorkshire, and a nice mix of playing football and cricket next to air raid warnings and war facts. 'Had tooth out. Saw Jerry chased off by Spitfire. Late night raid Berlin and Ruhr ... 103 enemy planes down. 22 British. Saw German planes with shells bursting around.'

The war formed many of my father's values. And looking back I'm surprised at how much of an Essex Man he still was beneath the middle-class veneer. He embodied many of the characteristics written about by Simon Heffer in 1990. My father was fiercely right wing and would get angry at the mere mention of a minimum wage. In later life he fell in with Northern Ireland Protestants and, much to my embarrassment, became an admirer of Ian Paisley and advocated no surrender to the IRA. He was an ardent monarchist too and admired titles. He believed that hard work and free enterprise were the solution to all problems and that people who went on demonstrations didn't have enough work to do and the unions were trying to bankrupt his business.

Like most Essex Men he loved his motor and driving down country lanes. His views on race were as dodgy as most other men of his time. The sight of a black policeman, or the Bermudan Clyde Best playing for West Ham, surprised him. He was suspicious of what he termed 'poofs' too.

My father was sent to the independent Brentwood

School, another major upwardly mobile move by his parents. Yet he never convinced as posh. He didn't have the manners or soft skills of the Old Etonian. He would have been what the true toffs refer to as 'a first-time buyer'. He was sent away to one boarding school, where he was bullied, presumably for his humble origins, although he had a happier time as a day-pupil at Brentwood.

After a stint at an experimental farm near Stoke where he met my mother Sheila Hughes, my dad returned to Essex to farm, first in Dunmow and then two miles down the road by Upminster Common. He worked hard, got up at 4 a.m. to do the milking, felt he was supporting his family and helping to feed the country. He was spiritually in tune with Essex all his life. And now I'm starting to see where that inbuilt love of work came from – the generational struggle of his family to rise from a saddler in Commercial Road to white-collar jobs in a garden suburb.

I turn away from Little Gaynes Gardens with its stained-glass windows and two-car families and walk the streets where my father cycled to school and went on day trips to Southend, where he looked for work on farms in the holidays and sheltered from explosions as the sky was pitted with German bombers.

For both Ian Dury and my father's family, Upminster was a refuge for those who decided that the only way is Essex – be it posh Essex or mockney. My dad's family wanted to get out of the working class and Ian Dury, a disabled middle-class lad, was desperate to get back into it.

Yes, Upminster hides much behind its leafy gardens, mock-Tudor beams and bay windows.

13

CANVEY ISLAND: OIL CITY RESIDENTIAL

Canvey Island will forever be associated with Dr Feelgood. The self-styled 'best local band in the world' brought Essex humour to the bloated music scene of the 1970s, claiming to come from the Thames Delta in homage to the rhythm and blues of the US. They played searing R & B while looking like out-of-work accountants in their ruffled suits. Lee Brilleaux, Wilko, John B. Sparks and the Big Figure were invariably photographed by the seawall and recorded albums such as *Down by the Jetty*, full of Canvey references.

The Feelgood factor was immortalised in Julien Temple's film *Oil City Confidential*, released in 2010 to glowing reviews. At the film's premiere, Dr Feelgood's manager, Chris Fenwick, emphasised how Canvey shaped the band:

> Both band and island shared the same uncompromising
> and distinctive qualities. It's Canvey Island and a bunch
> of take-us-as-you-find-us people that gave us the songs

and shaped the attitude of Dr Feelgood. And through
their songs, the band has repaid that debt by putting the
name of Canvey Island up in lights all over the world.

Like Canvey, Feelgood were full of idiosyncrasies. In the
1970s era of Yes, Genesis and Emerson Lake and Palmer,
the Feelgoods eschewed progressive rock and played
simple, menacing, R & B. They wore suits and had unfash-
ionable shortish hair. Along with bands like Southend's
Eddie and the Hot Rods, they spawned a burgeoning pub
rock scene.

So perfect was their Essex bloke credibility that three-
quarters of the members were really called John: Lee
Brilleaux was born Lee Collinson, Wilko's full name
was John Wilkinson, the Big Figure was John Martin,
and John B. Sparks played bass.

Incredibly, Dr Feelgood reached No. 1 in the album
charts with 'Stupidity' in 1976. Feelgood's on-stage
energy, with Wilko machine-gunning the audience with
his guitar and Lee Brilleaux performing press-ups and
star jumps, laid much of the groundwork for the punk
explosion of 1977.

Back in 1987 I interviewed the late Lee Brilleaux for
LAM magazine in a pub by Euston station. He was
waiting for a train to the Brilleaux pad in Southend.
The interview took place over four pints of real ale;
Lee's penchant for milk and alcohol had been immortalised in song, but the dairy industry appeared to be
losing out to the latter.

In a scenario that might have come from a Feelgood

song, which invariably featured hard-done-by men, upon my return to the office I discovered that I had been sacked. Unable to write a blues song about it, but inspired by Lee's Canvey grit, my best option was to file a case for an untrue statement of dismissal (subsequently won) and flog the Brilleaux interview to rival *Midweek* magazine.

Lee was thirty-four at the time, but died of cancer seven years later, aged forty-one. He told me: 'A lot of people tell me I look older, I say so would you mate, if you had as many miles on the clock as me … People might say, "Who's that old tosser?" but I can still give a pretty good account of myself.'

He spoke fondly of his home town: 'Canvey was a brilliant place to have a childhood, before they put housing estates on all the rural areas … Every Sunday I still walk down to Leigh beach and have a pot of cockles, pure protein, great for hangovers.'

Memorably, Lee was wearing a Barbour jacket, apparently unaware of its Sloane Ranger connotations: 'This bloke in Scotland said it's great for grouse shooting. I said we don't get many grouse in Southend!'

Even the other band members' semi-retirement appeared to be the result of them becoming too Essexy for their ruffled, sweaty shirts. 'The Big Figure has got a gearbox repair company in London, Sparko got fed up and is a builder in Southend with his brother. Gypie Mayo is wasting his remarkable talents just messing around in Southend,' Lee explained. 'As for Wilko, I hardly ever clap eyes on the man. He only lives about a mile from me, but he's not a pub person. I sometimes bump into his missus shopping in Southend and that's the closest we get.'

Most rock stars sold out and moved to Hampstead or LA. The closest Lee Brilleaux and Wilko came to selling out was moving down the road to Southend.

Indeed, Canvey has had a disproportionate influence on music. The Canvey Goldmine nightclub was a hugely influential soul club from 1973 through to the 1980s. On Channel 4's *The Tube*, Paula Yates described it as 'a little club at the end of the pier with fairy lights outside'. DJ Chris Hill told Yates that the club owed its success to 'being at the end of the world – there's nowhere else to go once you get here. There's an element of danger that the petrochemical terminal might explode and it's below sea level. The whole thing could end tomorrow. Plus it's a committed musical audience, they're not into the current trends, they're into contemporary black music of the day.'

Joshua Hayward (formerly Joshua Von Grimm or Joshua the Third), guitarist of The Horrors, hails from Canvey, which he told quietus.com was 'a horrible island in the Thames Estuary … Have you ever been to Canvey? It's a strange place. I always kind of stood out a bit there. They didn't really like kids that wore make-up. It was a fight just getting out your front door, so I wanted to move somewhere that was a bit more open-minded.'

British Sea Power recorded a song about the 1953 Canvey floods, 'Canvey Island', on the 2008 album *Do You Like Rock Music?*, with the memorable line:

'In 1953 many lives were lost and the records of the football team.'

Canvey tends to inspire strong opinions either for or against the place – although, in its defence, most of the oil refineries are at Coryton and not actually on the island, as many believe.

The Romans had a small settlement and lighthouse here, but must have found it a pretty bleak place. Canvey was largely uninhabited until the seventeenth century, when Dutch engineers drained the area. In 1900 Canvey had just 300 people. There were only 1,500 or so inhabitants here at the end of the Second World War. Yet now there are 37,000. Despite the 1953 floods, the place has grown at a phenomenal rate, along with the refineries and accompanying jobs.

The name Canvey Island derives from the 'Island of Cana's People', Cana being some geezer from the Iceni tribe. It's a matter of some historical debate whether Cana wore Burberry, but on the Chavtowns website someone has nominated Canvey, writing:

The only redeeming features of Canvey are: a) It's an island, therefore we know if the chavs get too rowdy we can just cut them off from civilised society by taking out two bridges and b) It's below sea level and sinking fairly rapidly, so in thirty years they'll need to start investing in Burberry water-wings.

Several Canvey Islanders have commented in defence of the place. Jordan writes:

What you have written is absolute rubbish. I Live in Canvey Island and it is a great place to live. Yes there's the odd few chavs here or there and youths hang around but they don't cause any bother. The only few that do, ask for cigarettes but not mobile phones and wallets! Every time I go to the beach the sea is fine and I always see sand everywhere. CHECK THE FACTS! The thing about coming back in an ambulance is a step too far, you are pushing ur luck BIG TIME. I Seriously Feel Like you are practically trying to make us live in our own world away from everyone else.

Although another comment reads, 'I am a Police Officer, I always have trouble with people born on Canvey, the only thing they seem to be able to recall is "No Comment" or "F**k Off!"'

Similarly on the 'Beer in the Evening' website, one comment on The Lobster Smack reads: 'Great Pub, great food shame about the narrow minded mainlanders who think of Canvey folk as "Inbreds". Even with our webbed feet we consider our gene pool to be of the highest quality and most diverse, so there!'

Music fans still come from all around the world to look at the home of Dr Feelgood. Which doesn't mean 'the island', as the locals refer to it, is easy to get to, even from London.

Getting to Canvey Island involves my family and Vulcan, our dog, taking the Fenchurch Street C2C line – only this Saturday it's a replacement bus service between Basildon and Benfleet, gateway to the island.

We narrowly escape an incendiary incident when ten-year-old Nell asks loudly on the train, 'Does Joey Essex really think there is a horse in the back of his car? Are all people in Essex stupid?' Luckily the man in the seat behind us reveals he's from Yorkshire, visiting his children in Laindon. 'Yorkshire's better when you leave,' he tells us. 'You grew up in Essex? I don't think anyone from Essex ever grows up, do they? I love it down here now.'

The double-decker rail replacement bus from Benfleet hits gridlock on the A127. 'Why is there so much building work going on?' asks Lola. Ah, but this is Essex, where the road-building never stops, a bit like the perpetual painting of the Sydney Harbour Bridge.

By the motorway a solitary house on the Essex tundra flies a cross of St George flag. The kids are strangely unmoved when I tell them there's a motorboat museum at Pitsea. After half an hour we arrive at Benwell. It's starting to feel less like a rock-and-roll pilgrimage and more like a penance getting to Canvey.

From Benwell station bus stop we catch another bus to Canvey, at a cost of £8.60 for four fares, travelling past Benwell Creek and onto a roundabout that bears the logo 'Welcome to Canvey Island' painted on what looks like the tail fin of an aircraft. Did the locals shoot it down?

My wife and kids appear to be joining the anti-Canvey side as the bus travels on through endless post-war homes. Some are mock-Tudor palaces, others more basic. We pass Dr Feelgood's old local, the Admiral Jellicoe, in the High Street. Eventually we disembark at Leigh Beck. We ask a solitary passer-by for directions to a dog-walking area and she suggests going up Wall Road 'and then you can get on the wall'.

Here we find the concrete seawall defences, by the evocatively named Smallgains Creek. Across the creek stands Canvey Heights, a park reclaimed from a landfill area. The nomenclature is an example of local humour, as although it's the highest point in Canvey the land is only marginally above sea level.

The girls walk on top of the wall, but from the landward side you can hardly see over it. It feels like we're incarcerated in Canvey. Boats in various stages of disrepair litter the creek as we walk round to the Thames-side defences.

Here, by the Estuary Canvey Island's seawall, is 10 feet or so of uncompromising grey concrete. It stretches for fourteen miles and looks like something from the Cold War – Essex's answer to the Berlin Wall, minus the Brandenburg Gate.

Inland from the wall, there's a downward slope towards numerous streets of below-sea-level, post-war houses. Many of these are Canvey's 'upside-down houses', where the living room is on the top floor to facilitate a sea view.

From here, looking down into the houses, you can easily imagine how the terrible floods of 1953 occurred. It would have been like filling up a washbasin with freezing Thames water. The floods killed fifty-eight people on Canvey, many of whom died of hypothermia that January night.

The original seawalls were made in 1623, possibly by

Cornelius Vermuyden, the Dutch engineer who drained the Fens. Two further islands towards Southend are marked on seventeenth-century maps, but have since been submerged and are now sandbanks.

After the defences were overwhelmed by the 1953 floods, the higher concrete walls were created. Every few hundred metres open sluice gates lead to steps going down to the seaward side and offer an escape to a sea view.

We step down and stroll by the grey waters of the Thames Estuary. 'Stop this nigger shit cunts,' reads a lone piece of graffiti on the seawall. Not a great introduction to Canvey – its writer's ability to use three taboo words out of five shows a horrible proficiency in obscenity. And as the island is 98.2 per cent white, it's not exactly multi-racial yet.

'Good afternoon!' booms a tannoy announcement from an unknown destination. It adds to the sense of being in *The Prisoner*, the classic 1960s series beloved of Dr Feelgood. Turns out it's coming from Canvey Island FC, whose stadium is just a free kick away from the defensive wall.

Disconcertingly the beach is black. Maybe that's why it's called Oil City. We pass two men on the rocks look-ing for cockles and the odd dog-walker, as well as many unretrieved canine poos. As Nicola picks up our dog's doings, she wonders aloud if she's the only person on the wall ever to pick up their dog's poo.

The council has made some effort to gentrify the wall, with shiny black seats in shelters, each with a nautical emblem such as a crab or salmon. There's another piece of graffiti, a crossed-hammers West Ham crest.

'They should get everyone to do a mural on the wall,' suggests Nicola, stopping to take a photo of a yellow plant that matches the brown stains leeching out of the concrete.

A huge DFDS ship passes by, just as the big ships did in Dr Feelgood's epic song 'Paradise'. There's a welcome change from grey wall as we pass Concord Beach; this wall is painted sea-blue and there's an area of sand by an ocean paddling pool.

A sign by a small brick building celebrates the Canvey Island drainage scheme in May Avenue. Five million pounds has been spent on three pumps to remove surface drainage water from the island.

Inland stands a moribund set of seaside amusements. There's a funfair playing loud music, where you can enter all day for £5; Parkins Palladium, Fraggle Rock Bar, snooker at Vi Bowl. Not so long ago East Enders came here for their annual holidays.

But Canvey is a place of surprises. After all that utilitarian concrete comes the art deco white concrete, glass and curves of the Labworth Café. It opened in 1933 and was designed to resemble the bridge of the *Queen Mary* by Anglo-Danish engineer Sir Ove Arup. As Canvey's tourism declined, the café fell into disuse, and it was nearly demolished when the sea defences were rebuilt in the 1970s. Thankfully, it was awarded Grade II listed status in 1996. In 1998 the Labworth was bought by Chris Topping, a local businessman who had won the Lottery. It is now the grand-sounding Labworth Restaurant and Beach Bistro. The café featured in *Oil City Confidential* and on the film's publicity postcards. Beneath an iconic shot of Dr Feelgood in front of the Labworth was the strapline: 'OIL CITY IS 100% PURE BELOW SEA LEVEL, CANVEY ISLAND NOIR.' For me, it feels like a great Essex R & B moment to be here.

Meanwhile, away from my musical reverie, we're told by a polite waitress in the Labworth that they stopped serving food at 3 p.m. so the girls have no chance of chips.

We cross Labworth Park to head back towards the town centre. Bizarrely, there's a silver sculpture of a giant fly in the park. There are warnings of anti-climb paint but no words of explanation. A fly, but why?

We move up Furtherwick Road, past a house painted bright yellow, and among the shops find Islanders Fish and Chips. A poster in the window explains how the shop stocks sustainably harvested Marine Stewardship Council approved fish. The kids just want chips, but Nicola wants to discuss ethics in Essex, asking how selling cod can be sustainable. The proprietor is remarkably helpful. 'Because we only buy cod from boats that fish in a sustainable way,' he explains.

Nicola asks him what other fish he has.

'Pollock,' says the chippy.

'Never mind the pollock,' I suggest in a lame joke.

'Would you like some pollock instead of cod, girls?' asks Nicola, ignoring me. They chat some more. 'He really knows his stuff. This is a good chip shop,' says Nicola. She asks him where the 'triple SI' (Site of Special

Scientific Interest) is, and he says it's down the road near Morrison's.

Nicola minds the dog outside and a local woman in a wheelchair admires our border terrier. 'It's not a dog, it's a human in furry clothing,' she coos at Vulcan.

Our fish and chips arrive and we sit down on a patch of green grass opposite. It's superb: freshly made batter, chips cut from new potatoes in the shop. We've stumbled upon the best chippy in Essex. Vulcan gets a bit of fish skin and a chip too.

Fortified by chips we head to the bus stop and ponder whether to try and see Canvey's famous Site of Special Scientific Interest. Canvey Wick is an unlikely haven for invertebrates and has even been billed as 'Britain's rainforest', as it allegedly has more biodiversity than anywhere else in the UK.

As there's only one bus that goes near Morrison's, we ask directions from a woman at the stop. She points to a taxi rank located, bizarrely, in the middle of the adjacent car park. A car from Steve's Taxis arrives immediately and we ask for the SSSI near Morrison's.

The driver is happy to give us a Canvey briefing. 'Yeah, I've lived on the island all my life. It gets a bad press, I don't know why. My family's been here for 100 years. They were here in the floods. You can still see the water mark on North Street. Look, there's one of the Dutch houses down there.'

Sure enough, there's a small octagonal thatched house nestling among the semis. We rapidly pass another. There's more to Canvey Island than you think, once you look beyond the oil refineries. 'Dunno why they moved here, it might have been the salt.' Salt was first removed from Canvey by the Romans and the remains of a Roman bridge to Benfleet have been unearthed.

Mentioning Dr Feelgood elicits more local colour from our driver: 'They used to play the Canvey Club, and there's a new Oyster Fleet, now. You going to the Wilko gig? And there's the Admiral Jellicoe. I've taken people from Canada and America there. What's it like as a pub? It's a bit lively, put it like that.'

We draw up at a gravel car park on the roundabout where there's a sign for the park. We walk down a gravel path and come across a children's playground. Lola and Nell are delighted to climb up the wooden structures. We lie on the grass with the dog and a crane fly lands on me. There's a sense of space and massive skies. Here are fields of long grass surrounded by reeds and drainage ditches. The refineries lie to the north and the white cottages of Benwell to the south, across the muddy island boundary of Benfleet Creek.

'I feel like I'm in Scotland,' says Nicola, suddenly warming to Canvey. 'That's a curlew I can hear.' Could it be she's a Canvey convert?

We walk further into nothingness, feeling completely alone. Or are we? Suddenly a park ranger's Land Rover appears on the track. Are they going to chastise us for having a dog? No.

'Hello, we saw you arrive with our binoculars. We are closing the park gates at five o'clock,' says a friendly blonde woman with a high-pitched European accent. 'I am afraid we have to do this because some of the local youngsters took stuff away from the playground.'

Nicola asks if she is from Holland. 'No, I am from Germany, but I got a job here at the park. I have lived here on the island for two years and I think the people here are very close. They do not like to hear the place criticised…'

She then answers a question about wildlife from Nicola with anecdotes about five-banded weevil wasps, Canvey Island beetles and the shrill carder bees prospering on the brownfield site of the old Occidental oil works and how they hope they will colonise the whole marsh.

'Are you a Dr Feelgood fan?' she asks, looking at me.

What? I'm a bloke walking in an SSSI… 'Erm, yes I am, how did you know?'

'You're a man of a certain age,' suggests Nicola. And perhaps the only people who ever visit Canvey Island are Feelgood fans.

'Dr Feelgood's manager Chris Fenwick comes walking here once a week. He says it's his favourite place,' she adds.

'Are you going to see Wilko Johnson?' she asks.

'Yes, I've booked two tickets,' I answer, trying to envisage if Dr Feelgood were actually early eco-trippers.

'What about you?'

'This is my boyfriend,' she says, gesturing to the man in the four-wheel-drive alongside her, 'and his parents are coming down that weekend, and I do not think they would like it.'

'I'm sure they would,' I suggest.

We discuss maps a little more and decide to walk to Benfleet. She shows us the route along the seawall, under the bridge and back to the station on her OS map. 'I hope you make the Wilko gig,' I say to our new German friend.

We walk along the path and turn right on to the seawall. To our left is the old brownfield site of the infrastructure for the Occidental oil works. The Occidental infrastructure was built on soil dredged from the Thames. The silt, gravel and crushed shells have, you might say, Occidentally created an ideal habitat for insects and birds. Because of high oil prices in 1973 the refinery was never completed and the area became a haven for bees and butterflies. Here lies the lengthy, unused jetty that Dr Feelgood wrote about.

The sea wall is a simple earth bank next to East Haven Creek. There's very little water in the creek, just an expanse of grass and grey mud. The wall feels like some Neolithic structure as we walk on top of the bank. This must be the very wall where Wilko Johnson described walking with Irene in the long grass in 'Paradise'.

We hear the cries of curlews and admire the sloe berries and plants like ox's tongue and wild cabbage. A flame flickers on the tower at the distant oil refinery. The rotating sails of two wind pumps give the marshes a Dutch feel. Only three cows standing on top of the wall bar our way.

'I'm not going any further!' says Nell. We have perhaps an hour till darkness. And here we are stranded in the middle of a marsh. With a dog and mad cows.

After some debate, I pull a small white sapling from the ground. It looks pretty pathetic, but will have to be my drover's stick. I never thought we'd be facing life-threatening cows in Canvey Island. Why are there no songs about cows in Dr Feelgood's repertoire? Or is that what 'Milk and Alcohol' is really all about?

I advance calmly on the bovines, flanking to the river-side of the bank, using all my experience of growing up on an Essex farm and hoping to drive the cows back to their companions. 'Come on, girl, come on!' I say. Two of them stumble down but the third cow, which is starting to look rather bulky, just stares at me as if I've knocked over its pint in the Admiral Jellicoe. This stick will snap as soon as I wield it. 'Come on, girl, go on!' When I'm a few feet away it veers away like a reluctant teenager. Phew.

'Pick the dog up, Lola, and follow me.'

'Daddy, I'm scared,' says Nell.

'Just keep calm and look straight ahead,' I counter.

'Daddy, is that a bull?'

Bugger, I think it is. A large brown bull with sides of pure muscle and some very masculine testicles dangling beneath its haunches.

'Erm, just keep going and keep the dog quiet. Good boy, Vulcan ... It won't want to come up here.'

We seem to walk agonisingly slowly. Somehow we make it to the next field, where an electric fence warns off the cows.

'Nobody's concerned about me, I was scared too,' says Lola, still holding the pesky dog.

'Lola, you did well,' declares her mum.

'Well done, Lola. Lucky I'm a farmer's son,' I declare, pleased by my bovine victory.

The earth wall seems interminable, but eventually a motorway on stilts comes into view. It looks like a weird concrete snake travelling across the blankness. Please let there be no more cows. We scramble beneath the flyover and follow the earth wall to the right across the marshy inlets of Benfleet Creek. Boats lie at all angles in the mud as if victims of some Canvey apocalypse. It's taken an hour, but eventually we emerge on to the B1014. It seems we've been walking for miles in a deserted landscape halfway between sea, earth and, erm, petroleum.

A group of boys on cycles swoop past on the pavement and are polite as we step out of their way, saying, 'Thank you!' So much for Canvey being a chavtown.

We walk a few hundred metres to the station bus stop, where we wait for the rail replacement service. There's a helpful man from C2C directing passengers to the service.

'That was enjoyable when we went through the cows,' says the previously terrified Nell. Oh dear. Maybe she's going to grow up to be an adrenaline junkie.

Night is falling and the angular towers and cylinders of the refinery and the streetlights across the marshes look like a strangely beautiful city from a science fantasy series.

Sadly, in 2012 it appears that the Coryton refinery is about to close with the loss of 850 jobs. In *Oil City Confidential* Wilko Johnson quotes *Paradise Lost* and 'darkness visible' when talking about the influence of Coryton. 'The closer you get, the uglier it gets,' he reflected as news of the closure emerged. 'But just across the creek it is a thing of beauty … It pisses over the Pompidou Centre.'

There's something beguiling about Canvey Island, isolated, urban yet rural, full of surprises, unique habitats and the urban poetry of Dr Feelgood, standing down by the jetty, the wall and the long grass.

The locals are right. 'The island' has been unfairly maligned. You start off wondering what you're doing at the end of the world, but by the time you leave Oil City you're quietly fascinated by the place.

A fortnight later I return to the island to see Wilko Johnson perform at the Oyster Fleet Hotel. I'm with my mate Robert in his motor. We've driven down the A13 in an inverse version of one of Dr Feelgood's London heists. He comments on the density of the housing and the tiny gardens. We stop the car, attracted by a sign advertising 'the cheapest fireworks in Essex'. Entrepreneurial Essex likes a bargain.

'I would have thought just being the cheapest fireworks in Canvey would be enough, as it takes so long to get off the island,' muses Robert.

'It's like Santa's grotto in here, lads, we've got everything,' says a friendly bloke in white trainers and denims, standing in a hastily converted white room by a sandwich bar. Next door the shop is burned down. Hopefully not by fireworks. We look at the £100 selection box of giant rockets.

'You can't import them ones any more, they changed the regulations, but you can still sell 'em!'

Robert opts for the cheaper £20 pack and leaves a happy man.

Fortified by the cheapest fireworks in Essex we head for a pre-gig drink at The Lobster Smack. It seems to have the cheapest drinks in Essex as two pints of EPA are just £3.48. The fish and chips are agreeably priced too.

The Lobster Smack is past the gas silos down Haven Road. It's a lovely old pub, clad in white weather-boarding and nestling at right angles in the shelter of the huge earth banks topped by the concrete seawall.

A sign outside reveals how the pub was used by smugglers, who could nip out of their boats through the back door and take their dodgy goods to Hadleigh and Rayleigh. So nothing much has changed there then.

It's featured in *Great Expectations* as The Sluice House, the riverside pub where Pip and Magwitch stay when they attempt to return the transported felon to Australia. We feel a frisson of Dickensian fervour and both vow to read the ending of *Great Expectations* again. The pub still has low ceilings and old beams and, apart from the laminated menus, can't have changed much since Dickens's time. A photo on the wall shows it looking just the same in the early 1900s, apart from having a horse and cart outside instead of cars.

From the pub you can climb up on to the seawall and view the tide lapping impatiently at the other side, waiting for a breach. You can see the tremendously long and useless old jetty designed for the never-completed Occidental oil works and the marshland stretching off towards Coryton. It's a great place to have a drink.

We drive back to the Oyster Fleet Hotel and head upstairs to where Wilko is set to play in a glorified function room with a smallish stage and mock chandeliers as lights.

The room is full of mainly older blokes, some with shaved heads, some in denim jackets. As Wilko takes the stage, a female Mohican and her similarly coiffed mate from the local support band Eight Rounds Rapid are in the front row.

Wilko comes on with a minimum of fuss. He has the most amazing face these days; a bald, veiny head, huge eyebrows and mad stare. No wonder he recently got a part as the mute executioner Ilyn Payne in fantasy series *Game of Thrones*. All he had to do was look dangerous, which comes easily. His first song, 'Everyone's Carrying a Gun', adds to the general feel of lunacy as he careers across the stage with his trademark guitar bursts.

An added plus is that we also get Norman Watt-Roy on bass, famed for his time with another Essex legend, Ian Dury. He performs some amazing funky solos and you realise just what a good musician he is. He also has a bald head, staring eyes and, like Wilko, looks like he would make an admirable villain in *Harry Potter*. Meanwhile, there's Dylan Howe, a younger drummer working admirably hard to keep up with the old codgers.

The room is sweaty and packed with 300 people. The old Feelgood favourites are there, starting with 'Sneakin' Suspicion' and the Canvey lyric of Wilko looking at the flares by the river. It's not quite the same without Lee

Brilleaux of course, but Wilko is a great performer in his own right.

Wilko brings on a harmonica player for a storming 'Roxette'. 'This is a song I wrote in those stunning seventies,' he says before performing 'Back in the Night', scatter-gunning riffs into the crowd. There's 'She Does It Right' too, with Wilko holding his guitar up by his head and machine-gunning the audience. Then a great 'Paradise' and an impassioned cry of 'Irene Irene Irene!'

It feels like some mad convention of Essex eccentricity with electricity as Wilko puts his guitar behind his head and plays it backwards. What's also striking is how hard the band are working; they're all covered in sweat – it's a very Essex characteristic to put in a proper shift in your night job. Wilko says that when he's asked how long he's been touring, he replies, 'Twenty-eight years!' Somehow the seawalls hold as Wilko encores with 'Johnny B. Goode'.

It's a special moment to have seen Wilko in his home town, where he's still very much loved. Like Canvey, he's in a place apart, a geezer metaphorically a few feet short of sea level, but strangely addictive and still adored by the locals. And at £15 it's probably the cheapest guitar strafing of an audience you'll find in Essex.

14

CHELMSFORD SISSIES

Travelling to Essex in a car with Radio Essex emblazoned on the side – it doesn't get any better than this. Mark Syred, a Radio Essex researcher, has kindly picked me up at six in the morning in London to appear on the *Ray Clark Show*. It's as close as this Essex exile will ever get to feeling like a member of *TOWIE*.

We head round the darkened M25 and then onto the A12 to Chelmsford, passing a 'Welcome to Essex' sign. We're going to be discussing the twentieth anniversary of Essex Man, inspired by my piece for *The Independent*.

Inside the corridors of Radio Essex, Mark offers me the obligatory instant coffee as Ray hosts the *Breakfast Show*. I'm ushered into the studio after an item about Professor King on Lord Hutton, ready to broach a subject of equal gravitas. Ray has many a question about whether the public are learning to love Essex Man. The station has a radio car travelling through Woodham Ferrers looking for Essex Men, sending in excited soundbites about a house with a Doberman and finding the odd builder called Steve who says people in Essex 'get off their bum' and work.

Ray says he lives in Burnham-on-Crouch and we get on to Ian Dury, so he finds a live version of 'Billericay Dickie' for the airwaves. After my stint, fellow DJ Dave Monk comes in and laughs, 'The council hate all that Essex Man stuff. They've been trying for years to get rid of the image. Are we culturally barren as Simon Heffer wrote? I've always been quite proud of that whole Essex thing; I think it's a slight compliment.'

Monk then confesses that he fears Essex Man might be getting a bit soft as 'Mark Wright has been known to moisturise', though he likes my suggestion that Wright should cover 'Billericay Dickie' as a Christmas single.

I'm big in Essex this morning. After the radio slot there's an interview with Gareth George from *BBC Look East*. I tell him: 'Whatever the origins of Essex Man, he's no longer seen as nasty, brutish and short. He's cuddlier today, no longer exclusively right wing, and a lot funnier.'

Then it's a short journey to the HQ of the *Essex Chronicle*, where Alan Geere whisks me into his office, gives me voluminous copies of various papers and then suggests a picture with all the Essex Men in the adjoining open-plan office. This is just about every reporter, so we pose for a nice snap with me in an armchair and the lads all around.

By 10 a.m. I'm away from the media frenzy (well, at least a scrum of three news organisations), hungry for breakfast and real coffee on the streets of central Chelmsford. Can it match the hype I've just helped generate?

Chelmsford was awarded City status by the Queen to mark her Diamond Jubilee in March 2012. Tellingly, the

Queen dumped Reading in favour of her beloved Essex. *The Sun* called it 'TOCIE (The Only City in Essex)' and claimed it was famous for 'stilettos and Bacardi Breezers'. My pal Nigel, a Brentwood man, commented on the news: 'Seventy-four years after the football club was christened Chelmsford City and ninety-eight years after it got a cathedral!'

So Chelmsford City FC had it right all along. The Romans knew it was a proper city too. Chelmsford was originally called Caesaromagus, meaning 'Caesar's market place' (where maybe he sold used chariots?) and has the distinction of being the only town in Britain ever to be named after Caesar.

In 2006 Simon Heffer, author of the original Essex Man feature, wrote in the *Sunday Telegraph* of the 'increasingly charmless aspect of the towns of inland Essex, like Chelmsford, whose heart was ripped out by developers in the early 1970s'.

That's a little unfair, although walking from the station to the town centre you do realise why Chelmsford was designated a 'clone town' a few years ago. All the usual chains like Debenhams, Starbucks, HMV and Waterstones are present, plus two rather bland shopping malls and a bar called Decadence. Decadence, in Chelmsford?

My wife recently asked a Chelmsfordian where to go to find something exciting to do and the local replied, 'Anywhere but Chelmsford!'

Thankfully, though, there's still the cathedral, the Shire Hall, the county cricket ground, a railway viaduct over the park and a little touch of Essex individuality and directness in shops like Nosh and a hairdressers entitled Blow, which must make for some interesting phone bookings.

The new marketplace is made of ugly concrete, but does offer *Doctor Who* videos for £3, and nearby is a rare section of the river Chelmer that is grass rather than concrete-lined.

At the Market Square Café I partake of a fine full breakfast for just £3.49 and am treated to more margarine than I've ever seen on a plate of toast. Inside the caff are three older women who sound like former East Enders. They're discussing the poor job prospects of their grandchildren and how terrible it is with those foreigners coming here to claim benefits: 'Well, I mean you'd come for free money, wouldn't you?'

They then cheerily hug the waitress as they leave, saying, 'See yer next week, darlin'!' The waitress is black and presumably born of parents who'd migrated to the UK. This seems to capture a little of the Essex Man/Woman conundrum; sometimes ferociously right wing in their views at the debating table, but friendlier and willing to take as they find face to face.

There's no sign to the museum, but after asking at the Town Hall I'm directed to Moulsham Street. At the end of the high street there's Chelmsford's not very impressive answer to the Sydney Harbour Bridge straddling the river Chelmer and then traffic lights crossing over the five-lane A1060. Chelmsford's other problem is that it is dissected by major roads.

Moulsham Street shows more individuality and has some old-style Essex weather-boarded buildings. There's a vintage shop with a small Goth section and even an Adult Discount Store. Although, this being Essex, even here there's a madly entrepreneurial air – an ad for the same sex shop in Chelmsford's *The Edge* fanzine offers 'Over 2,000 DVDs exchange old for new'. You'd think Essex porn watchers might want to keep their viewing furtive, but no, they're busy doing deals on used razzle films as if it's the Record and Tape Exchange in Notting Hill.

Way down Moulsham Street, past the college and suburban homes, the museum finally emerges in Oakland Park. It's sited in the rather grand Oakland House and struggles manfully to make something of Chelmsford. There's plenty on radio pioneers Marconi and a video of ball bearings on a production line. Yes, the UK's first mass production of ball bearings was at the Hoffmann factory in Chelmsford. There's a Roman temple here too; only it's under the roundabout.

In the museum's music section there's a picture of Keith Flint of the Prodigy, who grew up in Braintree, struggling to start a fire in his county town. Much is made of the Chelmsford Punk Festival in 1977. There's a picture of eight rather middle-class-looking Chelmsford punks and a description of a wonderfully *Spinal Tap*-esque festival. It rained all day, the crowds didn't turn up, the scaffolders started to dismantle the stage before the concert was over and The Damned refused to play. An inadvertent vision of anarchy in the commuter belt.

But what's this? Not only has Chelmsford produced

Rod Stewart's missus Penny Lancaster and West Ham goalkeeper Mervyn Day. It's most famous son of all is the dress-wearing artist Grayson Perry. A very unlikely Essex Man indeed. In the museum's pottery room, the cross-dressing geezer has a vase on display entitled *Chelmsford Sissies*. On top of his vase is an upturned car crashing into a Chelmsford sign and on the side of it is a picture of a Barrett-style home and parked car.

It's proper art, and it's proper Essex, with motors and new houses on a great vase. The rest of the vase is covered in pictures of bearded men wearing skirts. This is a reference to a mythical transvestite festival invented by Perry, based on a group of Civil War gentlemen who were forced to wear women's clothing and parade through Chelmsford. The adolescent Grayson must have spent days thinking up that one in his bedroom.

Cross-dressing in the commuter belt? That bar name was right – there really is Decadence in Chelmsford. Grayson Perry, eh? But then for somewhere so apparently homogenous, the county has produced an awful lot of mavericks, I reflect on the walk back to the station.

Shortly after my visit, Grayson was in the press declaring he gets most of his ideas 'sitting in front of the telly with a beer, watching *X Factor*'. So far, so Essex. He denounced the art establishment as disengaged 'with the real world', adding that he preferred Banksy, Scottish painter Jack Vettriano and Beryl Cook to the works on display at the Tate. 'I have a pot called *Boring Cool People*,' he said. 'It's decorated with pictures of the sort of people who go to contemporary art galleries.'

Is he really that different to the Chelmsford Sissies he grew up with? You can take the cross-dressing out of Essex, but you can't take Essex out of cross-dressers like Perry.

As Phill Jupitus tells me of Mr Perry: 'He's a man in a dress with a bear, but you hear him talking and it's like you've bumped into a bloke in the pub! I've always thought the most fascinating people in Essex are what Ian Dury described as "arts and crafts".'

Caesar and Sissies – all can be found by the banks of the Chelmer.

A month or so later, I'm in Chelmsford again, this time catching the bus to Maldon with my daughters. The half-hour bus journey from Chelmsford feels like you're going into another land and the sense of otherworldliness is compounded by the fact that on the bus are two people, a nineteen-year-old student and an older woman, wearing backpacks and returning after a stint teaching in Africa.

My old school friend Alison O'Brien lives in Maldon, which is proper posh Essex. She's lived in Spain, Coventry, Manchester and Liverpool, but decided Essex is the best place in the world. She fell for Maldon after day trips there with her parents, who had moved from Laindon to East Hanningfield.

We meet Alison in town and walk down the high street, full of old pubs and churches, towards the Blackwater Estuary. There's plenty of history here; the name Maldon is a corruption of the Roman Camalodonum.

And the Battle of Maldon in AD 991 is certainly still big here. In the Plume Library at All Saints' Church we find the Maldon Embroidery commemorating the 1000th anniversary of the battle. It's Essex's attempt at the Bayeux Tapestry, done by local schoolchildren.

The Blackwater Estuary is rather magical. On Hythe Quay Maldon feels more like north Norfolk or Cornwall. Around ten Thames sailing barges are moored on the muddy banks, their rigging flapping in the breeze. These sailing barges used to work the east coast rivers and sail to London in the nineteenth century. They would carry hay, straw and grain to London to feed the growing numbers of horses and return with the 'London mixture' of manure and straw, which seems a neat summation of the way London has often thought of Essex.

We find pubs, mudflats, seabirds, a playground and a funfair. My kids are delighted to stop at a stall selling chip butties and chips and cheese. Over tea in foam cups, Alison reminds me that a crew of us once visited Maldon when we were in the sixth form, back in the days when we'd motor off to Mersea Island for a bonfire and hippie songs.

She says Maldon has been a great place to bring up her son Scott, now a sixteen-year-old West Ham fan who can demolish a big breakfast in Ken's Café, Upton Park, in a millisecond. And no, she's never been to Maldon Sea Salt factory.

We chat about how Alison's sister has left Sociology-on-Sea (Wivenhoe) and is now reunited with her first-ever boyfriend in Basildon. Then we get on to the subject of *TOWIE* and Alison reveals that she knows Debbie, Lydia's mum. My children are impressed.

Lola and Nell are happy to find a mini-funfair, where

they play on bumper cars and roundabouts. The estuary seems to extend for miles. It's here that Maldon has its famous New Year Mud Race. Loads of Essex folk try to gloop through the cloying mud to the other side and end up looking like mud monsters.

The path terminates at a statue of Saxon loser Lord Byrhtnoth at the end of the Blackwater Estuary. He has his hand in the air in a pretty heroic posture for a bloke who lost. Lola and Nell pose for a picture underneath the sword-wielding Saxon.

Alison tells us the story of how the Vikings were trapped on Northey Island, out in the river. The Norwegian Olaf's forces couldn't get across the small causeway to the mainland so Olaf sent a messenger to Byrhtnoth asking him to allow his warriors onto the shore for a fair fight.

Showing all the military acumen of *TOWIE*'s Harry Derbidge and Joey Essex, Byrhtnoth agreed to this. The Saxons duly got a right hammering. It all got a bit *Monty Python*-ish as a geezer called Godrīc nicked Byrhtnoth's horse and decided to run away. Godrīc's brothers, Godwine and Godwīg, followed him and then many other English soldiers scarpered too, as they recognised the horse and thought it was Byrhtnoth fleeing. Maybe they were all Chelmsford Sissies?

Poor old Byrhtnoth ended up losing his head in the battle, though his gold-hilted sword was found alongside his body. Rumours that his descendants later managed West Ham can't be discounted.

They're not great at battles in Maldon, but they do know how to brew a nice beer. We walk back along the

river and our day ends with a pint of Maldon Hotel
Porter in the Queen's Head, watching the waders at
work in the river mud as we eat. It's a refreshing, muddy
antidote to the more clonetown aspects of Chelmsford.
Who needs Penzance or St Ives when we have the Essex
Riviera right here?

Yet Maldon offers more than just losing battles and
Thames sailing barges. It can now add the Northern
Lights to its attractions after the Aurora Borealis
was spotted over Maldon and the Heybridge Basin
in July 2012 – proof that Essex has everything the
Scottish Highlands can offer and more. Though, like
most Maldonians, Alison and Scott slept through
the display.

'Good sky you got here, McIntyre...' The lights had
rarely been seen so far south, but significantly they
chose Essex for their debut, giving a purple-and-green
hue to the early morning sky. Just as well they didn't hit
Brentwood, where they might have been mistaken for
the lighting at one of Joey Essex's Reem nights. Aurora
Borealis would have been thought to be Mark Wright's
latest date. Perhaps *Local Hero* will now be re-made
in Maldon.

15

HAVING YOUR PHILL OF LEIGH-ON-SEA

Phill Jupitus meets me at Leigh-on-Sea station and escorts me to his Cherokee Land Rover in the car park. He's with his dog Chester, a black Staffie, and clad in off-duty jeans, green parka and scarf. We take the short drive over the bridge to the car park on Two Tree Island. Phill laughs approvingly when I say it sounds like a track from a *Joshua Tree*-era U2 album.

'If the tide's in and it's the right sort of day, it's achingly lovely here,' says the *Never Mind the Buzzcocks* and *QI* star and former Radio 6 breakfast show DJ. 'And you don't see many people, though when the wildlife trust has an open day there's hundreds.'

Two Tree Island was built on reclaimed land in the eighteenth century. It was once a sewage works and then a landfill site, but is now a rather striking place, covered in grass and reeds. Though the car park does have an unfortunate nocturnal reputation for dogging, reveals Jupitus.

Indeed, there's a memorable exchange on worldseafishing.com where one fisherman warns: 'Two Tree

Island is not safe to fish at night. Often cars from Southend seafront turn up there to see who can be the fastest in the car park. It's been used for drug deals, is also known as a dogging site and the island is notorious for people trying to commit suicide by using a pipe connected to the exhaust pipe.'

To which someone called Ron replies: 'Sounds like a proper night out. Fishing, smoking a spliff, getting a gobble while the racing is going on and at the end of the night watching some loonie top himself! ... Anyone going tonight? :)'

In the daytime, though, it's a peaceful, idyllic place full of eelgrass and birds. 'This reminds me of my childhood in Stanford-le-Hope, really grubby salt marsh,' says Phill as we take a path through the long grass. 'I'd leave home in morning and my mum would say don't go further than her whistle radius point. She has this incredibly loud whistle. We were remote controlled kids.'

Jupitus's mother was from Collier Row. As a kid, Phill grew up with his mum and stepfather, close to the oil refinery. 'Do you know that's where they filmed *Quatermass 2*? That terrifying industrial complex is the Shell Haven oil refinery at Coryton. It was always my grandfather's rather bleak assessment that if there was a nuclear bomb we'd all die rather quickly as there was only four miles of flat farmland between our house and the oil refinery!

'As kids we'd run around in the Coalhouse Fort and Tilbury Fort. Queen Elizabeth built it. Now Tilbury, there's bleak! It's docks – any town in the world that has docks, people say stay away. But there is a long, cresting hill across the marshes down into Tilbury and a good pub. On the train my favourite thing is Tilbury station when people are wrong-footed, you go in and come out backwards.'

We've walked out onto the island proper. It's wind-swept here and my DMs start to squelch on muddy ground. 'People think Essex is flat but this ridge is where the ice age stopped,' Phill continues, pointing out the long ridge along the coast on which Leigh-on-Sea and Hadleigh Castle are situated.

He clearly loves life in Leigh, enthusing about the local shops, the coffee houses and the art scene. 'I also like the conceit of the "on-sea" when it's an estuary. On sea is when it's a flat horizon, not Canvey and Kent in the distance!'

When the Royal Festival Hall had an exhibition on the seaside, Jupitus made them a bright red beach hut with all the coastal areas of Essex on it. 'There's a lot of it! Walton, Bradwell, and people come from Cape Cod to try the seafood at the Company Sheds at Mersea. When you go there it's a shed with two picnic tables outside and you bring your own wine. My mate met people from Boston in the United States who had come specifically for the seafood.'

He tells me that Joseph Conrad wrote *Heart of Darkness* in Stanford-le-Hope. It's possible his line 'The horror! The horror!' may have resulted from Conrad's early exposure to watching West Ham. Author John Fowles and Viv Stanshall of the Bonzo Dog Doo Dah

Band are other local luminaries. 'I like the fact it's got culture rubbing together with London and that East End thing,' says Phill.

It soon emerges he's no fan of *TOWIE*, though he admits to never having actually viewed it. 'There's more positives than negatives to Essex, but I don't like *TOWIE*, as that's the first thing people associate with Essex now. That poor girl who had her salon firebombed … they've made a rod for their own backs. What I hate are the people who came up with the idea. It's like the people that built Lakeside saying, "That's Essex."'

Jupitus observes birdlife with the enthusiasm of an Essex Attenborough as they glide over the water. 'That's oystercatchers. No one comes this far down normally. I've been here and seen hundreds of thousands of geese, it's all you can hear. Five thousand flew out round the other side of the island. It's weird to be walking the dog and move a tonne of wildlife.'

Phill was brought up in Barking from the age of five until seven, going to the same school as Billy Bragg, before moving on to Stanford-le-Hope. As with many an Essex childhood, his early memories are centred around the car.

'My local was The Bell in Horndon on the Hill, which was pretty, but we'd be walking two and a half miles from Stanford to get there. Then we got cars and found Essex littered with beautiful villages like Herongate, Hanningfield and Danbury.

'A lot of Essex is predicated on the car. There's kids in nothing-going-on towns, where everyone gets in a Subaru and tear-arses down to Southend at night. There's that sense that you gotta get mobile. I remember the first one of my mates who learned to drive at seventeen. He was the first to get a car, the plastic pig we called it, and he'd play this game in his Reliant Robin. We'd drive down single-lane roads late at night and turn the lights off. We used to laugh about it but I could have died!'

Chester the Staffie is enjoying his romp through the mud as we reach the end of Two Tree Island. Phill stops for a mobile phone snap of one man and his dog with Old Leigh in the background across Leigh Creek. It's halfway between land and sea, reminding me of one of those liminal places that were so important to Neolithic man.

The view of Leigh has Jupitus telling me about one of his favourite pictures of the Leigh flyover crossing Leigh Creek. 'It's by local artist Jenny Eccles and it was only fifty quid. She said she couldn't sell it and it was lying up against the wall, but it makes Leigh look like Van Gogh.'

There's a boat seat lying in the marsh and a splendid sense of isolation. We also have a fine view of the low-lying Canvey Island, rising out of the estuary like an Essex Atlantis. 'That seawall on Canvey, now that's hubris,' says Phill. 'I've always had that feeling people weren't supposed to live there, especially with what the climate's doing, but also it defines their character being an island too: because people say it's a bit of a shithole, they say, "No, it's not."'

Walking back across the island towards Phill's car, we discuss our old spoof membership of the Essex Liberation

Front and advocacy of 'Freedom, liberty, equality, Tiptree jam!'

'I remember as a kid being taken around the Tiptree jam factory. If we ignore petrochemicals, I imagine jam is Essex's principal export,' opines the well-preserved comic. 'I was in Tokyo and there was Tiptree jam, there on the other side of the world. You couldn't even grow me a strawberry, Japan … it was probably on the same plane as me!'

Had we based the economy on Tiptree jam there would surely have been no credit crunch, just a bit of credit stickiness when the toast economy landed buttered side down.

We drive on to Hadleigh Castle. Having only ever seen this landmark from the train, it's impressive to be up here at last. It was once vital for defending the Thames. Work started on it in 1230 but it was given an Essex makeover by Edward III in the 1360s. The round tower is hollow and has two large cracks down it, but is relatively intact on three sides, while other bits of wall survive around the rest of the area. From the castle summit there is a fantastic view of Canvey Island and the reclaimed flat, muddy fields below us. 'You can see from here that Canvey wasn't really meant to be there,' explains Jupitus.

We read the board describing the castle's history and how it was built on unstable ground. 'It had subsidence! They had cowboy builders even then!' I suggest. 'There, you've got your story!' says Phill.

From Hadleigh Castle we return to Phill's gaff. It's a modern house in an affluent but normal street and he says here the neighbours take no notice of him. Generally, people in Southend treat him as part of the furniture, he says.

Above the mantelpiece there's a fantastic picture of sunset over Leigh by Phill's mum and his living room is something of a homage to Essex, with several other paintings on the walls. In the kitchen there's his fifty quid picture of the Leigh flyover above minivans and boats. Phill shows me a picture of Bobby Moore and a World Cup Final programme in a window-shaped dark wooden frame made by his friend Billy Bragg. Before we leave, he insists on giving me a framed abstract of Canvey Island gasometers.

We leave Chester the dog at his house and return to the motor, driving through Old Leigh. Phill remembers visiting the Peter Boat on the seafront as a child. Two police cars are parked beside the Crooked Billet pub and quite an elderly man is being arrested outside. 'Now that's a very Essex scene,' says Jupitus. He recommends the splendid ales of the Crooked Billet and the bacon sandwiches of the Strand Tearooms. He shows me the astonishing fourteen coffee shops in Leigh town centre and says The Coffee Bean is the best.

We drive past a converted public toilet that's now a restaurant called Toulouse (an Essex pun on 'two loos') and head towards the Arches on Southend promenade, which Phill says 'have to be seen to be believed'.

The Arches is a row of thirteen, yes thirteen, cafés crammed under Shorefield Road in Westcliff. They've been going for a hundred years in arches that before that were storage spaces for fishermen. We enter the Riverside Restaurant and sit at a table topped with menus, ketchup, salt, pepper, sugar and various sauces. The radio is playing songs like 'Hot Hot Hot' and 'Working My Way Back To You'. The plate glass windows give a panoramic view of the high tide.

'I'm very tempted by the Christmas Day breakfast they do here,' admits Phill.

'It's a great view,' I say.

'Not being funny or anything, but that view, that flatness...' muses Phill. 'I was a latecomer to Dickens and when I read *Great Expectations*, his description of North Kent and the Thames as "the low lead line", that's what it looks like – like lead. Me and the missus say when this county's at its most beautiful it's like it's in black and white. The grey of the river, the grey of the sky and Kent. I love it. I can relax so much here...'

Our Dickensian reverie is interrupted by a waitress and Jupitus orders fried breakfast with double beans, two toast and some marmite, while I opt for the mushroom omelette and chips, accompanied by a pot of tea.

As he pours the tea, I ask him how Stanford-no-Hope earned its moniker.

'There was a beautiful stone facade at the station and the name was engraved on it. In the mid-1970s someone just sprayed "no" over "le". My old mate Brian used to say, "We've got three hopes in life, Bob Hope, no hope and Stanford-le-hope." With Stanford people there is an acceptance of the negative aspects of it. It can go from begrudging to fully embracing, but I've never encountered loathing, because the people that don't like it, they leave.'

When quizzed about the iffier places in Essex he ponders on Tilbury, Aveley and Ockenden as possibilities, before opting for the trains from Fenchurch Street after the Christmas office parties as the worst place to be for 'complete and utter intoxication'.

'Best place ... I'd have to give it to Leigh. It's got everything I need. I love it, love my house, love the people. I can come out of my front door and that view ... I go to the end of the road and sometimes the sun setting over Canvey ... It's a weird thing to get pastoral about, but that's my mum's picture you saw, sunset over Canvey. The variation in the view of the refinery, Canvey, Two Tree Island, the Kent marshes and the river and the differences you see in it, tide in, tide out, sunny, cloud, windy. Quite often if I want to clear my head I just go to the end of the road. I remember seeing twenty Thames barges in full sail tear-arsing up the Thames. It's a sight Dickens would have seen – timeless.'

I'm now imagining Phill in an Estuary English version of The Proclaimers crooning, 'While the Chief puts sunshine on Leigh...' Lunch arrives and it's damn fine fare. My omelette is perfectly burnished and the chips gold and crispy. After we've enjoyed a hearty scoff, Phill reflects on who most embodies Essex Man.

'If I had to pick a classic Essex Man it's Jonathan Ross, even though he comes from Leytonstone. There's a sense of fairness, but at the same time an edge to it. If I was to pick one person to define the modern Essex state of mind

I think Jonathan's as good a shout as you've got. He's bright. He transcends class and I think the county does.'

Outside the tide is leaving the mud exposed with astonishing speed. We discuss Wilko Johnson's theory that estuaries encourage creativity and Phill thinks there's something in this. While not having any grand theory of why Essex spawns so many comics, he speculates:

'Essex is constantly in motion. It throbs with daily movement. There's rhythms, people moving in and out of London and the tide going in and out. You see change all the time. The place is in a state of flux and in an odd sort of way that affects your mind set and makes you quite mercurial, it leeches into the humour.'

At which point a lady leans over and asks to borrow the ketchup. We then banter about the less cerebral matters of West Ham and how Jupitus is proud to be the man who first started barking at 'Mad Dog' Martin Allen, sparking a crowd craze. Phill insists on paying the bill ('I'm on the telly, mate') and chats happily to the proprietor as he does so.

Fortified by the finest fare in Southend, we're back in Phill's Cherokee and riding the Promenade towards Shoeburyness.

We drive beyond the amusement arcades and pass the Kursaal. Phill is impressed that I saw Rod Stewart and the Faces there. He's seen Status Quo and Thin Lizzy at the Kursaal in the 1970s and Aswad at the Cliff's Pavilion, plus Siouxsie and the Banshees at the Chelmsford Odeon ('I still have the badge!').

He points out the other restaurant that used to be a

loo and some of the more expensive houses that overlook the sea beyond the tackier amusements end of town.

Then it's along the deserted seafront to Shoeburyness. There are no shops, just the Sealife Centre, where Ian Dury filmed a section of his cancer charity advert, and a few windswept palms, some very expensive houses and the omnipresent greys of sea and sky.

Shoeburyness town centre has a few quiet shops and a pub called The Garrison. Phill tells me that Shoeburyness has the lowest crime rate in the UK because it's a garrison town, and it's got the lowest rainfall too. We drive past the station. 'Ah, now that's an Essex rite of passage. Falling asleep on the train and a guard saying, "Wake up, mate, you're at the end of the line!"'

Jupitus confesses that he's always dreamed of visiting the military ranges on Foulness Island. 'I can hear the guns when I'm walking the dog at Hadleigh Castle. If I ever do a gig with the armed forces maybe I can fix something up. When I was a kid there were rumours they were firing nuclear shells...'

We drive back along the seafront and Phill recalls seeing a Maestro bobbing in the sea after being driven onto the beach by drunks. Happy days.

'You have to try the Rossi's ice cream,' he says, pulling up at the Rossi's shop. It's another dreamy venue, packed with retired folk looking out at the sea through huge glass windows. There's a bloke with a bucket looking for bait, which is a very Southend sight. Jupitus recommends the vanilla cone as the Rolls-Royce among the numerous flavours on offer.

Isles of dogging, castles, chips, ice cream ... perfect. We take a seat by the window and discuss his favourite place in Essex.

You don't expect a comedian to be full of eulogies to Essex, but spend some time with Jupitus and you soon discover that there's more to him than the *Never Mind the Buzzcocks* persona – and he's a great advocate for the most maligned of counties. Like one of his heroes, Ian Dury, he's finding Essex and drugs (OK, the odd shot of caffeine) and rock'n'roll are very good indeed.

We discuss how quickly the tide is going out. It's gone from waves lapping at the esplanade to a huge grey sweep of mud, sand and beached boats. 'I can say, hand on heart, that I've looked at the Grand Canyon and thought this is not for me. Here the beauty is so subtle. There's physical changes, millions of tonnes of water where it wasn't an hour ago,' reflects Phill, a man who's toured Route 66 for TV, but is utterly happy in Leigh-on-Sea.

16

SOUTHEND'S PIER PRESSURE

Jamie Oliver claimed to have been conceived at the end of Southend Pier in his TV series *Jamie's Great Britain*.

It sounds like a great starting point for an Ian Dury song. You can imagine those posthumous lyrics arriving via some dodgy Southend medium: 'I wouldn't be here if it weren't for Southend Pier / and too many beers / a lark on the planks with grateful thanks...'

Jamie was filmed with his dear old mum and dad and Nan sitting in deck chairs on Southend beach – his mum denied the pier story, as she would, while his dad merely smirked.

Oliver is not the only famous son of Southend. Wilko Johnson is still a resident, having moved the few miles from Canvey Island, to a house complete with a rooftop dome for his telescope. 'Sitting in my dome when it's raining is really great. Especially if you've got biscuits,' he reflects. His neighbours haven't objected to the dome as it's hard to see from street level. He told me at the launch of his autobiography, *Looking Back At Me*,

'Funnily enough there's a rather nice-looking woman who's moved nearby who keeps asking if she can come round and use my telescope...'

These days Wilko, previously John Wilkinson, is an old bloke on a bicycle having an unlikely epiphany on the seafront as he remembers his younger self shifting guitars and amps in the very same place. 'What if somebody had come up to me then and said to me, "One day you're going to be an old geezer with your bike looking at the Moon, that's how far you're going to go!"?' he writes in *Looking Back At Me*.

'Someone told me he had a theory that estuaries and places where boats come in produce more bands than elsewhere,' Wilko said at the launch of *Oil City Confidential*. 'With Southend it had something to do with the fact that it was a seaside town for East Enders. There were always Teddy Boys there through all the eras with Jerry Lee Lewis booming out, so there was always a feeling about that kind of music and maybe that's got something to do with it.'

Indeed, Southend is almost in danger of trending. The hero of David Nicholls' very funny novel *Starter for Ten* is a character called Brian from Southend. The opening scene sees Brian and his two old mates from school on the end of Southend Pier, drinking beer and contemplating his imminent departure to university.

Would Mr Darcy now come from Essex? I ask Nicholls if he set the first chapters of *Starter for Ten* in Southend because Brian was supposed to be a bit like people perceive the county to be, a little unsophisticated and out of his depth when confronted by naked bohemian parents, but genuine, funny and down to earth, and basically a nice guy who gets the girl at the end (even though it's not who he thought it would be).

'I think that's exactly what I was getting at,' says Nicholls. 'It was really a stand-in for the small town I grew up in, Eastleigh in Hampshire, a suburb of Southampton and a lot less lively than Southend. Brian is, initially, a little bit of a snob about his home town, and its lack of dreaming spires. But it's also where he runs back to when things go badly wrong.'

'*Starter for Ten* is very much a traditional coming-of-age novel, and Brian feels the same way about Southend as Adrian Mole feels about Leicester, or as Pip feels about the north Kent coast, or as Billy Liar feels about Leeds. He likes to think he's too big and smart and sophisticated for the place, though in reality he's entirely a product of it.

'I was so sorry that they couldn't shoot the film of *Starter for Ten* on Southend Pier, which is quite something. Someone, I can't remember who, said that a pier was a disappointed bridge, but Southend is long enough not to feel too disappointed. In the end I think the sheer length of it was the problem.'

Southend has starred in many films, even if it did miss out on *Starter for Ten*. Southend Pier, Adventure Island and Eastern Avenue appeared in Mike Leigh's *Happy-Go-Lucky* when Poppy visited her sister Helen in Essex, and the town's derelict Esplanade House doubled as war-torn Iraq in the film *Screwed* (OK, maybe that's not too flattering). Southend airport featured in the 2006 film *The Queen* and the James Bond classic *Goldfinger*, while the seafront appeared in *EastEnders* in 2011 and the pier made the closing credits of *Minder* when Ray Daley joined Arfur in 1991.

'We can be Hollywood-on-Sea,' Southend council's Lisa Ferne told the *Basildon Echo* in 2011. The tourism and events manager enthused: 'Southend has a lot of advantages over London. Crews only have to deal with one council and the town is less busy, so it's easier to close roads and other buildings for filming. We had one Hollywood studio which wanted to use the office blocks in Victoria Avenue for filming because it looked exactly like the financial district in a big American city.'

The one place I didn't explore in Southend with Phill Jupitus was the pier, because he didn't fancy walking to the end of it if the trains weren't running. So I'm returning with my daughter Nell.

The best way of approaching Southend is to walk along the beach from Leigh-on-Sea. Old Leigh is a proper working seaside town with boatyards, cobbled streets, stalls selling seafood and a fine history of smuggling and fishing. Nell takes a particular interest in the mini-octopuses on sale. And here are the hangover-curing cockles as advocated by Lee Brilleaux.

It's got some brilliant pubs. We stop at the Peter Boat, serving fish, and I buy a J2O for Nell and a drop of Crouch Vale Brewery Gold ale for myself.

It's good to see local beer on sale. Crouch Vale is a small independent brewery based in South Woodham

Ferrers. Its Brewery Gold won the CAMRA Champion Beer award in 2005 and 2006. Other Crouch Vale beers include Willie Warmer (named in honour of William de Ferrers) and Essex Boys.

Boats bob in the choppy waters and Nell sees a shark, only it turns out to be a sunken wreck. When we emerge from the pub the rain has lessened and the tide has departed.

Suddenly, a vast expanse of oozing mud and sand has appeared and also the channel of Leigh Creek. Moored boats are everywhere and so are pubs. Leigh is well served for boozers with the listed Crooked Billet, Olde Smack Inn (sounds a little dodgy), The Mayflower and The Ship coming into view, as well as a chippy and lots of seafood restaurants such as The Boatyard and Simply Seafood. Mick Norcross from *The Only Way Is Essex*, being a classy gentleman, took Maria on a hot date to Leigh. We encounter a small boat with the name *There's Klingons on the Starboard Bow* emblazoned on it. And there's a giant iron hulk that houses Essex Sailing Club.

Nell is excited to discover oyster shells, groynes, paddling pools and a dead seagull. We find turnstones and Brent geese.

We walk out to the Crow Stone, a mysterious monolith rising from the middle of the beach. A green plaque on it reveals that it was erected in 1837, replacing an earlier stone from 1755. The line between the Crow Stone and the London Stone at Yantlet Creek marked the end of the City of London's authority over the river Thames. A marker has stood here since 1285 and there's a similar marker stone on the other side of the estuary at the Isle of Grain.

Chalkwell station is next to the beach. Through the salt-ravaged window frames on the platform you see nothing but sea. It's the sort of place you'd rave about were it in Devon. Who needs the Settle–Carlisle line when you have the C2C Fenchurch Street to Shoeburyness commuter route?

At Chalkwell I resist the urge to move inland and start looking down drains. In February 2012 drain cleaner Aaron Large struck gold when he found four designer watches down a couple of drains in Chalkwell. It's draining Rolexes. They were worth around £60,000 combined and since no one claimed them he was set to become the legal owner. It seems a particularly inept tea-leaf might have stashed the watches down the drain without reckoning on the vigilant Mr Large. It's a very Essex story and one iffy drain; though police are said to be looking into it.

After a couple of miles of beach walking we hit a promenade of balconied hotels, grand green public toilets, white bathing cabins and closed ice cream kiosks. We pass someone on a bike singing 'Yellow Submarine' – though the sky is not so much blue as grey.

Finally Nell and I emerge in Southend central and buy some fish and chips by the pier. We're eating fish and chips on the gravel beach in the rain. Typically British, but the food is good and we're just about sheltered by two deck chairs.

For my then ten-year-old daughter it's a real adventure.

And after eating chips she then finds three dead baby crabs and we dip a toe in the grey ocean. It's hard to believe we were in London an hour or so ago.

It's less enjoyable for the Essex family with teenage kids behind us on the front. 'What a shit day ... only cos you made it shit ... move your fat arse ... shut up! ... But I've got a soaking wet arse!'

Still, the weather clears up and it's pleasing to see Southend being used by so many 'new' East Enders, we spot families who are black, Bangladeshi and orthodox Jewish in a few hundred metres on the seafront.

The listed front of the Kursaal is still there, which, as I mentioned to Phill Jupitus, brings back memories of Rod Stewart and the Faces and Steve Harley gigs in the 1970s. Today it's full of no-hope-of-grabbing-a-soft-toy machines, ten-pin bowling and staff sporting electronic illuminated bunny ears.

Nell loves Adventure Island, the fun fair by the pier. We avoid the chuck-a-ball-at-something-for-two-quid stalls and my daughter tries the massive slide and crooked house. It's staffed by friendly studenty types and is obviously hugely popular with families.

There used to be a replica of the *Golden Hinde* with waxworks on it at the foot of the pier. In *Looking Back At Me*, Wilko Johnson recalled how, after his friends had a particularly good night out, Paul McCartney's wax head appeared in a box at his house as a birthday present.

But the real highlight of any trip to Southend is the pier – although sadly the nearby Pier Bar where my mate Nick used to bop in his Teddy Boy days appears to have disappeared.

There's a newly rebuilt entrance hall with *Doctor Who*-style futuristic lifts. We buy walk there/get the train back tickets (£3 adults, £1.60 kids). Nell decides to walk only a little way because she says she'll be scared walking over water and even more scared on the train. She tackles her fear by crawling on the planks and looking through the gaps at the water below. A splinter in her finger puts a halt to this but at least takes her mind off being scared. I entice her onwards by revealing it's the longest pleasure pier in the world at 1.33 miles.

Southend Pier has had a battered history, but it refuses to die. A pier was first built here in 1830. The expansion of railways in the late nineteenth century meant Southend was suddenly accessible to East Enders and the pier needed to expand. The current pier's iron structure was first built in 1890 when the electric train became a huge attraction to East Enders. Then it was just the longest pier in Europe, but it gained its world record status in 1897.

Once Southend was known as Whitechapel-on-Sea. The peak years of the pier came after the Second World War, when the train carried an astonishing 4,713,082 passengers in the 1949/50 season, and an extra million visitors walked the planks after coming through the turnstiles.

It might have been a good idea to ban smoking though. The pier suffered devastating fires in 1959 (when 500 day-trippers had to be removed by boat), 1976, 1995 and 2005. Oh, and in 1986 the MV *Kingsabbey* sliced through the pier and left it with a 70 ft gap. But as Sir John Betjeman said, 'The pier is Southend. Southend is the pier.' And they just keep on rebuilding it.

It's calm out at sea after the busy promenade. We wave at the passing train named the *Sir John Betjeman*. And stopping at the shelters on the way, fortified by a shared Mars Bar at the vending machine halfway out, we find ourselves edging towards the pier head.

'Look, we've come a really long way. You can't see the name of Adventure Island any more!' says Nell.

It reminds me of my own excitement as a child when our family first ventured down the end of the pier after a drive down the A127 in my dad's Ford Zodiac. Back in the 1960s that pier seemed to stretch on forever, the train over the water was a thing of wonder and there were lights and amusements and pennies teetering over the edges of metal precipices at the end of this watery grail. My dad worried about the prices, my mum thought it a bit lowbrow and their son loved everything about it.

The Isle of Grain and the Isle of Sheppey are vivid and enticing across the estuary. The sea is flat and now the rain has gone there's a pleasing breeze. Boats sail past, tantalisingly close.

Finally, we reach the rectangular platform at the end of the pier. There aren't many places where you can stand 1.33 miles out to sea. It's much better than, say, Brighton Pier. The tacky amusements have gone and there's just a reasonably priced café and a new lifeboat station with an RNLI shop and the lifeboats on display through glass windows.

I drink tea from a foam mug and admire the view. From the café, Nell rings her sister: 'Lola, I'm 1.33 miles out in the sea!' she excitedly proclaims.

People fish from the end of the pier, or sit and gaze at Kent and Cooling Marshes in the distance. Nell looks through a pay-and-display telescope and watches the cargo ships heading towards Tilbury.

It was here at the end of the pier that Jamie Oliver was conceived when his mum and dad took the term pleasure pier a little too literally. Southend Council should surely capitalise on Oliver-mania. One of the world's greatest chefs was cooked up here, back in the days when olive oil was a character in *Popeye*. A blue plaque to mark Jamie's conception – was it a thirty-minute recipe? – should be placed right here, 1.33 miles out to sea.

We take the train back to the seafront and when we get home Nell sums up the day with some alacrity: 'I remember having a juice at the café and looking out and it was really scary and high up and there were lots of benches to sit on and a mini train and I remember thinking imagine if the train fell into the sea and I could see the funfair park at first and it was a whole mile and I felt really triumphant when I walked to the end of it and I liked it, thank you.'

So that's been a success, then. Perhaps we should succumb to pier pressure a bit more. In the 'staycation' era there's still something special in Whitechapel-on-Sea. There aren't many places that have a world record anything, yet so close to London we have the world's longest pleasure pier.

Southend in Essex has seen off the piers at Blackpool, Cromer, Weston-super-Mare, Eastbourne, Llandudno, Southport and Hastings at home and all the other pleasure piers on the planet. As that mad Norwegian football commentator Bjørge Lillelien might have put it: 'Brighton Pier! Pete Townshend! Leslie Ash! Toyah Wilcox! Sting! Phil Daniels! Can you hear me Phil Daniels with your mods and *Quadrophenia* soundtrack! We gave your pleasure pier one hell of a beating!'

17

JAM TODAY IN TIPTREE

'Liberty! Equality! Tiptree jam!' So read the caption on a picture of the spoof Essex Liberation Front in *Midweek* in 1990. My friend Richard Edwards, a chef from near Colchester, had invented a party manifesto calling for independence for Essex and an economic policy based on selling Tiptree jam to the world. The man who wrote the caption, David Cheal, who is now at the *Financial Times*, still regards it as one of his most memorable creations.

The quality conserves of Wilkin & Sons have made the town of Tiptree famous throughout the world. Even the Queen is a fan. *The Apprentice* has filmed there too – hapless would-be entrepreneurs created new conserves for the aptly named Lord Sugar. And for this Essex Man it's rather an emotional moment to finally be taking a tour of the finest of jam makers.

It's a very English scene at Kelvedon station. Weeping willows droop over the winding river Blackwater and the sound of wood pigeons cooing comes from the woods.

The Railway pub has an idyllic beer garden with tables overlooking the water.

Kelvedon is a sleepy place with a One-Stop shop, an estate agent and a butcher near the station. It's a classic ribbon development built around the busy A12. Kelvedon has a more rural feel than Estuary Essex though, with old houses and cottages painted yellow, pink, white and green. There are few shops, though it does have the Essex perennials of the King's Fish Bar, Cutting Edge hair design and the Indian Cottage takeaway. It's a little schizophrenic politically: there's a Conservative Club flying a flag of St George's Cross and nearly opposite is the Kelvedon Labour Club and Institute, advertising a gig by Filthy Habits. A quick check of the Co-op supermarket reveals a full three shelves of Tiptree jams and marmalades.

The next bus to Tiptree is two hours away, so after asking in the One-Stop shop and the Sun Inn, I'm given a taxi number by the barman and take a cab. Three miles down the B1023 we pass through Tiptree, which is busier and larger than Kelvedon. The name Tiptree comes from an Anglo-Saxon leader called Tippa and a tree that became known as Tippa's Tree.

The taxi drops me off at the reception for Wilkin & Sons, on the edge of Tiptree. Clouds of steam issue from pipes jutting out of the factory sheds and there's a smell of sugar and citrus fruit in the air. Staff wearing white hairnets and white coats disappear through doors.

Claire the receptionist has a photo of a jar of Little Scarlet jam surrounded by bright red strawberries on top of her customised laptop. Tiptree is the only place in the UK where Little Scarlet strawberries are grown, and the jam is so rare it doesn't become available until July. Little Scarlet is also James Bond's favourite jam, mentioned in Ian Fleming's novel *From Russia With Love*.

It's friendlier here than it used to be. The early workers at Wilkin & Sons carried sticks to ward off undesirables. Tiptree Heath used to be regarded as a 'great wild', frequented by vagabonds and smugglers coming up from the tributaries of the Blackwater River. Some local farmers used to help the smugglers, and would find a barrel of contraband on their doorsteps in the morning in thanks.

The Wilkin family has farmed in the area for nearly 300 years, but it was in 1885 that Arthur Charles Wilkin, fed up with his fruit perishing on the train journey to London, set up the Britannia Fruit Company, later to become Wilkin & Sons. It has had a Royal warrant since 1911.

Arriving at reception, director Chris Newenham gives me a tour of the farm in his four-wheel-drive. He looks like an upmarket fruit farmer should, wearing yellow brushed cord trousers, a checked shirt and tweedy checked jacket.

He tells me the company has 850 acres over five sites. We drive around a fruity array of crops set over the 450 acres behind the factory. This farm employs six full-time staff and around 400 seasonal pickers, including caravaners who have visited for forty years. Chris points out the organic plum orchard, with Victoria plums, damsons and greengages. We see 45-year-old quince trees (which reminds me of the line 'they dined on mince and slices of quince' in Edward Lear's *The Owl and the Pussycat*) that are set at a 45 degree angle, the after-effect of the 1987 hurricane.

The thinking is always long term, he says. 'We have 150-year-old mulberry trees and these mulberries here that were planted two years ago. They won't bear any meaningful fruit in my lifetime,' he says matter-of-factly. 'It will be twenty-five to fifty years before they're ready.'

Ironically, the location is not great: 'If you were an alien landing here the last place in the world you'd want to grow fruit is Tiptree, it's got heavy clay and because we've been growing fruit so long every pest and disease known to man, and it's also the driest county in Britain! But the Wilkins made history on the back of it,' enthuses Newenham.

It's taken years of dedication to become a worldwide brand. Tiptree has had to be very efficient with its water use, recycling water from the factory and keeping its own reservoir. There's one organic section and the rest of the farm is run on integrated crop practice, where pesticides are used sparingly. Oranges have to be imported but the company is self-sufficient in many other fruits. Then it's the 'flagship crop' of Little Scarlet strawberries, medlar, apricots, plums and fresh strawberries grown in polytunnels for supermarkets.

We drive past the fine old Georgian building of Tiptree Hall, where Peter Wilkin, from the founding family, still lives. It was built by John Mechie, a merchant banker who made his fortune inventing a new type of razor and had a penchant for inventing new methods of model farming and land drainage.

As we drive back to the factory Newenham reveals that his family farmed in Ireland and he studied agriculture at Writtle College in Essex. He was living in Sussex eleven years ago when he was approached by Wilkin & Sons and said he couldn't possibly live in Essex. Now he couldn't leave, he says: 'Since we moved to Goldhanger, where there's another Wilkin farm, we've made the best friends we've ever had and we wouldn't move for all the tea in China.'

Chris drops me off back at reception where PR person Katie Mumford leads me to the factory. We don white coats and ridiculous-feeling hairnets for the factory tour. I'm not allowed to take in a digital recorder, or a pen, though they do allow a small notebook and a pen – presumably vetted for germs – from the office. It feels a bit like going inside a secret nuclear facility, or a Bond film set, where Q will reveal a secret marmalade that can disable a rival operative in sixty sticky seconds. The only person who has ever been excused wearing a hairnet is the Queen, when she visited in 2010 as part of the celebrations accompanying 125 years of jam-making in Tiptree.

My guide is production manager Mike Smith, who has worked at Wilkin & Sons for thirty years. First we visit the Christmas pudding building, where they have already started working on this Christmas's batch in May. Every pudding has the name of the person who made it handwritten inside. 'We get letters from people saying thank you for a lovely pudding,' explains pudding-maker Margaret.

All the factory workers are also clad in white coats and hairnets, and Chris has cheery banter with people standing over trays of oranges and shiny metal hoppers. The happy working environment is perhaps reflected by a video you can view on YouTube of a worker juggling oranges.

The Wilkin family has always been progressive in its employee relations. Founder Arthur Charles Wilkin was a 'non-conformist radical liberal' who campaigned successfully for a railway from Kelvedon to Tollesbury and gave land to his staff, while his son, C. J. Wilkin, built twenty-nine cottages in Tiptree for employees.

Workers have received a share of the profits since 1917, when the Wilkin Provident Trust was set up with the motto 'by their fruits shall ye know them'. In 1989 an Employee Benefit Trust was established similar to that at John Lewis. This was the idea of Peter Wilkin, who is now seventy: without any biological children of his own, he decided that the company should be given to its workforce. Today the employees have 48 per cent of the voting rights and will eventually own the whole company. That old caption on my *Midweek* article of 'Liberty! Equality! Tiptree jam!' might be more appropriate than it seemed.

We enter the building devoted to Wilkin & Sons' sister company from Devon, Thursday Cottage, where conveyor belts of lovely-looking yellow lemon curd are being filled. Chris says the factory produces 50,000 jars of conserves a day, with the 170 staff working shifts from 8 a.m. to 4 p.m.

Then we pass workers sifting trays of oranges and orange peel for the Old Times marmalade and also blackcurrants, followed by the production line of tomato sauce, where the bottles are blasted with hot water to clean them.

A worker with a hopper shows us how to mix up the fruit for marmalade before it is heated to boiling point and sent to holding tanks. There's some technical stuff about pH levels. We move on to the filling line, where clear glass jars of orange marmalade head towards the labelling section. I'm starting to fancy a slice of toast.

In fact, it's all getting a bit surreal. I'm wearing a hairnet and stepping over the odd stray strawberry and pools of water on the floor where jars and machinery have been steam-cleaned. It's like a fruitier version of Willy Wonka's Chocolate Factory.

Another machine sends out countless mini-jars of marmalade for hotels in Saudi Arabia. Chris points out a counter that reads '128,000' – the amount of mini-jars they've produced today.

We pass the honey section and redmoped.co.uk home delivery service and enter the warehouse, where endless pallets of preserves are stacked up. Fork lift trucks move the pallets. And no, they've never had a heist, which would presumably be more of a jam raid than a ram raid.

The packing label reveals the batch we're standing by is heading to Italy. Wilkin & Sons exports to forty countries. Maybe the Essex Liberation Front was right: the Essex economy really could be run on jam. Tiptree is a huge industry; if we'd stuck to preserves instead of derivatives and futures then Britain's economy would be a lot more fruitful.

'We had *Midsomer Murders* filming here a few years ago,' remembers Mike. 'The chap was crushed by what was meant to be a pallet of pickle, though it was really tawny marmalade.' Crushed by a conserve – a very British murder indeed.

He adds that during the filming of *The Apprentice* Karren Brady was in his office, not looking too happy to be wearing a hairnet, while Katie says that Nick Hewer had a good dry sense of humour. The BBC's *Countryfile* has also filmed at Tiptree.

So, after thirty years of jam-making does Mike still enjoy Tiptree jam? 'Oh yes, I have it for breakfast!' he says, enthusiastically.

Taking off my hairnet and white coat, which have to be put down a chute for washing, I thank Mike and head off to Tiptree tearoom with Katie. There's a coach party in and it's packed with people ordering dishes such as skinless chicken breast, macaroni cheese and a sausage bap with caramelised red onion relish.

There's a plaque on the wall marking the Queen's visit in 2010. We find the only empty table and sit down for a cup of tea. Katie reveals the joy of working at Tiptree: 'It's really lovely in the middle of winter to come into work and smell citrus fruits.'

Then we explore the shop, which is a jam anorak's delight. The shelves are stacked with pots of Tiptree jams, jellies, marmalades, savouries, honey, relish, chilli mustard and Tiptree tea. Plus a tea towel featuring

Tiptree labels that I decide I have to buy. After a long debate, my red Tiptree plastic bag is filled with lemon curd, strawberry and loganberry jams and marmalade with malt whisky.

We move on to the museum, where there's a display of antique jam-making equipment, photos of the German Zeppelin that crashed in the area in the First World War and several early jam jars. The classic Wilkin & Sons logo has remained virtually unchanged throughout the firm's history.

'That's Mr Peter there, he's such a lovely man,' says Katie, as we look at framed photos of the Wilkin dynasty. There's something charming and English about the way Peter Wilkin is still referred to as Mr Peter. Wilkin & Sons Ltd has retained its values of 'quality, fairness, integrity and independence' through the years and Mr Peter should be rather proud of that.

That evening my family hold a Tiptree conserve tasting session with bread, crackers and jars of lemon curd, strawberry and loganberry jam. The marmalade with malt whisky is reserved for breakfast. It's the most popular tea I've ever provided. 'This has to be the finest moment of my career,' I tell my wife. 'Finally, I've provided you with jam today.'

18

LET'S SEE CLACTON

Essex starts to feel distinctly East Anglian as the train heads towards Clacton. Giant skies, flat land, rippling green fields, cow parsley-flecked embankments and tumbled-down old maltings, completely ungentrified, at the tiny Thorp-le-Soken station. My wife Nicola, my youngest daughter Nell and our dog Vulcan are with me and we're heading for Essex's Riviera, or at least what was once Butlin's version of it. The train is agreeably slow as it completes the one hour forty-four minute journey from Liverpool Street to Clacton on the Tendring Peninsula.

Clacton didn't exist until 1871, when the pleasure pier was built with one solitary hotel alongside it, though in pre-Victorian times there was the nearby village of Great Clacton, renowned for its smuggling. Victorian tourists would be ferried to the pier by steamboat from Woolwich and Tilbury. Clacton expanded rapidly as a tourist resort, the pier was lengthened and it became famed for the Butlin's holiday camp that closed in 1983, and also infamous for the 1964 riots between mods and rockers. Now it's more popular as a retirement and day-trip destination and has 53,000 residents.

From the station we walk past numerous estate agents, chippies and the Wimpy café, towards the AA four-star Chudleigh Guest House. Proprietors Carol and Peter, who was born in Italy, are a very friendly couple. They've run the place since 1963, having heard it was up for sale and fallen in love with the building. They also welcome dogs, and Carol laughs at Vulcan's name and tells us about her friend in Germany who has a dog named Ripley, after the *Alien* movies.

On the wall by the reception desk there's a poster of Ken Dodd, the veteran comedian, which is signed with 'How tickled I am to be here again!' Carol says that Doddy, now in his eighties, has been staying there for nineteen years and is coming again in July. 'He's a lovely man and Peter helps him with the pronunciation of his Italian in his act. He asked us how we first met and I said I was working as a radiographer. Ken said, "So he saw right through you!" Quick as that!'

We're staying in the same hotel as Ken Dodd, one of those weird surprises that hit you in the backwaters of Essex. Dodd still performs a three-hour act and his preference for a family-run B&B over something plusher in Colchester suggests Ken and Clacton are a good match, both enduring despite changing fashions.

We deposit our cases in the top bedroom and walk the couple of hundred metres to the pier and seafront. Prominent on the horizon is Gunfleet Sands Offshore Wind Farm. Built by the memorably named Danish company DONG – well, it is a saucy seaside town – the wind farm has forty-eight turbines set mainly in rows of seven, which at certain angles look like one multi-bladed entity. They loom like a weird forest out in the sea mist. For all the controversy surrounding turbines, I rather like them.

By the pier is a sign on the beach that reads: 'KEEP OFF THE GROYNE: YOU HAVE BEEN WARNED.' It seems very Essex in its directness.

Nicola, Nell, Vulcan and I walk to the seafront looking for the part of the beach where dogs are allowed. 'It's at the disabled access steps halfway between the two Martello Towers,' explains the Essex *Baywatch* man in the Beach Control Hut. The Martello Towers are impressive relics of the Napoleonic Wars, large round defensive towers with bricked-up windows and doors. The three-storey towers could resist cannon fire and a piece of large artillery could be placed on the flat top. The closest tower to Clacton is now a children's zoo.

The beaches beat Southend's pebbles. A swathe of yellow sand stretches from Walton to Jaywick. The beach is lined by a concrete promenade with cafés, and wind shelters are cut into the earth embankment behind. Today they're needed. Groups of people in coats huddle inside bathing huts, drinking cups of tea in English style on this breezy summer day.

We unleash Vulcan on the dog-friendly beach and he happily chases seagulls. Nell runs to the sea and looks for shells. A couple of boats bob in the sea and an aquamarine tractor sits on the shore as we stop at a spit and sit down by the large rocks of the sea defences. Nell wants to mine the rocks for the sparkling minerals she can see in them and asks for her mum's penknife. 'My penknife won't go into the rock,' Nicola says. 'Can I have an axe please?' asks the persistent Nell. She then builds a sand castle with a shell flag on top.

We watch a wetsuited father and son kite-surfing on brown waves full of churned-up sand. When the wind picks up the kite lifts them right out of the water. The son has just been whacked in the face with his kite and struggles to hold it down on the beach. It reminds me of Australia minus the sun, with the bungalows inland, the clear rolling sand and the beach sports.

'Come on, Boudicca!' commands a woman dog-walker in a pink coat and blue boots. Boudicca is a Staffie in a pink collar. An impressive name for an Essex dog. Perhaps the real Boudicca sacked Colchester in a pink chariot. Boudicca is with a male dog called Diesel, sporting a blue collar.

The sand dunes are sprouting vestigial grass here. Nicola spots sea holly, marram grass and a striking but unknown purple flower.

We pace on past a large golf club inland with a mesh fence and 'keep out' signs. Soon we are in Jaywick Sands – officially the most deprived area in the snappily titled *Britain in the Indices of Multiple Deprivation* league table. This measures income, employment, health, disability, living standards and crime.

Jaywick started off as part of the plotlands move-ment in the 1920s, where urban dwellers bought strips of land from Fabian property developer Frank Stedman and built dream chalets by the sea. Some were knocked down after the Second World War but the locals went to court and preserved many of the bungalows. But today the majority of them are empty or have been rented to housing benefit tenants and people escaping problems in big cities. The area lacks street lighting and road maintenance and was only put on the main sewage system in the 1980s. Shops have closed and the Mermaid Tavern was burned down, while 62 per cent of those of working age were on benefits in 2011.

'That label is a terrible stigma,' admits councillor Dan Casey in our copy of the *Clacton Gazette*. The paper reveals that Tendring Council is to get a £1.3 million government grant to bring 800 empty homes in the Jaywick region back into use. The area's notoriety even inspired the short film *Jaywick Escapes* in 2012, where directors Karen Guthrie and Nina Pope detailed the problematic lives of some of the incomers.

But walking by the bungalows on the seafront it's clear the place has potential. The houses look weather-beaten but cosy and the locals still have a sense of humour; in one porch window are several models of Shrek and a *Fawlty Towers* sign.

The beach is superb and it's only a mile and a half to Clacton along the seafront. Yet houses are going for fifty grand. The boarded-up bungalows in the back-streets are depressing, but those that are still occupied are detached with small gardens and don't look bad places to live.

Put some money in, start some shops, set up a water sports centre or a YHA and get some beach huts and it could be the next Southwold. There's a golf club next door and light aircraft taking off nearby. It shouldn't be more deprived than the worst areas of Liverpool or Sunderland.

It starts to rain as we walk back to Clacton. 'Don't worry, Tendring Council says this is the Essex Sunshine Coast,' I tell Nicola.

'Don't you mean the Sun Once Shone Coast?' she quips.

Our party takes shelter outside a café and orders ice creams with flakes. A DVD plays on the monitor above the counter with images of the old Butlin's holiday camp, opened in 1937. It closed in 1983, as the old working-class punters discovered cheap package holidays abroad. The waitress points out the car park and housing estate where it used to be. At its peak it was full of *Hi-de-Hi* campers and Spike and Ted Bovis types entertaining East Enders by the sea. And talking of *EastEnders*, in an inspired piece of scriptwriting Pat and Frank Butcher first met at the Clacton Butlin's in 1958.

We make our way back along the redeveloped sunken gardens by the front, with lots of foliage, blue benches and red asphalt paths. Several girls in hoodies coo at Vulcan and ask what breed he is. This happens several times during our stay, as border terriers seem to be virtually unheard of in Clacton, the locals preferring Staffies.

Back at the guesthouse, Carol tells us that Clacton has improved generally since Butlin's closed, although Billy Butlin used to put a lot of money into the town and funded an open-air swimming pool. Now the place struggles for investment.

It's a Bank Holiday so the rain is setting in and in seaside towns on public holidays everything tends to close early. So just before six we head out clad in Gore-Tex coats to Geo's Fish Bar and enjoy some excellent cod and chips, as Nicola admires the Victorian tiles and fresh fish.

Rosemary Road appears to have much of Clacton's life, only everything is closed; Italian and Indian restaurants, a tanning shop, a pie and mash, an adult shop and ViceVersa nightclub.

We find a pub that Nicola has researched in CAMRA's Real Ale Guide, the Old Lifeboat Station. A large clock on the wall illustrates the pub's former incarnation. It's a blokey type of pub with a TV playing a documentary about the Thames and blokes in England tracksuits chatting over pints. 'You've bought the weather with you!' they say to a T-shirted man coming in from the rain. 'Look, he's waterproof!' As we leave a man behind us looks at Vulcan and asks, 'Doesn't he get an umbrella?'

Nicola goes back to the guesthouse and I take Nell to the amusements. We have a lot of fun wasting two pences on what the Australians call 'pokeys', the machines where coins are perched precariously on the edge of a precipice. A five-pound note lies right on the edge and we wonder if it is blue-tacked on.

The pier is delightfully tacky, with dodgems and amusements and a helter-skelter at the end. It doubled as Southend Pier in the film *Starter for Ten* and also featured in the Pet Shop Boys video of 'West End Girls'.

The roof of the covered section is transparent corrugated plastic, green with mould and held down by the same pegs that were not very effective on our back extension. Nell is like a child in a warren of amusements. 'Look, I could win that iPod, Daddy!' she exclaims. 'And that giant tiger and the chocolate…'

'But Lord Sugar would think a better business plan would be to make the grab 'em machines rather than play on them. You never win…' I try to explain.

She liberates my spare cash with undisguised glee, and miraculously discovers a grabbing machine that for 30p allows her to win a set of Fizzers, a fruit-flavour sherbet and a sweet in the shape of a sandwich, worth about ten pence each. 'Daddy, I won, I won!' She carries them in her pocket for the next week.

We return to the hotel and have a bath before huddling up in our very comfortable king-size bed, while Nell has a single bed under the eaves. Lucy Worsley is talking about Restoration women on the flatscreen TV. The rain patters on the skylights and the wind whooshes through the windows. It feels like we're at sea, or possibly in the middle of the Gunfleet Sands Wind Farm, and it's all rather cosy and enjoyable, being in Clacton on a typically deluged British bank holiday.

Breakfast at the Chudleigh sees a pleasing amount of Tiptree miniature jams and marmalades on the table. There are Australians in the dining room and the Chudleigh often has guests staying before flying from Stansted or taking the ferry to Holland from Harwich. Carol reveals that she's been on exchange visits to Germany and had great trouble explaining what 'tawny' marmalade is. Nell's bacon and the scrambled eggs, mushrooms and hash browns are all excellent and there's a hint of blue in the sky.

Nell has a morning session on the pier amusements, trying the helter skelter twice ('it goes over the sea!') and the trampoline, and grabbing some more sweets from the machines.

The tide is lapping the sea defences and the beach has disappeared, so we walk along the concrete esplanade towards Frinton, watching yachts and the shifting lines of wind turbines out at sea. After a mile and a half we reach Holland-on-Sea, which is pretty good going, and find a café that welcomes dogs where we have coffee and ice cream. The woman serving us gives some complex instructions on how to find the bus stop to Frinton, which is set a long way back from the seafront. In Holland, we wait for the bus by the Roaring Donkey pub. This sleepy town was once the unlikely childhood home of Sade, the 'Smooth Operator' jazz singer.

The No. 7 bus is packed with silver surfer pensioners. Hearing our conversation the man next to me gives me directions on where to get off. 'It's a lovely place, Frinton, just head up from the level crossing and there are lots of cafés. It's the only seaside town in the world where there are no amusements. And it didn't have any pubs until 2000. You should try the Hat and Mouse, that's a really nice café.'

The inland route to Frinton takes us past green hedgerows, woodpiles and cottages across the flat peninsula. We disembark at the level-crossing gates by Frinton station. The BBC filmed a *Wonderland* documentary on the campaign to save the old wooden gates, which were replaced, in the middle of the night, by automatic ones in 2009.

In a kind of Frinton Spring, one hundred people gathered at the gates to protest the morning after their removal. Frinton is triangular in shape, bordered by the sea, the marshes and the railway. Anyone entering the town has to go through the level crossing. Thanks to local heritage campaigners, the iconic gates that marked the border between posh Frinton and the outside world are now on display in the railway gardens. Less Watergate and more Frintongate.

'Look, a fruit shop!' declares Nicola in wonderment after the fast-food-dominated environs of Clacton. Along Connaught Avenue we find a sort of Fulham-on-Sea, with shops like Grape and Grain, Jade, Charlie and Oscar, Koko, Zen Art Ltd, Art Deco and Antiques, Wright's deli (selling home-cooked ham) and an Oriental rug specialist. It's so upmarket that the hairdresser has a simple name rather than a pun, something unheard of in the rest of Essex. The one chip shop is hidden in a back street. Frinton is losing its old image of 'Harwich for the continent: Frinton for the incontinent' and appears to be going for the Southwold set.

It's a friendly place. At the cashpoint a man in paint-spattered work clothes is chatting to a Scotsman. I ask if he's in the queue. 'Don't worry, you go first, mate, I was gobbing off about the Scots and how good they was in the war!'

At the Hat and Mouse we order takeaway sandwiches with homemade bread. It's a proper foodie place with bread mice in the window display. The Hat and Mouse is run by Jasmine (a Jasmine in Essex!) and Jonathan Fraser, who have returned to their native Essex after twenty years in Bath.

Inside the loo is a framed promo piece revealing that Jonathan has worked with all the celebrity chefs and for royalty, as well as Cary Grant, Alec Guinness and Frank Sinatra.

The rain starts to cascade down again and we rush for a shelter above the beach, eating our tasty sandwiches on a green seat in the wind. Beach huts line the front but, as the brochure says, there's no amusements anywhere, which rather disappoints Nell. It's very different to Clacton. Here are mums with cloth bags and kids in Boden shirts. You can tell it's well posh because they call the front 'the Greensward'.

The mile-long beach is still beneath the waves, though we can see the pier at Walton-on-the-Naze, so we return to Connaught Avenue, once dubbed 'East Anglia's Bond Street'. Judith in the Caxton Bookshop and Gallery happily discusses border terriers and literature with Nicola. When I ask if there's a discount for Society of Authors members, she says, 'There is now!' and offers me £3 off a copy of *Up Pohnpei* by Paul Watson. Now that's service. At the greengrocers Nicola is given a free punnet of raspberries.

It's time to explore Frinton's only pub, the Lock and Barrel, famously established in 2000. There's a wine bar in Connaught Avenue as well now, though, indicating that Frinton is rapidly heading towards complete alcoholic stupefaction.

It's a Shepherd Neame pub and, as you would expect from a discerning town like Frinton, serves a decent pint of Master Brew. 'Has the town been completely corrupted by your opening?' I ask.

'It depends who you talk to…' the barman replies. He says Wetherspoons were initially interested in starting the pub, but were put off by the licensing restrictions. 'It wasn't like you couldn't get a drink before – there was the golf clubs and the yacht clubs and the hotels. But the word public house did instil a certain fear in some people…'

About fifteen people sit around distressed tables in the homely pub and another ten or so are in the garden. All appear to be sober. There's a copy of *The Times* on the bar. It doesn't seem that Frinton has, as yet, become a town of alehouse brawlers.

We are held up by a train at the level crossing, but just make the No. 8 bus back to Clacton. It takes us past the weird cranescape of Harwich docks across the Stour Estuary.

In breezy Clacton Nicola appears to be coming round to the town's charms: 'It's not all greensward and jam sandwiches here.'

The beach has reappeared. Nell insists on going paddling by the pier. At first she gets her shorts wet jumping the waves and then her top too. She's having a great time getting soaked, as kids do, but luckily we are able to collect our cases from the Chudleigh and change her clothes there. Carol and Peter show us pictures of their two dogs, drawn by a very talented chambermaid, and give us a friendly sendoff.

'Tendring is the night...' I whisper to Nicola, trying to evoke the spirit of F. Scott Fitzgerald as we roll our cases to the station, while Nell fondles her pier booty of sweets.

The Tendring Peninsula has a bit of everything. It might have slipped out of fashion but it still has plenty of interest: once publess, posh Frinton with its greensward, art deco shops and hallowed level-crossing gates; the most deprived part of Britain in Jaywick; and the amusements, pier, chips and Martello towers of Clacton, with Ken Dodd a happy visitor, all linked by miles of sand.

19

WHAT HAVE THE ROMANS EVER DONE FOR COLCHESTER?

The taxi driver taking us from Colchester North station to our B & B isn't exactly positive when Nicola asks her, 'What are the top three attractions in Colchester?'

'Dunno, it ain't got a lot going for it really,' she says. 'There's not a lot apart from shopping and people going about their lives. The pubs ain't great, what with the students and army; you wouldn't want to go in them. And the traffic's getting worse…'

Our driver is not a great fan of *TOWIE* – 'It's other people's lives, innit, makes you feel better about your own' – and when we ask her where she'd live if it wasn't Colchester she replies, 'Somewhere hot!'

With some prompting, she concedes the new art gallery might be OK and that the castle is worth seeing if you like that sort of thing.

Sometimes you don't notice what's right under your cab's air freshener. Just being in Britain's oldest town feels like an achievement to us. We're on a romantic mini-break to celebrate our wedding anniversary. As soon as we get out of the taxi in the busy high street we are accosted by historical re-enactors in ruffs, advertising Tudor dancing at the Holy Trinity Church.

We're staying at Trinity Town House, which has a blue plaque on its wall revealing that it was the home of John Wilbye, composer of the first Madrigal in the sixteenth century. He was the muse of Lady Cornwallis.

Malcolm, who runs the boutique B & B with his partner Helen and her children, shows us the rooms and tells us that the church opposite, the pre-Norman Holy Trinity Church, is the oldest building in Colchester and was built from recycled Roman bricks. When I mention my upbringing in Brentwood, home of *TOWIE*, he speaks of the show in the manner of someone referring to a sad death in the family.

Trinity Town House is full of white carpets and wobbly black beams and has a shelf of books upstairs featuring Oscar Wilde. Yes, Oscar Wilde in Essex. There's a real fire in 'the Column Room'. We stay in the Wilbye Room, which has a four-poster bed and the biggest ensuite bathroom we've ever seen. It was here that Wilbye showed Lady Cornwallis his madrigals, so to speak.

We head out towards the promise of Tudor dancing in Holy Trinity Church. It's a café in the week, run by the Youth Culture charity, and is designed to give NEETS (an acronym for 'not in education, employment or training') mentoring and training.

We sit down at a table and dine on homemade vegetable soup and coffee. Women in huge dresses and chaps in ruffs and Guy Fawkes hats take to the floor and find their partners for the 'Earl of Essex Measure', played on a violin.

'It's like a sort of Tudor Sugar Hut,' I suggest, as the couples gyrate.

'They probably used to discuss the drainage in the lower field between reels,' says Nicola.

There are more men with white beards than Nicola has ever seen in Essex before, accompanied by women carrying Past Times laminated shopping bags. Then there's 'Ding Dong Merrily on High' (originally a dance) and something on the bagpipes.

After the performance we enjoy the anachronistic double-take of watching women in voluminous Tudor dresses sitting drinking mugs of latte and checking their mobiles. Might Tudor dancing in a country house have inspired Colchester lads Damon Albarn and Blur?

In the back streets, full of overhanging wooden wattle and daub medieval buildings, there are both classy shops like Karen Millen and a pleasing amount of independent shops. The only signs of *TOWIE* are bags reading, 'I've been vajazzled' and 'Let's go glamping' in a shop called Fun 'n' Games. In the high street we find a splendid old department store named Williams & Griffin, offering Christmas hampers of Tiptree jam. Genius.

At the Minories arts centre by Love Bistro there's a pop-up craft market. It's all very upmarket compared to Brentwood. There are men in leather bush hats and pastel shades, people discussing pensions and a woman with a plummy accent selling bramble jelly. Nicola buys some, of course.

We move on to Colchester Castle. It's still an imposing building with huge 12-foot walls built by the Normans with recycled Roman stone, tiles and septaria.

Colchester is surprisingly hilly for Essex, and the castle is on the town's highest point, overlooking the river Colne. The castle is built on the 2,000-year-old foundations of the Temple of Claudius, which was burned down by Boudicca and her tribes in AD 60 or 61, then rebuilt by the Romans. Even in Neolithic times it was regarded as a special spot.

'It's a long time, 2,000 years ago,' says Nicola.

'What, since we've been married…'

It's the warmest castle ever as there's a roof, put on in the 1930s, and lots of 21st-century heating. By the entrance is a deep well and 'the largest diameter castle staircase in Britain', which reminds me of 'the largest mirror in Essex' at Sheesh in Chigwell.

We pay our £6 entry fee and immediately there are two superb Roman mosaics on the wall, found under someone's kitchen garden. They're very bling, and when pristine and shiny would not have been out of place in Harry Derbidge or Mark Wright's lounge. The Romans were not as far from *TOWIE* as we think.

The Colchester Vase has gladiators on it and is not too dissimilar to a West Ham souvenir mug. We discover the huge Sheepen Cauldron from Colchester and the wooden Dagenham Idol, the oldest human depiction in Britain.

'It's not often Dagenham and culture are linked,' I suggest.

There's a large selection of axe heads from 4000–2000

BC. Wheeling and dealing seems to be an age old Essex occupation, as they were bought to Essex from places like Cornwall and distributed from Colchester.

'We sell any axe!' suggests Nicola, thinking of the *Horrible Histories* sketch 'We sell any monk!'

There's plenty of information on the run-up to Roman invasion. When the Romans invaded in AD 43 they regarded Cunobelin, the king of the Thinovantes tribe of Essex, as the king of all England. Before the Romans arrived Colchester was Camulodunum, meaning 'the Fortress of Camulos', the Celtic god of war. Proof indeed that Essex is well hard and should still be the capital of the UK.

It's moving to see blackened pottery and fused glass from the massive fire when Boudicca attacked the town. Her forces were said to have killed 20,000 people. The Romans had conspicuously failed to win the hearts and minds, as those army chaps term it, of the local tribes.

Boudicca was understandably traumatised by her whipping and the rape of her daughters by the Romans, and responded with great cruelty, leading the Iceni, aided by the Thinovantes, when they destroyed Colchester, St Albans and London. She committed suicide after her eventual defeat, somewhere on Watling Street in the Midlands.

The museum has the replica chariot used in the TV film of Boudicca, in which Alex Kingston (River Song in *Doctor Who*) played the feisty Queen.

It's hard not to feel some sympathy for the retired Roman soldiers, women and children who for two days took refuge in the temple on this very site, before it was burned down and everyone slaughtered.

The Romans responded to their previous complacency by building huge town walls around Colchester, rebuilding the temple and Romanising Britain for 400 years. A Roman circus was recently discovered beneath the town, where chariot races took place, with the horses travelling at 45 mph. Possibly it was an early equivalent of Romford dog track.

On the upper floor of the castle huge fireplaces are lined with Roman tiles in a herringbone pattern. Still the history comes at you. The near-abandonment of the place after the Romans scarpered, the Norman castle-building, the Black Death, the role of local priest John Ball in the Peasants' Revolt, Witchfinder General Matthew Hopkin running his show trials in Colchester, the castle's use as a prison and then an air raid shelter in the Second World War.

Drunk on history, we finally leave the castle at the 5 p.m. closing time and walk to the Purple Dog for a fine pint of Brewers Gold from Crouch Vale and a glass of sauvignon blanc.

From the high street, numerous buses head towards the University of Essex and also Wivenhoe, known as Sociology-on-Sea due to the high proportion of academics that live there. My old school pal Roz – yes, a sociology graduate – lived there for a long time and many a weekend was spent in the Rose and Crown pub on the quay by the river Colne. Her gardener was Martin Newell, for a long time *The Independent*'s poet in residence and now a columnist covering Essex bohemia in the *Anglian Daily Press*. He'd be showing her his latest stanzas, when probably she just wanted the roses pruning.

All those sociologists on the lash certainly add something to the nightlife of Colchester. Everywhere seems packed on a Saturday night and we just manage to book a table at the Lemon Tree, one of Colchester's best restaurants in St John Street. It's packed out and there's a huge office party in the gazebo section, but the service from our student waiter is instantaneous.

The city walls run under the street. In the basement of the Lemon Tree we dine next to a large chunk of Roman wall. What an underrated place Colchester is. Goat's cheese tart, stuffed mushrooms, risotto, pumpkin curry and shared cheese and biscuits, washed down with a bottle of white from the Adelaide Hills round off the evening nicely.

Our sleep is slightly disturbed by the squaddies and students or descendants of Boudicca, singing 'Who let the dogs out? Woof woof!' as they walk up to the high street. But at least it's a town where people enjoy themselves.

The next morning Lady Cornwallis and myself have breakfast accompanied by one of John Wilbye's madrigals with no woofing at all. Told you. Essex is cultured.

We have plenty more things scheduled. Firstly we walk towards the Roman wall, only we're distracted by an absolutely gigantic castellated water tower next to the Mercury Theatre. What is it, we ask a woman passing by.

'That's Jumbo,' she answers. 'It's an old water tower,

but it's just going to waste. It was sold to someone, but I don't know if they'll do anything with it.'

Jumbo was built in 1883 and nicknamed Jumbo by the Reverend John Irvine, who was peeved that it dwarfed his rectory. At present it's sadly underused. It's 116 ft high and contains more than a million red bricks. Most recently a planning application to turn it into penthouses was turned down in 2011.

We move on and find the best-preserved Roman gateway in Britain at the Balkerne Gate, by the aptly named Hole in the Wall pub. The arch is complete and there's a guardroom next door. It's 15 ft tall and you get a real sense of what an imposing entrance it must once have been. The Iceni were not going to mug Rome off again. We walk along some more of the wall and despite being next to a busy road it's better preserved than much of Hadrian's Wall. You can do a complete circular walk of Colchester around the remnants of the wall.

Back in the high street there's a Christmas market and we buy chestnuts while admiring Dunmow pork pies, Mersea oysters and Mersea wine. Nicola purchases a huge piece of mistletoe for some reason, sparking some banter from the stallholder.

'You'll need some oysters and the sofa, it's going to be a long afternoon,' suggests the earthy mistletoe seller.

Meanwhile mummers are walking up and down the high street, with blacked-up faces meant to resemble chimneysweeps, bells on their legs and costumes made of flapping pieces of brightly coloured material. It all feels a little pagan.

We continue through the high street and over the loop in the river Colne to East Street. The river is green, leafy and much more East Anglian in feel than the rest of Essex. Some whiteboarded maltings lie next to the river, converted into flats and standing on thick black iron supports.

Here is the fifteenth-century Old Siege House, now a restaurant. Bullet holes from the Civil War battle of 1648 pepper the exterior timbers of the lovely old building. That is unless they're just the result of spilling someone's pint. The bullet holes are marked by red circles of paper and help you visualise the fierce battle as the Roundheads took the town from the Royalists after an eleven-week siege, executing Sir Charles Lucas and Sir George Lisle round the back of the castle. The spot is still marked by an obelisk.

We have a coffee inside the Old Siege House, in comfy chairs by a grand piano, where we can admire the bowed white walls and black timbers. The Eastern European waitress shows us more bullet holes in the roof timbers by the bar. What a place for *Time Team* buffs. I've got some real archaeology here for you, Tonee.

We move on to something much more futuristic, the £28m Firstsite art gallery. It was over budget and late opening and has attracted criticism in the local press. But it's a striking building, covered in golden metal and nick-named 'The Golden Banana'. It's a weird crescent shape, and looks a little like an upturned Sydney Opera House.

When the gallery opened the *Daily Telegraph*'s Rupert Christiansen opined:

How can you lure people to poor old Essex, with its chav-stained public image, the clichés of which were all unfortunately confirmed this year by the hugely successful and dismally moronic *The Only Way Is Essex* and the Dale Farm saga? There's not much you can do with a marvellous but scattered heritage of parish churches, but a lot is being invested in the city of Colchester, the one place in Essex with a bit of cultural clout, based on its Roman past and its admirable repertory theatre, the Mercury. Now it also has its 'iconic' piece of new architecture... I hope I am wrong, but I have a sinking feeling that like the Baltic in Newcastle... the golden banana could turn into a white elephant. Essex just isn't Sussex.

Which is a little unfair, as this is the posh side of Essex, Rupert, mate. Inside Firstsite it's full of white space and huge ceilings. Impressively it has a work by Andy Warhol, and pictures of Damon Albarn as a child with a pony in an extended photo montage by Aleksandra Mir. Plus pieces by Sarah Lucas, Ai Wei Wei, Henry Moore and Barbara Hepworth, some chalk and mirrors on the floor and a set of pictures of naked bodies from the Neo-Naturists, a group of exhibitionists featuring Grayson Perry and Leigh Bowery, among others. Yes, it's next to the bus station, but there's an upmarket restaurant selling Essex oysters too and Colchester is at least trying with Firstsite. We rather like it.

Next we travel back to the castle for the guided tour we missed the previous day. Our well-groomed and outgoing guide Claire takes us to the chapel on the roof, which has fantastic views over the town's rooftops, and shows us a garderobe and some medieval graffiti on the stairs. Then we descend to the Roman vaults. Musty white mortar and local stone septaria line the ceilings while bizarrely there are green carpets on the floor. These foundations have stood here for 2,000 years. We're standing in the temple that was ransacked by Boudicca. Blimey. People go to Rome for this but it's all here in Essex.

Clare tells us that 'although 20,000 people were meant to have died in Colchester when Boudicca razed the town only one body from that period has ever been found'. Possibly there are mass graves somewhere outside the town or the fire destroyed the bodies. Or could the eventually victorious Romans just have exaggerated the death toll?

The vaults used to be full of sand. In 1683 a prototype Essex Man, local ironmonger John Wheeley, bought the castle and decided he could make a nice bit of dosh demolishing it and selling it off to the building trade. Thankfully it proved remarkably difficult to dismantle. When Wheeley tried blowing up the foundations in an attempt to blow up the castle, he discovered the vaults full of sand and was convinced that Roman treasure lay within. He spent ages digging them out (they're still half full of sand) only to go bankrupt and find nothing.

As we check out of Trinity Town House we tell Malcolm how much we're impressed by Colchester. He in turn reveals some more nuggets. *Humpty Dumpty* was a cannon set on a tower near the Balkerne Gate at St Mary in the Wall during the Civil War, and the rhyme is a celebration of it being toppled by snipers. And there's the Dutch Quarter where in 1806 Jane Taylor is claimed to have dreamed up *Twinkle Twinkle Little Star*...

Why Colchester has even attracted a Timelord in *Doctor Who*. Matt Smith's Doctor rooms with James Corden's Craig Owens in 'The Lodger'. In 'Closing Time' the Doctor and James Corden are mistaken for gay dads, in what must surely be Williams & Griffin department store. The Doctor and Craig also see Amy and Rory out shopping at Williams & Griffin and presumably happily living out their post-Tardis days in Essex.

Meanwhile there was a crashed cyberman spacecraft underneath the store and the cybermen were having to rebuild themselves with bits of Essex men and women and possibly some old Roman septaria too.

Nothing would surprise you about Colchester. It's bidding for World Heritage Site status, yet few people think of it as a tourist destination. Even the cybermen were only there because they crashed.

'I'm sorry I made a fuss about your choice of desti-nation,' says Nicola at the bus stop. 'Colchester turned out to be fab and even better for being so easy to reach by train. There's nothing like following an Essexologist around their natural habitat. Thank you.'

'That taxi driver was right. What have the Romans ever done for Essex?' I answer. 'Apart from the city walls, the temple, the castle, the pre-Norman church, the best arch in Britain, drains, central heating, pottery, olive oil, several giant mosaics under kitchen gardens and prob-ably some great nightclubs.'

We sample some steaming mulled wine in the high street and then prepare to take the bus to the station, carrying a large sprig of mistletoe. Boudicca might have misjudged the place. Colchester has turned out to be rather a fine destination to celebrate our wedding anniversary. The bus arrives as night draws over the hills, the Roman walls and Tudor architecture and we prepare for the hour-long train journey to Liverpool Street.

'I guess we'll always have Colchester,' I suggest.

20

THE OTHER WAY IN ESSEX

What do they know of Essex, whom only Essex know? Returning to the county after years of exile in London has made me realise I hardly knew the place.

In its own way it's been just as interesting as a visit to some remote outpost of the planet. It's got indigenous people, marshes, malls and some of the world's most dangerous highways. There are many signature items in Essex, such as the fact every town appears to have a Wimpy bar, a franchise the rest of the world assumed expired thirty years ago; a preponderance of fine fish and chip shops; more nail salons than can ever be filed and an obsession with wheels and road rage. There's that entre-preneurial zeal too: every town has a market and walk into any coffee bar or pub and someone somewhere will be discussing a money-making scheme.

There's humour everywhere, a particular kind of self-deprecating comedy that is often insulation against the gap between expectation and reality. Dreams coexist beside motorways, flyovers and starter homes.

It's also a place of surprises. There's a marvellous

nature reserve on a never-built refinery at Canvey Island that has more biodiversity than anywhere else in the UK; a station on the beach at Chalkwell; castles overlooking the Thames; swathes of nothingness and cement lorries by the river in Dagenham; bluebells in Billericay; a ruined garden at Great Warley; sailing barges at Maldon; the great defences of Tilbury Fort; Roman walls in a Colchester restaurant; Hollywood signs at Basildon and a not-very secret nuclear bunker in Kelvedon Hatch.

The most entertaining part of the county is undoubtedly Estuary Essex with its East End overspill parents and their children with *TOWIE* values. Yet much of Essex is upper middle class, or as we say in Brentwood, well-posh.

Close to the Hertfordshire border lies Audley End House, a proper Jacobean stately home that's not been done up with mockodile floors or zebra-patterned carpets. The grounds are divided by the river Cam and were designed by Capability Brown. It all feels very *Brideshead Revisited*. It has sea monsters on the ceiling friezes and the largest ballroom in Essex, designed by Robert Adam – not very different to Sheesh's largest mirror in Essex.

There's also Oliver Country, on the Hertfordshire border. Jamie Oliver's parents run the Cricketers at Clavering. An idyllic village pub, it serves real ale called Jamie's Tipple (though it's brewed by Nethergate not Oliver), is packed with diners and has a sign that creaks in the wind. Though for all Jamie's Essex-speak, Clavering feels distinctly more Hertfordshire with its old church, thatched cottages, Georgian houses and modern bungalows.

A few miles from Clavering is Saffron Walden. It's full of Tudor houses (it has twenty-seven Grade II listed buildings), two mazes and a castle and at one time it was Oliver Cromwell's headquarters.

You know it's posh because it has a tourist office with a list of dates for tea dances. As Her Indoors noted as we drove through Saffron Walden: 'The houses are painted in shades of ice-cream flavours and the rubbish gets put out in Waitrose bags.' Even the YHA is 600 years old.

On the way to the castle there's a crossroads that has timber-framed buildings on all four corners. One of the buildings here, the Old Sun Inn, was Oliver Cromwell's headquarters in 1647. Here Oliver and his Roundhead army made big efforts to ban dancing, perhaps including the reem Cavaliers at Sugar Hut (or was it the Zero 6 or Canvey Goldmine in those days?).

Saffron Walden's museum reveals how the town took its name from the fields of saffron used to dye wool. It has a mammoth tusk, a couple of skeletons and geological anomalies on sale called the Devil's Fingernails, because they look like, well, Devil's fingernails. Next to the museum is the atmospheric ruined keep of the old castle, built by Geoffrey de Mandeville the first Earl of Essex in the early twelfth century, but trashed by Henry II in 1158.

The parish church of St Mary the Virgin is more like a cathedral and is an early example of a bling church reflecting the wealth of the town. In the churchyard lies the grave of the famous Tory politician R. A. 'Rab' Butler, 'the best Prime Minister we never had'.

Another attraction is the Victorian Hedge Maze at Bridge End Garden and the Turf Maze by the short-stay car park. Yes, mazes in Essex. The Turf Maze could be 800 years old. It's cut into the ground and one of only eight turf mazes surviving in England and is circular with seventeen circuits in a labyrinth design, the sort of thing that in my youth the hippies at the Castle pub in Brentwood might have come up with.

Posh Essex has tearooms. Tiptree's Wilkin & Sons Ltd alone now has The Essex Rose at Dedham, The Lock at Heybridge Basin and The Lordship at Writtle. Near Kelvedon is Layer Marney, the tallest Tudor gatehouse in Britain. Not far from the lovely estuary of Manningtree is Constable country – even if that phrase sounds disturbingly similar to something you might hear shouted out of the window of a moving car in Billericay. The great painter was based at Dedham Vale on the Essex/Suffolk border, where his old man owned Flatford Mill. In the Stour Valley he painted masterpieces such as *The Hay Wain*, voted Britain's second favourite picture. And we've even got the village of Ugley for lovers of cheap jokes.

Yet it's Estuary Essex that has been the main focus of this book, that fascinating intersection where the children of escaping East Enders go rural and rub up against old Essex. It's given us Essex Man and *TOWIE* and who knows what else is to come?

Essex remains the journalist's dream county. It inspires humour and headlines in a way no other county does.

Where are the Hollywood roundabout signs in Kent? The image is tacky, downmarket, but also earthy and affectionate.

The county's as high-profile as ever. Russell Brand introduced the Dalai Lama on stage in Manchester as part of the Tibetan spiritual leader's tour, with the pair forming a bizarre double act with the Dalai Lama tugging Brand's beard. 'Going from junkie to Shagger of the Year... three times... to now introducing the Dalai Lama... it has been an interesting journey,' reflected Brand.

The Apprentice has virtually decamped to Essex with one task set at Wilkin & Sons in Tiptree and another episode devoted to Lord Sugar's 'old manor'. The teams had to go to a cash and carry and buy £150-worth of goods to sell at a destination of their choice. Strangely the teams eschewed bound sets of Milan Kundera novels and opted for the fake spray-tan.

Lord Sugar's aide Nick Hewer was impressed by the choice of Romford as a venue: 'There are 70 per cent women here and 70 per cent of them are from Essex!' he enthused about the likely tan sales.

The other team chose Ilford and Pitsea to flog their gear. 'Ricky was very vocal that Essex likes a tan,' commented Nick in the boardroom. 'You're not giving Essex a great name, you lot!' suggested Lord Sugar, after being presented with an Essex kit of fake tan and nail wraps. One team bought bottles of fake tan for £2 and sold them on for £10 in Romford shopping mall. When the other team added false eyelashes, Lord Sugar suggested 'they're having a good day in Essex!' playing up to all the stereotypes around his manor because Essex sells TV.

Tuesday 8 May 2012 proved to be an extraordinary day in the annals of Essex political history. Labour leader Ed Miliband visited Harlow in the morning to counter David Cameron and Nick Clegg's appearance in Basildon that afternoon. With Labour having made key gains in the Thurrock and Harlow local elections, the leaders of all three parties believed that appealing to aspirational Essex really would shape the destiny of the coalition. Joey Essex was right: they all wanted to be the Prime Minister of Essex.

David Cameron and Nick Clegg's visit to the Fiat-owned New Holland tractor factory in Basildon was broadcast live on *BBC 24 News* and *Sky News*. Two posh boys who may or may not know the price of a pint of milk got down and dirty with a set of tractor-making blokes in yellow and blue polo shirts. The factory makes an impressive 26,000 tractors a year. Cameron even took off his jacket to get physical. *The Guardian*'s Michael White compared the Basildon Q and A session to 'the Soviet-era of heroic five-year tractor plans and targets regularly smashed, at least on paper'.

The duo spoke of immigration controls, apprenticeships, petrol prices and school standards without saying anything particularly newsworthy. But what they really wanted, you suspect, was the macho backdrop of the tractor plant for the TV pictures. The workers just looked grateful for some time off the production line.

The Essex tactic worked with the press. *The Independent*'s editorial ran 'The Only Way Isn't Essex, Prime Minister', while the *Indie*'s Andy McSmith revealed that house prices had gone up three times faster than incomes in Essex and that youth unemployment in the county was soaring too. *The Sun* went with, 'The only way to win is Essex.' On the *BBC News* Nick Robinson revealed that in Harlow Ed Miliband felt the Tories had 'lost touch with Essex Man'.

In *The Guardian* it was 'The only way is Essex as party leaders go in search of aspirational voters.' Michael White contrasted the setting with the Downing Street Rose Garden tryst of 2010. 'Where better to shake off the taint of matrimonial metaphor and renew their alliance on a more business-like footing than in Basildon? No one goes on honeymoon in Basildon. Southend perhaps, but not to the '60s new town, home patch of the legendary reality TV show *The Only Way Is Essex*. So Essex it was yesterday.'

Which is a little unfair, as you can get a room at the Basildon Premier Inn at the Festival Leisure Park for just £19 and then visit Bas Vegas. Where better to rekindle Dave and Nick's bromance than under the Essex neon?

It's not just politics, is Essex now art, darlin'? At the launch of his six Hogarthian tapestries on class in June 2012 Grayson Perry announced to *The Guardian*: 'I have a thick crust of Islington but if you cut me, you find Essex there. The tone of my taste decisions is often very Essex, but I put an Islington spin on them. That might be the deciding fact in my entire oeuvre.'

Grayson Perry, we salute you for being possibly the only man from Essex to use the word 'oeuvre'. Telling the story of Tim Rakewell, a working-class lad done good, the tapestries have a distinctly Essex take on class and pomposity. They make you laugh too. Grayson fills Tim's home with Agas, cafetieres, organic vegetables, iPads, Cath Kidston bags, Le Creuset casserole dishes, framed pictures of Steve Jobs and Bill Gates and Penguin Books mugs with titles like Class Traitor by Chip E Prole. 'If you cut me, you find Essex there.' Grayson Perry has hit on a nice way of describing how Essex shapes its sons and daughters.

If ever proof was needed that Essex was satirical gold it came with the glorious escapade of the Essex Lion. In August 2012 the news arrived that a lion had been seen in a field near a caravan site in St Osyth, close to Clacton. It was reportedly spotted by a man who shouted, in true Essex style, 'It's a fucking lion!'

Police took the sighting seriously as a circus had recently been in the area (or was it a trophy pet?) and a team of marksmen were dispatched, followed by the national news crews. The public was less impressionable. Soon jokes were going round social media that the lion should be easy to spot, as it would be one of the few things in Essex not wearing leopard-print. The spoof Essex Lion Twitter account, set up by voice actor Eddie Bowley, gained an astonishing 40,000 followers in twenty-four hours. The Essex Lion was soon trending. The best of the tweets included, 'I'M GOING TO LAKESIDE FOR A NANDOS AND PERHAPS A YOUNG FAMILY'; 'I'M

HIDING IN JD SPORTS. POLICE ALWAYS HAVE IT IN FOR ME JUST COZ I'M A LION'; 'ON ME WAY TO THE CARPARK FOR A PROPER FIGHT. BRUVS GOING DOWN. LISTENING TO CIRCLE OF LIFE TO GET PUMPED'; and, best of all, 'LEAVE HIM ALONE SIMBA, HE AIN'T WURF IT!' All stereotypical nonsense of course, but rather funny.

Two days later it appeared that the Essex Lion was, in fact, an overfed cat. The papers revelled in a superb silly season story. *The Sun* had three pages on the 'Essexy beast'. The *Daily Mirror* ran a front-page story, 'Revealed: The Lion of Essex', next to a picture of Tom, the ginger cat who had sparked a two-day lion-hunt. It also exposed a fake picture of the lion on Twitter with the memorable headline 'You can't hide your lion eyes'. The story also made the front page of *The Guardian* and the paper included an internet image of the lion superimposed on a picture of the *TOWIE* cast in front of their Essex logo. Another Twitter hit was a picture of the lion with a reem haircut. The *Big Issue* had a photo of Ray Winstone on the cover with the headline, 'The real Essex Lion'.

Meanwhile, *The Independent* opted for the moral high ground with a piece by Patrick Strudwick lambasting anti-Essex snobbery. 'Essexism, it seems, is the last unchallenged prejudice,' he wrote. 'There's no moral difference between laughing at people simply because of where they were born and mocking people because of the amount of melanin in their skin, their chromosomal make up or their inability to walk.'

His viewpoint rather ignored the fact that much of the internet commentary was very amusing and that most Essex people can laugh at themselves. Indeed, it was probably them making the jokes.

What the Essex Lion undoubtedly proved was that – wanted or not – Essex had a stronger image in the public mind than any other county. Would the Bedfordshire Lion have caused anywhere near as much of a media lion-feeding frenzy?

While writing this book it's become apparent just how little I knew of my home county. The first eight months of my life were spent in Dunmow and the rest of my childhood in Brentwood. My family never fully explored the new towns, the islands, the jam factories, the castles or the coast – and the diversity of the place has been a huge surprise. Now I'm proud to come from Essex.

David Nicholls compared his Essex character of Brian to Pip in *Great Expectations*, feeling the same way about Southend as Pip does about the Kent marshes. Yet experience teaches him that Joe Gargery and his larks back at the forge are not something to be ashamed of, in fact they're the most solid thing in his life.

And what of the people of Essex? Yes, there's materialism, belligerence, road rage, xenophobia and intolerance, but also warmth, humour, a desire to better themselves and a total disdain of pomposity. You don't want to wind the locals up, but my Romford-born friend Jacqui Burke put it nicely when asked to sum up the county: 'Cheap and cheerful. The people are the kindest in the world though.'

You can wander into their boutiques and talk to the stars of *TOWIE*. The barmaids in King William IV and Sheesh in Chigwell are as friendly as the taxi drivers in Canvey Island. And behind the commuter facade, in the pubs there's banter and piss-taking and warmth.

And what a diverse set of characters it's spawned. Russell Brand in Grays, Ian Dury in Upminster, Sally Gunnell in Chigwell, Jessie J in Romford, Phill Jupitus, Joseph Conrad and Denise Van Outen from Stanford-no-Hope, Sir Alf Ramsey, Terry Venables and John Terry from Dagenham, the Prodigy from Braintree, Griff Rhys Jones and Douglas Adams at Brentwood School, Blur from Colchester, Grayson Perry and Dougie Poynter from Chelmsford, Wilko Johnson and Lee Brilleaux from Canvey Island, and *TOWIE*'s Mark Wright, Joey Essex and Amy Childs.

In *Gavin and Stacey*, set in Billericay, the characters embody what the public wants to love about Essex. Gavin's mum Pam, played by Alison Steadman, is blonde and strident, but also welcoming and doing her best to expand her cultural horizons with veggie sausages and differentiating between 'men gays' and 'lesbian gays'. They eat in an upmarket Italian restaurant rather than a burger joint, although this being Essex there's always the chance they'll run into Dawnie and Pete trying to spice up their sex life.

Like most Essex men James Corden's Smithy has gone slightly upmarket. When something traumatic happens such as West Ham losing the play-off final or discovering he's the father of Nessa's baby, he retreats to the golf driving range.

Yet when it matters Smithy does the right thing and decides that he's going to be a good father and wants to see his kid even it means dressing up in a Batman suit. Smithy is like Essex as a whole. A bit rubbish, but genuine.

The week after the original Essex Man appeared Simon Heffer went to Australia for two months. He recalled those days on the blog *Iain Dale's Diary*:

My wife would ring me up from home saying: 'Oh there's endless stuff about "Essex man" in the papers and people want to talk to you and they're saying you've fled the country', and I had fled the country but not quite in that way. I wish people would go back and read it because it's actually very complimentary...

I don't want people to be kept in servitude for the rest of their lives. I'm delighted that people could get good jobs, buy their own homes, buy shares, provide for their wives and children and what it was celebrating was that ethos... I still live in Essex now and I love it.

Heffer put it nicely in 2006 when in a *Daily Telegraph* feature he referred to Essex's 'down-to-earth people, ex-denizens of the East End and old sons of the soil, who rub along in a remarkably affable way, unpretentious and welcoming. Who could want to live anywhere else?'

Unpretentious is a good word to use for today's Essex. It's what people liked about all those reality TV winners like Stacey Solomon, Dougie Poynter, Matt Cardle, Harry Judd, most of the cast of *TOWIE* and numerous other Essex celebrities.

Today Essex Man is a much more subtle beast than the cropped Rottweiler-holder with a blonde bird in white stilettos of 1990, more Cameron's cuddler than Maggie's mauler. Through comedy, film and literature God's own county is making a real contribution to the cultural zeitgeist – although in Essex you'd probably still get a slap for using such a phrase.

Twenty-plus years on you might even be able to share a vomit-free train journey home with Essex Man, just as long as he hadn't been to a *TOWIE* wrap-party. It seems we've learned to love the county as well as satirise it. And that is the joy of Essex.